The Abiding Presence

The Abiding Presence

Hugh Martin

Copyright © Christian Focus Publications 2009

ISBN 978-1-84550-469-4

10 9 8 7 6 5 4 3 2 1

Republished in 2009
in the
Christian Heritage Imprint
by
Christian Focus Publications Ltd.,
Geanies House, Fearn, Ross-shire,
IV20 1TW, Scotland, Great Britain

www.christianfocus.com

Cover design by Daniel van Straaten
Printed by Bell & Bain, Glasgow

All rights reserved. No part of this publication may be reproduced, stored in a retrieval system, or transmitted, in any form, by any means, electronic, mechanical, photocopying, recording or otherwise without the prior permission of the publisher or a licence permitting restricted copying. In the U.K. such licences are issued by the Copyright Licensing Agency, Saffron House, 6-10 Kirby Street, London, EC1 8TS. www.cla.co.uk.

CONTENTS

INTRODUCTION *by Sinclair Ferguson* 9

Part One: The Principle or Main Idea

1 THE PRINCIPLE STATED: THE CONJUNCTION OF THE PRESENCE AND THE HISTORY 15
    Give Me His Biography Alone 17
    Give Me the Promised Presence Alone 18

2 THE PRINCIPLE ARGUED: THE PRESENCE—BY THE SPIRIT 21

3 THE ARGUMENT CONTINUED: THE PRESENCE—IN THE HISTORY 29

4 FURTHER ILLUSTRATION 41

5 AN INFERENCE: THE INSPIRATION OF THE GOSPELS 51

6 THE GOSPELS—THE GALLERIES OF THE KING 55

CONTENTS

Part Two: Special Instances Examined

7 THE GALLERIES OF THE KING VISITED 63
   I. The Baptism, and its Perpetual Testimony 64
      Our Lord's Baptism 65
         The Baptism of Water 65
         Baptism of the Spirit 68
      The Father's Testimony 70
      Meet The Living Head 74
      Hear and Receive His Father's Testimony 75
   II. The Temptation, and its Perpetual Triumph 78
      The Identity of the Assault 80
      The Identity of the Defence 90
      The Identity of the Victory 98
         Increase of Comfort 99
         Increase of Usefulness 101
   III. The Synagogue, and Its Perpetual Sermon 103
      The Inspiration of the Scriptures 111
   IV. The Cross, and Its Perpetual Sacrifice 119

Part Three: Additional Elucidation

8 CHRIST'S PRESENCE,
   REAL AND PERSONAL—BY YHE SPIRIT 145
      Would You Have a Real Religion? 159
      Would You Have a Personal Religion? 160

9 THE TWOFOLD REVELATION 163
      Revelation—External or Objective 165
         The Glory of God Must Be Revealed to Us 166
         This Glory Must Be Revealed in Christ 167
         The Gospel History Is the Glass in
         Which this Revelation is Given 169
      Revelation—Inward or Subjective 171
         Have You Seen the Light? 175
         Have You Seen This Glory? 177

CONTENTS

10 CHRIST'S PRESENCE IN HIS PEOPLE   181
    I. Causes of Christ's Presence in His People   183
        Christ Himself   184
            By the Holy Spirit   184
            By the Word   187
        Believers Indispensable yet Subordinate   188
    II. Consequences of christ's presence in his people   193
        Holiness Secured   193
        Mutual Love   195
        Persecution   197
        Hope of Glory   199
    III. Cautions Concerning Christ's Presence in His People   203
        Its Bearing on Their Responsibility   204
            Conscience   205
            The Will   207
        Its Bearing on Their Humanity   211
        Its Bearing on Their Individuality   212

11 THE VIRTUAL CONTEMPORANEOUSNESS OF ALL SAINTS   223

'The book of the generation of Jesus Christ' (Matt. 1: 1).

'Lo, I am with you alway, even unto the end of the world' (Matt. 28: 20).

INTRODUCTION

Hugh Martin (1822–85) lived at a time when spiritual and theological giants walked the streets of the Scottish capital city of Edinburgh. Perhaps simply for that reason he is not as widely known as some of his contemporaries. In addition, his public ministry was cut short by ill health while he was still in his early forties (although thankfully his pen continued to make significant contributions to the Christian church for another two decades). His works are less read today than those of William Cunningham or George Smeaton, but share many of their spiritual characteristics. It is therefore a great personal pleasure to introduce this wonderful study of the ministry of Christ originally published with the title *Christ's Presence in the Gospel History*.

Hugh Martin was born in Aberdeen. He graduated from University there with highest honours in Mathematics—in which he retained a lifelong interest, publishing a Study of Trilinear Coordinates (1867), and serving as a University Examiner in the subject. But under a sense of calling to the Christian ministry, he gave himself to the study of theology. In 1842 he came under the powerful influence of William Cunningham, and became convinced of the cause that, the following year, would issue in the Disruption and the founding of The Free Church of Scotland. He was the first student to be licensed as a preacher of the gospel in the new denomination, and was ordained to the ministry of word and sacraments at Panbride in 1844.

INTRODUCTION

In 1858 he was called to serve Greyfriars Church in Edinburgh, but five years later he retired on the grounds of ill health. During the years that followed, a steady stream of articles for *The British Foreign Evangelical Review* and *The Watchword* came from his pen, and a number of outstanding books. These included studies on *The Prophet Jonah* (1866) and a work on *The Westminster Doctrine of Inspiration* (1877).

It is, however, Martin's trilogy of studies in the person and work of Christ that have the most lasting appeal—*Christ's Presence in the Gospel Narrative* (1860, here republished), *The Atonement* (1870), and *The Shadow of Calvary* (1875). Each of these books is remarkable in its own right. Taken together they represent a treasure store of good things.

One of the things that will most strike a modern reader who works his or her way patiently through these pages is that Hugh Martin did not merely pour old wine (the insights of others) into new wineskins (his own books). While well-versed in the history of theology he was someone who himself thought deeply about Christ. The result is that he takes us to vantage points other authors miss, or never thought of ascending. In this way he leads us to a fuller and richer understanding of the person, ministry, and sacrifice of Jesus—and with that a deeper faith and a more fervent love for him.

There can be few greater needs in the church today than a recovery of thought about Christ. Correspondingly in the world of Christian literature there remains a profound need for books about the Saviour. In our contemporary world—sometimes described by social analysts as either a Narcissistic or a Therapeutic culture—the spirit of the age has also profoundly infiltrated the way Christians think. Books, sermons, studies, seminars abound—but too often they teach us only how to engage in the great project of the times—the enhancement of the self. Tragically even passages from the Gospels can be taught, studied and preached on in order to pursue the question, 'Where am I in the Gospel narrative?' rather than the more fundamental question, 'Where is Jesus in the Gospel narrative?'

In such a context Hugh Martin and his book possess exactly the qualities we need—careful, thoughtful, clear,

INTRODUCTION

biblical, Christ-centered and Christ-honouring teaching. This, then, is a work to treasure, one that repays reading and re-reading—a book about Christ that will stimulate thought and devotion in equal measure.

Sinclair B. Ferguson,
First Presbyterian Church,
Columbia, South Carolina.

PART ONE

THE PRINCIPLE OR MAIN IDEA

1

THE PRINCIPLE STATED:
THE CONJUNCTION OF THE PRESENCE
AND THE HISTORY

'The book of the generation of Jesus Christ' (Matt. 1: 1).

'Lo, I am with you alway, even to the end of the world' (Matt. 28: 20).

If the opening words of Matthew's Gospel—'The book of the generation of Jesus Christ'—might be regarded as a title prefixed not only to the first chapter but to the whole work they would be equivalent to the more modern expressions—the memoirs, or biography of Jesus Christ. But when we find these memoirs closing with such an utterance from the person who is the subject of them, as this—'Lo, I am with you alway'—we instinctively shrink from speaking of them as the memoir and remains of Jesus Christ. Such a designation, we feel would be indeed out of place as applied to the biography of him who cannot only say, 'I am he that liveth, and was dead and, behold, I am alive for evermore,' but who closes the record of his life upon the earth with the matchless declaration 'Lo, I am with you alway.' These are not the memoirs and remains of Jesus Christ; for, lo! He is with us himself.

The Abiding Presence

It is proposed, in these pages, to consider the exact value, the specific and distinct peculiarity, which the closing promise of his presence attaches to the biography of Jesus.

For, surely, the promise not merely exalts this history above all other histories to a place of unparalleled and unapproachable importance—the subject, the mere theme alone, would secure that. But it assigns to the history a use, a practical improvement, altogether singular and unique.

The biographies of others are valuable—the serviceableness or practical worth of them comes out—when the persons are themselves with us no more; when personal fellowship with them has become henceforth in this world impossible. The biography of Jesus—terminating as it does with the astonishing assertion: Lo, I am with you still; 'Lo, I am with you alway'—seems to be the very means whereby we are consciously admitted to his presence, and enabled to maintain with him a personal and living intercourse. I take up the memoir of any other friend with the melancholy feeling: Alas! He is gone, and this is all that remains; and, as I look upon it or peruse it, it reminds me of my loss and makes me feel my brother's absence. But this memoir I may rather take into my hands as the means of causing me to realize my Elder Brother's presence; for it breathes the closing promise that he will never leave me. By the necessary omnipresence of his godhead (but especially by the sovereign and gracious presence of his Spirit) He, whose biography is now before us, is himself with us; and the record of his doings and his doctrines, his life, and death, and resurrection, is thereby no dead history, but a living biography—a biography which, like him of whom it testifies, 'liveth and abideth for ever.' Rather, a biography in which he liveth and abideth for ever; 'with us alway' in 'the book of the generation of Jesus Christ.'

Let us ponder well the marvellous advantage of possessing this presence and biography unitedly.

Suppose them separate, and consider the two cases that arise. First, suppose that we had the biography, without the presence, of Jesus. And, secondly, suppose we had his presence, but not his biography.

Give Me His Biography Alone

Give me his biography alone. It is full of marvels. It is interesting beyond measure. I read, and re-read. And if I render it the tribute of my belief, I feel as if I never could have enough of it.

But if this is all, I feel also that I am dealing merely with a history, a record of what is long past and gone—of events that are very interesting in themselves, but in which I can assert or make out no direct, personal, present interest of mine. I may envy those who actually listened to the gracious words, or saw the glorious 'Works of power and mercy, here recorded. And, very specially, I may envy those to whom testimonies or messages of personal love were delivered, or on whom deeds of healing virtue and of sanctifying grace were achieved. Oh! would that I had been there! Thou Friend of grace, thou King of glory, will that I also may be clean! Command this evil spirit, this strong corruption, to come out of me and enter into me no more. This, also, I would that thou shouldst do unto me, even that I may receive my sight. Blessed Master, question me also, as with thy searching loving eye, thy piercing tender voice: 'Simon, son of Jonas, lovest thou me?' Enable me also to say unto thee, 'Lord, thou knowest all things, thou knowest that I love thee.'

Alas! it is but a fond imagination. It is but the keen and quickened action of the fancy. At the best, I can only form a very vivid conception of the scene which the record commemorates, and delude myself with the pleasing dream that I was there. And as I awake from my dream, I feel painfully that I am alone, with a dead history of the past in my hands.

Give me the biography alone—and the more my heart were adequately moved in reading it, so much the more mournfully would I regret that all these sayings and doings of Jesus are numbered among the things that were.

But do not give me the biography alone. Let me have the promised presence, 'Lo, I am with you alway'—and I am delivered from all these mournful regrets, and from all reasonable ground for entertaining them. Let me by faith realize that he of whom the biography testifies is himself actually with me while I peruse it; let me, in and with the biography, possess and enjoy the presence of Jesus; and then the biography is no dead history, serviceable at the utmost as a means of quickening my fancy to conjure up what, to me now, could be nothing more than an imaginary conjuncture, a shadowy, unreal scene. Instead, it has become replenished with all the original historical reality of that which it commemorates, instinct with present life and truth, lighted up with fulness of grace and glory. In the biography now, we have the very Christ himself—the living Saviour—still speaking to us as never man spake, still going about doing good.

Give Me the Promised Presence Alone

Or, secondly: Give me the promised presence alone. Let me know that a living, but invisible person is present with me. And suppose that this is all I have the means of knowing. I am solemnized. I am filled with awe. But how exactly to conceive of him who is thus with me, I am at a loss. Assure me merely of his presence—and all is vague and hazy, very solemnizing, and (if I have confidence in his friendliness) very encouraging and consoling; but very indefinite also; and, withal, somewhat ghostly. A weighty—almost an oppressive—sense of that unseen presence may be upon my heart: no clear, impressive view of it can be before my mind. I am left very much to my own discretion in trying to conceive of him who all the time is actually present with me. But then, it is just from my own discretion that I crave in so solemn a matter to be thoroughly set free. For I cannot consent to invest this unseen one with the forms of my thoughts which are not as his thoughts—my emotions, imaginations, and conceptions, which are not as his. I know that I cannot but fall over into mere pietistic, sentimental conceptions of his presence, and perhaps into fanatical emotions begotten of the belief that he is present with me. The more, therefore, I have cause to adore and love him; the more I need intelligently to appreciate and trust him; so much the more must I shrink from clothing him, to my own apprehension, with any ideal character of my framing—an ideal that could be framed only from the elements of my own character, and that could not possibly transcend the utmost of my own powers of conceiving the beautiful and good. To abstain, on the other hand, from seeking any clear conception of his presence, is to acquiesce in the painful alternative of regarding the most glorious privilege I can possess as the most indefinite, vague, and indistinct of all things.

Oh! would that I had but some means of forming an exact and worthy conception—an authorized and true idea of him! Would that there were but some mirror in which I might behold his glory well-defined; where I might see the exact features of his character; where, especially, I might read the outgoings, in precise and definite action, of his disposition and desire towards me—some radiant mirror where I might see the glory of God in the face of Jesus Christ; some lively oracle where I might hear his very voice in articulate discourse and converse with me!

With his sure and spiritual presence, then, let it be my privilege to possess his clear and definite biography. Give me the presence of the Lord—not vague, indistinct, and ghostly; silent, oppressive, and almost appalling—but as uttering the very sayings, and achieving the very works of grace and love that the biography details. Let me hear this Saviour, present with me, saying (as in this history) to Peter and James and John, 'What I say to you I say to all' so that I am entitled to hear it as said to me. Let the ever-present Christ make his presence with me definite, intelligible, and most distinct, by proffering to me—as still full of spirit and life, of grace and glory—the very words he uttered and the works he did in the days of his flesh. Let him enshrine his promised presence within the very lineaments and limits of the biography: and I no more complain that his presence with me is indefinite, intangible, vague; difficult of apprehension; destitute of use; incapable of being practically improved, or rationally conceived of and asserted, or validly defended. No, he is present with me now in all revealed distinctness and precision. His own blessed voice speaks with me in the lively oracles. His own blessed face looks forth upon me from the now living picture of his biography. By an arrangement that leaves nothing for imagination to attempt (and therefore no room for imagination to misconceive), and nothing for sentimentalism to supply (and therefore no scope for sentimentalism to pervert), by an arrangement that leaves me no discretion whatsoever, but calls on me simply to receive the heavenly revelation that is given, *the Lord himself is with me*—not to my fancy, not to my pious sentiment, but with me verily and in very truth; present with me for most intelligible converse, for most distinct and blessed action—to cleanse my leprosy; to cure my blindness; to save me in the storm; to rebuke me when my vigilance slumbers; to reprove me with his silent glance if I deny him; to restore me when I repent, restoring to me, also, the responsibility and privilege of feeding his lambs and sheep.

Thus the presence gives reality, present reality, and life, to the biography: the biography supplies to the otherwise indefinite presence distinct manifestation, action, and utterance. The biography is enlivened by the presence: the presence is defined by the biography. The biography is very life-like; but without the presence it is not living. The presence, on the other hand, is living; but without the biography it is far from life-like. Yet what Christ by his promise hath joined, let not unbelief put asunder. Let the biography and the presence be conjoined and coalesce. The biography, then, is not dead; the living one lives in it. The presence is not mysterious and vague; for he is present as in the mirror of the biography, and according to the well-defined, reflected glory there. The biography is more than a biography now. It is—*the life of Jesus*.

2

THE PRINCIPLE ARGUED:
THE PRESENCE—BY THE SPIRIT

Now, it is by the Holy Spirit that this conjunction, or coalescence, is achieved. The glorious arrangement takes effect, or holds good, by reason of the promise and gift of the Spirit.

Yes, it is the Holy Spirit who brings Jesus prominently and personally before us in the one and only way in which Jesus can be with us till he come again the second time, without sin unto salvation.

Jesus himself in his valedictory discourse—his paschal converse with the eleven—brings this out very beautifully and copiously; very elaborately, one is even tempted to say; certainly with great earnestness of feeling, and great variety of expression. On the one hand, he promises the Spirit, the Comforter, as a compensation for his own acknowledged and now imminent departure. On the other hand, while admitting in a sense his departure, and assigning it as the reason why he shall send 'another Comforter,' while admitting his bodily departure (or rather the withdrawal of his flesh, the bodily manifestation of his presence, from the eyes of their flesh) he protests that the removal of that manifestation of his presence shall not be the removal of his presence itself, but he shall be truly with them still. So that while he promises

The Abiding Presence

the Spirit as a compensation for his absence, side by side with this he promises his own presence too; and between these two promises a sort of singular action and reaction goes on, not unlike a series of collisions, till in the end they are found to coalesce into a harmony, or rather unity. For ultimately it becomes plain that the promise of the Spirit (the other Comforter) and the promise of his own prolonged presence (notwithstanding his admitted departure) are quite equivalent, or rather identical. The advent and the indwelling of the Spirit, as sent by Jesus, shall fulfil the promise that Jesus himself is to be with them.

It is in bringing out this equivalence, or identity, that our Lord's thought takes, oftener than once in this discourse, a train so singular that its continuity cannot be traced or evinced, except by recognizing this as the special drift or design of it.

As the first example, examine in this light the paragraph in the earlier part of the discourse (John 14: 16–26)[1] relating to the promise of the Comforter. It opens with this promise: 'I will pray the Father, and he shall give you another Comforter, that he may abide with you for ever; even the Spirit of truth; whom the world cannot receive, because it seeth him not,

---

1 'And I will pray the Father, and he shall give you another Comforter, that he may abide with you for ever; even the Spirit of truth; whom the world cannot receive, because it seeth him not, neither knoweth him: but ye know him; for he dwelleth with you, and shall be in you. I will not leave you comfortless; I will come to you. Yet a little while, and the world seeth me no more; but ye see me: because I live, ye shall live also. At that day ye shall know that I am in my Father, and ye in me, and I in you. He that hath my commandments, and keepeth them, he it is that loveth me; and he that loveth me shall be loved of my Father, and I will love him, and will manifest myself to him. Judas saith unto him (not Iscariot), Lord, how is it that thou wilt manifest thyself unto us, and not unto the world? Jesus answered and said unto him, If a man love me, he will keep my words: and my Father will love him, and we will come unto him, and make our abode with him. He that loveth me not keepeth not my sayings: and the word which ye hear is not mine, but the Father's which sent me. These things have I spoken unto you, being yet present with you. But the Comforter, which is the Holy Ghost, whom the Father will send in my name, he shall teach you all things, and bring all things to your remembrance, whatsoever I have said unto you.'

neither knoweth him: but ye know him; for he dwelleth with you, and shall be in you' (v. 16). In like manner it closes with a reiteration of this promise: 'But the Comforter, which is the Holy Ghost, the Father will send in my name' (v. 26). But Jesus does not reiterate the promise as if he were returning to it from a digression. He does not repeat it as if he were resuming the broken thread of an interrupted thought. The thought has been entirely unbroken through all the intermediate verses. And the continuity of it is very beautiful. But it is perceived only when we understand that Jesus is vindicating for the promise and advent of the Comforter a perfect equivalence or identity with his own true presence amongst them.

Mark, then, how, after the opening promise of the Spirit in verses 16 and 17, Jesus immediately follows on with a promise of his own advent, his own presence with them: 'I will not leave you orphans; I will come to you' (v. 18, margin). Strange contradiction! The Father will send the Comforter because I go away from you; you shall not be comfortless, because I will come to you!

Yet not a contradiction. Rather a very deep harmony. For by my Spirit coming to you on my departure, my presence shall be with you more intensively, more distinguishingly, in more powerful sovereign grace, than now. Now you have my presence—or rather, you have that particular means of perceiving my presence which you so much dread to lose—in common with the world. You are prizing only such a presence of your Lord as the ungodly world itself may share. But you shall perceive my presence then as the world cannot perceive it. 'Yet a little while and the world seeth me no more; but ye see me: because I live, ye shall live also' (v. 19). My death and my ascension—my going to the Father through the cursed cross and the spoiled and rifled grave—will remove me from the world's cognizance. But it will not remove me from yours. While the world is not seeing me, you shall see me. 'A little while and ye shall see me.' You shall see me again; and that, not at my second advent and glorious appearing unto judgment—for then the world also, yea, every eye, shall see me—but while the world is not seeing me you shall see me. And your sight of me shall be a function of such life and powers as you do not share with the world. It shall be the function of a life that you share with me: 'Ye shall see me; because I live ye shall live also.' It shall be spiritual perception; even such, in kind, as I have. It shall be knowledge, infallible and divine: 'At that day ye shall know that I am in my Father, and ye in me, and I in you' (v. 20). It shall be that sight of me in which you have scarcely yet perceived me. For how otherwise, Philip, could you say, 'Show us the Father?' 'Hast thou not known me, Philip? He that hath seen me hath seen the Father. Believest thou not that I am in the Father, and the Father in me?' (verses 9 and 10). This is precisely what you shall believe and 'know' (v. 20) when you have my presence with you as the world cannot have, and see me as the world cannot see me. Indeed, it shall be a manifest presence: 'He that hath my commandments, and keepeth them, he it is that loveth me; and he that loveth me shall be loved of my Father, and I will love him, and will manifest myself unto him' (v. 21).

This, however, is just what is beyond Jude's comprehension. 'Judas saith unto him (not Iscariot), Lord, how is it that thou wilt manifest thyself unto us, and not unto the world?' (v. 22). And our Lord meets his difficulty very beautifully by assuring him that the manifestation shall not be bodily, such as the world could receive and appreciate, but spiritual, such as the invisible Father may give of himself. Even thus will he manifest his presence with his disciples: 'Jesus answered and said unto him, If a man love me, he will keep my words: and my Father will love him, and we will come unto him, and make our abode with him' (v. 23).

Notice here the bringing in of the word: 'he will keep my words.' For the word—the record, the sayings of Jesus, the biography—has a part to play in this great arrangement for achieving Christ's presence. The theme is quite continuous. 'He that loveth me not keepeth not my sayings; and the word which ye hear is not mine, but the Father's which sent me' (v. 24). If my Father and I are to make our abode with you, and manifest ourselves unto you, give heed to my sayings, my word which you hear, which is my Father's word. To speak that word has been all my care hitherto. I have given you the word which my Father gave to me (John 17: 8). I have taken advantage of my bodily presence with you to speak unto you in the Word of God. 'These things have I spoken unto you, being yet present with you' (v. 25). And if I have taken advantage of my presence with you to speak the word, see that you take advantage of the word to secure my intelligible presence and fellowship with you still. To this very end the Spirit will come. By this very means his advent will be my explicit presence with you. Thus will I come unto you. Thus shall you see me. Thus will I be manifest unto you, as making my abode with you. Even thus: 'The Comforter, which is the Holy Ghost, whom the Father will send in my name, he shall teach you all things, and bring all things to your remembrance, whatsoever I have said unto you' (v. 26).

It is one continuous train of thought throughout. And the design of it is to show that he will himself be manifestly present with his church by the Spirit. The Spirit achieves Christ's presence with his people.

Again, in the *second* place, precisely similar is the tenor of another passage, another continuous paragraph, nearer the close of this blessed address to the eleven (John 16: 13–22).[1]

---

[1] 'Howbeit when he, the Spirit of truth, is come, he will guide you into all truth: for he shall not speak of himself; but whatsoever he shall hear, that shall he speak: and he will shew you things to come. He shall glorify me: for he shall receive of mine, and shall shew it unto you. All things that the Father hath are mine: therefore said I, that he shall take of mine, and shall shew it unto you. A little while, and ye shall not see me: and again a little while, and ye shall see me; because I go to the Father. Then said some of his disciples among themselves, What is this that he saith unto us, a little while, and ye shall not see me: and again a little while, and ye shall see me: and, Because I go to the Father? They said therefore, What is this that he saith, a little while? we cannot tell what he saith. Now Jesus knew that they were desirous to ask him, and said unto them, Do ye enquire among yourselves of that I said, a little while, and ye shall not see me: and again a little while, and ye shall see me? Verily, verily, I say unto you, That ye shall weep and lament, but the world shall rejoice; and ye shall be sorrowful, but your sorrow shall be turned into joy. A woman when she is in travail hath sorrow, because her hour is come: but as soon as she is delivered of the child, she remembereth no more the anguish, for joy that a man is born into the world. And ye now therefore have sorrow; but I will see you again, and your heart shall rejoice, and your joy no man taketh from you.'

Here, again, Jesus is not merely promising the Spirit, and indicating the nature of his work and functions, but he is very solicitous again to prove that the Spirit, by specific operations assigned to him as their Lord's ambassador, agent and representative, shall really accomplish and achieve among them a most manifest and glorious presence of their Lord himself. Hence the care, the elaborate accuracy, with which Jesus asserts that the Spirit's office shall in no respect be isolated from his own. 'Howbeit when he, the Spirit of truth, is come, he will guide you into all truth: for he shall not speak of himself; but whatsoever he shall hear, that shall he speak: and he will shew you things to come' (v. 13). He will not turn you aside from contemplating me. He will not so present himself as to obliterate or supplant your views of me. Far from it. 'He shall glorify me: for he shall receive of mine, and shall shew it unto you' (v. 14). And how infinitely more glorious shall this be than any bodily manifestation visible to your eyes of flesh! For 'all that the Father' (who dwelleth in light that is inaccessible and full of glory) 'hath is mine: therefore said I, that he shall take of mine, and shall shew it unto you' (v. 15),

Am I not entitled, then, to say that I will be present with you still, and that my presence shall be manifest? Yes. 'A little while, and ye shall not see me: and again a little while, and ye shall see me; because I go to the Father' (v. 16). My going to the Father shall be the cause of your not seeing me for 'a little while'; but the cause also of your seeing me in a higher mode, after that little while has passed away.

For Jesus went unto the Father by his shameful death—his death so shameful as a penalty endured, yet so glorious as a sacrifice offered. This going unto his Father concealed him for 'a little while' from his disciples in the sense in which they shared with the world in seeing him (14: 19). But Jesus went unto the Father also by resurrection and ascension. And this going unto the Father was the means of revealing him to his own, and enabling them, through the outpoured Spirit, to see him even as he is the revelation of the Father, and as 'it sufficeth' our souls to see him.

The Principle Argued

But it is all mysterious to them, exactly as the same thought formerly was incomprehensible to Jude (14: 22). 'Then said some of his disciples among themselves, What is this that he saith unto us, a little while, and ye shall not see me: and again a little while, and ye shall see me: and, Because I go to the Father?' (v. 17). They cannot understand what this 'little while' means, nor this 'seeing' of Jesus, nor this 'going unto the Father.' And above all, apparently, they are utterly at fault in their attempt to comprehend how there should be a presence of Jesus, and a seeing of him, which are not interrupted, but rather promoted (indeed, even produced or caused) by this mysterious departure to the Father. 'They said therefore, What is this that he saith, a little while? We cannot tell what he saith' (v. 18).

Jesus answers their unspoken inquiries; for 'he knew that they were desirous to ask him.' Accordingly, he again puts the case, and states the difficulty: 'Do ye enquire among yourselves of that I said, a little while, and ye shall not see me: and again a little while, and ye shall see me?' (v. 19). He admits that this will cause them sorrow (v. 20). But he shows them that their sorrow because of his absence from them by death, shall be like the very special sorrow of travail (v. 21), sorrow fertile of life and joy; while he adds: 'And ye now therefore have sorrow' (v. 22). Yes: 'Therefore'—with that special end and intent; even that your sorrow may be a pathway to life, and be turned into joy. Nor does he fail to set the joy before them, specifying exactly what it is. It is his own presence: 'But *I will see you again*, and your heart shall rejoice, and your joy no man taketh from you' (v. 22).

Now, assuredly, this promise that he would 'see them again' was not fulfilled and exhausted in his tarrying with them certain days between his resurrection and ascension. Then, indeed, were the disciples 'glad when they saw the Lord.' But this joy would have been 'taken from them' at his ascension, had this been all the 'seeing' which he meant to promise them. Instead, we read that they 'returned' from the mount of his ascension 'to Jerusalem with great joy; and were continually in the temple, praising and blessing God' (Luke 24: 52–3).

The Abiding Presence

Most manifestly the Lord is emphatically and elaborately teaching that the advent of the Spirit to glorify Jesus is the presence of Jesus himself.

Take all these expressions, therefore, in which Jesus is professedly treating of the promise and gift of the Comforter: 'I will come unto you'; 'Ye shall see me'; 'I will manifest myself unto you'; 'I will come and make my abode with you'; 'a little while, and ye shall see me'; and 'I shall see you again, and your heart shall rejoice.' Could stronger language be employed by Jesus to promise that he will himself be present with his people? And shall we say that for Christ to be present with us merely by his Spirit is a secondary, subordinate, shadowy, figurative presence? Shall we admit that we are disappointed when we come to understand that it is in this sense that Jesus would have us realize that he is with us alway?

Rather let us study its fulness of meaning and of truth, before we acknowledge or admit any feeling of disappointment, lest we disparage and depreciate we know not what.

Above all, let us see whether this be a shadowy, impalpable, ill-defined presence.

3

THE ARGUMENT CONTINUED:
THE PRESENCE—IN THE HISTORY

Take, then, into your hands the biography of Christ; and suppose its closing promise, 'Lo, I am with you alway,' is fulfilled by the Holy Spirit, the Comforter, being given to you.

The Spirit of light and truth shines in your heart while you read the biography. God who commanded the light to shine out of darkness shines in your heart, to give the light of the knowledge of the glory of God in the face of Jesus Christ. He cleanses and purifies your mental eyeballs. He sanctifies and warms your affections. He enables you to see in his own light (Ps. 36: 9) the character and doings, the utterances and affections, the mind and heart of Jesus. That eternal Spirit with whom Jesus, as God, is one in the undivided substance of the godhead—with whom also Jesus, as Messiah, was anointed without measure and above his fellows—is with you inwardly, dwelling in you, searching in you, shining in you. And outwardly, spread out before you, is the biography of him of whom the Spirit has come to testify. And he testifies of Jesus by that written word, quickened by his own Almighty power, shone upon with his own marvellous light. He invests the record of Christ's life and character with heavenly radiance, the glory as of the only begotten of the Father, full of grace and truth. He leaves no veil on the face of Jesus. The glory of God in the face of Jesus Christ he discloses to your view; even the glory of the Lord as in a glass—the glass of the word—with open face (2 Cor. 3: 18; 4: 6). Nor does he leave any veil on your face or your mind: 'Where the Spirit of the Lord is there is liberty' (v. 17). With eyes anointed of the Lord (Rev. 3: 18), and opened to perceive wondrous things (Ps. 119: 18), you are free, without fear, to 'look steadfastly' on what the Spirit, in his own light, is unfolding to your view.

And what have you now? What is it that you now see? What do you discover by the Spirit's light in the biography of the Son of God?

Some shadowy semblance of Jesus? Some memorials or mementoes of your beloved? Some fragments and remains?

No, indeed. A semblance? You behold the glory of the Lord. Fragments? 'All that the Father hath is mine; therefore said I, he shall take of mine and shew it unto you.' Remains? No; but Jesus himself: 'He shall testify of me' ; 'He shall take of mine'; 'He shall glorify me.' It is the living Saviour himself. 'Lo, I am with you alway.'

The precise value and astonishing uniqueness of this result may appear to us more strikingly, and with more conviction, if a simple question be suggested.

Does any other biography possess an advantage such as this, that the living Spirit of him whom it commemorates should adjoin himself to the record, and take possession of the mind and heart of those that read it?—I believe not.

No doubt, in a sense, the spirit of the master in painting or in poetry whom you chiefly study, or of the author you most admire, may seem, as the fruit of that cordial admiration and constant study, to descend upon you. You may insensibly assimilate your state of mind, or style of character, or strain of thought and of expression, to his; in so much that he may seem even to he risen from the dead in his pupil. But all this is ideal, and ideal only. However far it may be carried, and however much the very spirit of your favourite author may breathe in you, it is still after all nothing more than your own mind dealing with its own conceptions, memories, ideas of

The Argument Continued

the departed one. You are, in this process, really solitary and alone.

This communing with the mighty dead, what is it at the best but communing with your own heart in the reminiscences of them which you love to cherish, or in the ideas of theirs which their written remains suggest? The deeds of manly prowess or gentle beneficence they once performed you now recall and admire. The utterances of their noble intellect and tender heart you think you hear again; and they thrill through your frame, and do you good by their inspiration, as of old. The thoughts and feelings they once entertained and recorded, but concealed from all, until, after death, the hand of affection, entrusted with these rich remains, gave over to the world or the church a legacy of wisdom which the living voice had never uttered; these thoughts and emotions—most free, familiar, cherished, deep—may pass through your mind now, till your own thoughts and emotions beat in unison with those of the great departed. In this sense, and to this extent, you have communion with them. Intercourse with them you do not dream of now possessing. Their writings and remains are at the utmost substitutes for that.

But possessing the biography and Spirit of Jesus is something totally different both in kind and in degree. Others may inoculate you, in a sense, with their spirit. It means merely their genius, their enthusiasm, their individual style of thought and feeling. Jesus baptizes you with the Holy Ghost and with fire.

And then, you do not deal with reminiscences of Christ—memories and mementoes of him, however accurate; conceptions, notions, ideas concerning him, however true; no, nor even with mere doctrines concerning him, however truly divine and infinitely precious in their own place as these unquestionably are. You deal with him, and he with you. The true and living Christ, present with you—secretly and subjectively present in you by his Spirit—deals with you. And you in the Spirit deal with the true and living Christ, present with you—ostensibly and objectively present with you—in his own holy word and history.

The Abiding Presence

There is true communion now. There is personal and mutual intercourse. Yes, you have found Jesus. And he speaks unto you face to face, as a man speaks to his friend. He reveals his face to you without a veil; and you lift up your face to him without spot, and without fear or tremor save that of reverential awe. For he lifts the light of his countenance upon you; and he is the health of your countenance and your God. Behold! Jesus indeed is with you; shining on you; speaking to you—shining forth on you from the biography, resplendent now, through the Spirit, with the glory as of the only begotten of the Father; speaking forth to you from the biography, vocal now, through the Spirit, with the Chief Shepherd's voice. Jesus is with you, and you with him—the very Jesus of the Gospels; causing you to 'wonder at the gracious words that proceed from his mouth,' causing you to feel that 'Jesus Christ maketh you whole.'

Thus you have Jesus himself, presently revealing himself to you by the Spirit, as in his biography; so that he brings down to you, along the course of time, all that was essential and of lasting import, all that was of universal and eternal value, in the intercourse he maintained with others, and the services he rendered to them, now so many generations ago, in the days of his flesh. You have not merely what he once thought, and said, and did; but what he thinks, and says, and does now; for, Lo, he is with you alway. As revealed in that very record, the same yesterday, to-day, and for ever, he is with you alway. And you have not merely what he thought, and said, and did concerning others; but what he now thinks, and says, and does concerning you; for, lo, in the visible church—by his striving Spirit and stirring history—He is verily with you; weeping over you, if, with Jerusalem, you are still rejecting him; rejoicing over you, if, with Peter, you have seen his glory and confessed him as the Christ, the Son of the living God.

Ah! we have not the record of a past, but the revelation of a present Saviour. By the lively oracles and the perpetual presence, we may have true intercourse with Jesus. He will come in and sup with us and we with him, even according to the revelation of him in his history and in the revealing light of his Spirit.

The Argument Continued

For, without the Spirit you may know much about Christ. But it is impersonal knowledge; Christ himself you do not know, nor see, nor meet with. You may have the means of knowing him; but they are not effectual. You may have the means of intercourse with him; but intercourse itself you have not. You may have his perfect and all-sufficient biography; but without the Spirit of Jesus you cannot appreciate the life of Jesus; for you are not yourself quickened to live in the same spiritual world, or atmosphere and realm, with him. The truths and doctrines concerning him which you pile into your mind may be divine in themselves; but grappling with them in your own spirit alone, practically they are not divine to you; to you their divine excellence and beauty is concealed. From your own spirit they assume the hues and lights in which you see them—hues and lights, not of the divine Spirit, but of the human mind with its darkening and distorting prejudices—of your own mind with its peculiar evil set, its own particular bent of error. Higher than the character, or calibre, or capacity, of your own heart and intellect you cannot rise. The very biography and character of Christ, to your view, when seen only in the light of your spirit, will be limited and stunted to the size and tone of your spirit. The natural man will not receive it, for it is spiritually discerned. The very word of God you may put, like fuel, into the furnace of an earnest, excited, anxious mind; and the furnace may be heated seven times; yet, if you be not baptized with the Holy Ghost and with fire—if that divine fuel burn only with the strange fire of your own spirit—sparks only of your own kindling will fly from it. The light of the knowledge of the glory of God will not be yours. This only shall you have as the result: you shall lie down in sorrow; you shall still be in solitude; no living person, no personal and present Saviour with you.

But let the Comforter, the Spirit of truth, shine in your heart, and shine on the truth before you; let the fuel of

> *You may have his perfect and all-sufficient biography; but without the Spirit of Jesus you cannot appreciate the life of Jesus; for you are not yourself quickened to live in the same spiritual world, or atmosphere and realm, with him.*

divine truth, in general, in your mind be kindled and glow radiantly with a fire divine; let Christ's record, in particular, be illumined and opened by Christ's own Spirit; and then you shall have seen the Lord—you have seen him and heard him yourself. And have you not embraced your opportunity to claim him, as with Thomas, 'my Lord and my God'; to say to him, as with Nathanael, 'Rabbi, thou art the Son of God, thou art the King of Israel'; to appeal to him, as with Peter, 'Lord, thou knowest all things, thou knowest that I love thee'?

Ah! you are not now paying reverence to the manes and memory of a departed Teacher. You are not bowing before an ideal impersonation of departed moral worth and beauty, however ravishing. You are no more labouring merely to form a vivid mental conception of one whose life may well fire your spiritual ambition, and quicken and provoke, while it allures and encourages, your imitation. You are in no figurative sense communing with one of a bygone age. You are with Jesus—that same Jesus who was dead and is alive again—and, behold, he lives for evermore, speaking to you the very words he spoke when on earth; forgiving all your iniquities; rebuking all your corruptions; healing all your diseases; dealing very effectually, very intelligibly and precisely, very tenderly with you. He fulfils his promise. He does not leave you an orphan. He comes unto you. Lo, he is with you alway.

Oh! to what a singular and matchless utility does this exalt 'the book of the generation of Jesus Christ'! What meeting-places with the Saviour does it now afford! What personal meetings with him does it now effect! Not a word that Jesus uttered eighteen hundred years ago, suitable to any poor sinner that made application and appeal to him, but—if my case be similar, and that word be suitable to me—a Saviour still present makes it freely mine as it was free to him that first obtained it—freely mine; full, also, of all its light, and grace, and power to do me good, undiminished by the lapse of ages. Nor is there any work of mercy and of might which Jesus ever did, 'manifesting forth his glory,' but—if it could suit my case, benefit my soul, and promote my salvation and my comfort—that work is being prolonged in unattenuated efficacy up to this moment and on to my needy soul, by a Saviour the same

THE ARGUMENT CONTINUED

yesterday, today, and for ever, who in his marvellous biography is living with us still by his Spirit. The element of time is got rid of, and cast out. Jesus is with us. We are with him. In all the spiritual and permanent efficacy of what he said and did on earth, and left on record, he is with us. In the Spirit and in faith we are with him, having companionship with him, and personal interest, in all the doctrines and deeds he uttered, all the grace and glory he revealed, all the invitations he gave, and all the blessings he conferred, in those wondrous days of his flesh.

A striking illustration of this casting out of the interval or element of time may be drawn from that singular designation of our Lord, 'the Lamb slain from the foundation of the world.'[1]

On what grounds can the truth and accuracy of this title be vindicated? Was not Jesus Christ offered up a slain lamb in sacrifice to God in 'the fulness of time,' four thousand years after the creation of man? And how then can he warrantably be said to have been slain from the foundation of the world?

Not merely, I apprehend, as is usually said, from the prior certainty of the event. The ordination and appointment of God made the death of Christ certain from the foundation of the world, or rather from everlasting. But in the sure and all embracing purpose of the good pleasure of the will of God— which in reality is one, and comprehensive of whatsoever

[1] Here I am indebted to a singularly interesting passage near the close of Dr. Candlish's little volume on the Atonement, where he supposes the death of Christ to have been postponed to the end of time, and makes effective use of the supposition in dissipating, as a mere illusion, the notion that there is any inconsistency between a definite atonement and a universal gospel call: 'For certain purposes, and in a certain view, the death of Christ is ante-dated in Scripture, and he is spoken of as "the Lamb slain from the foundation of the world" (Rev. 13: 8). It is no bold fiction, or mere figure of speech, that thus assigns an era to this event, so remote from that of history. The truth is, the event itself, like the Godhead concerned in it—the everlasting Father ordaining and accepting, the only-begotten Son undertaking and accomplishing, and the eternal Spirit sealing and applying it—is "the same yesterday, to-day, and for ever." It has properly, therefore, no date; and if, on this principle, it may be held to have taken place "from before the foundation of the world," it is not doing any violence to its reality, or taking any undue liberty with its sacredness, to conceive of it as delayed till the world's close.'

comes to pass—the death of his martyr Stephen was as certain from the foundation of the world as the death of that Jesus for whose testimony Stephen died.

Nor is it a sufficient answer to say that the blood of Jesus was shed according to a covenant, an everlasting covenant, ordered in all things and sure. For the sacrifices of the Levitical priesthood were slain, and the blood of bulls and of goats shed and sprinkled, according to a covenant; and yet the efficacy of such blood—for it had an efficacy to remove ceremonial guilt and disability, and to cleanse from ceremonial pollution (Heb. 9: 13)—lasted only for a very short time after it was shed, and did not exist at all before that. Certainly such blood, having transient worth and power, could not seal into perpetuity the covenant to which it appertained. The covenant Christ died to seal is indeed an everlasting one that passes not away. But it is confirmed into its perpetuity by the blood of that great Shepherd of the sheep. It receives this attribute from the sacrifice of Calvary rather than bestows it. So that still we have to look for the solution of the question.

In the sacrifice of Christ our passover, besides the sure decree appointing it, and the everlasting covenant sealed by it, there was a specific and unparalleled element whereby the efficacy of his death was unshackled—relieved and set free—from all consideration of time, and in virtue whereof it traverses, with unchanged intensity, all epochs of our chequered history as a race; from the very first moment of time when its application became needful or possible, down even to the last; from the fall to the restitution of all things. And that element is this: 'He, through the *eternal Spirit*, offered himself without spot to God.' The conducting power of the eternal Spirit (if we dare use the expression)—of the eternal Spirit dwelling in Christ's person without measure (as, of course, in none but a divine Redeemer he could have dwelt), and glorifying to the uttermost the moral excellence and spiritual glory and legal meritorious efficacy of Christ's obedience unto death—fills all time, past, present, and to come, with the divine well-pleasingness and reconciling energy of that single sacrifice of the cross. On the wings of the eternal Spirit the sin-expiating, saving power of the death of Jesus reaches backward from the hour of his crucifixion to the consciences and the salvation of the fallen pair in Eden; and forward, in like manner, all-undiminished, to the last soul that shall be cleansed and made whiter than the snow. The element of time has no influence at all on the efficacy of the sacrifice. As to past time, he may be called 'the Lamb slain from the foundation of the world.' And to the end of time, he is 'the Lamb as it had been slain.'

A blessed consideration! infinitely precious to me a sinner!

For when, as a guilty and conscience-stricken sinner, I come, at whatsoever time, drawn to the cross by that same eternal Spirit, through whom Jesus offered himself there, a spotless sacrifice of sweet-smelling savour unto God, do I find the cross empty and void? the crucifixion, a thing over and gone—wound up, put by, and set aside—the power and might gone out of it? True, indeed, I find that the crucifixion is over and completed. In one sense it is past. Yes; blessed be our high priest for ever! in offering himself a sacrifice, he exclaimed, 'It is finished.' But that very finishing implies and celebrates the triumph and the presence of what can never pass away. In that very finishing there is eternal perfection—a perfection of redeeming preciousness and saving influence traversing all time, the same yesterday, to-day, and for ever—lighting up the ages with the only real glory that has ever gilded them. For what was transacted in the passing moments of the sacrificial work, was transacted in the permanent perpetual might of the eternal Spirit and is therefore permanent and eternal. It is 'eternal redemption' that he achieved 'through the eternal Spirit' (Heb. 9: 12, 14).

Hence Paul does not say, 'I *was* crucified with Christ.' He might have said so. He would have stated a great truth in saying so; even that, Christ being the federal head of his elect, virtually and legally they *were* crucified with him. But this would have been an abstract and impersonal truth, no expression of Paul's own experience; a truth that might be asserted in disjunction from anything pertaining to his own consciousness, even as it may be asserted of the yet unborn elect. He meant to utter a personal experience and consciousness of his own. He meant to indicate that, by vital union with

Christ, and living faith in him, the abstract and doctrinal fact that Christ died for him as his legal representative, had been translated into the sphere of his own experience; that what was true in point of law at the epoch of the cross, had become efficient in point of fact in the present estate of his own inner man. And so, drawing the cross to himself over the intervening years, he says, 'I *am* crucified with Christ.'

But this casts out the element of time. It means, Christ and I *are* crucified together; *are* crucified, even now; both Christ and I—I with him, but he also with me. Christ's crucifixion and mine are virtually simultaneous. They are, both of them, present and continuous.

For the virtue, the efficacy, is continual—continually present; unaltered by lapse of days, unaffected by consideration of time, or date, or epoch. In respect of its sacrificial virtue, its expiating power, the crucifixion is the same, through the Holy Spirit, as if it were even now in progress. Nor is this mysterious, when we think that the one Spirit through whom Christ offered the sacrifice to God, and through whom also God applies the sacrifice to us—that one Spirit who was concerned in the shedding of the precious blood, and who is concerned now in the sprinkling of it—is the eternal Spirit, with whom the element of time can have no weight; through whom, therefore, Christ is the true continual burnt-offering, the Lamb slain from the foundation of the world, and slain till the world's end.

Now, what is thus true of the death of Christ, namely, that it is unshackled from the mere element of time or date, is true equally of his whole biography, or rather of all that it records. All that it records it perpetuates.

There is an 'outward action performed by Jesus of Nazareth—it may be in Nazareth where he was brought up (Luke 4: 16-21), or elsewhere—an outward action performed by him in time, in the days of his flesh, while he was a pilgrim and a stranger on the earth, not having where to lay his head. And that time is gone by eighteen hundred years and more. The time is gone by, and the outward action—rather, shall we say, the outwardnesss of the action?—is gone with it. But in the action, inwardly and secretly, there is a prolonged, permanent,

The Argument Continued

endless efficacy, which to those to whom Jesus says, 'Lo, I am with you alway,' never passes away.

For the bodily presence of our Lord on the earth for a time was as the setting up of a temporary dial-plate, on which indications might be given of the permanent glory of his person, and of the ceaseless dignity and efficacy of his office; of his perpetual power and wisdom for our salvation; and of his changeless love unto the sons of men. And as the days of his flesh passed by, while the marvellous movements on that dial of the 'light of the world' told off to a darkened race the things that must have otherwise remained in the 'light that is inaccessible,' a spiritual mind might have mourned to see them in swift succession flit rapidly away, replacing each other with ever-changing marvels and glories that were gone ere their full import could well be seized.

But do not mourn, said Jesus. The Spirit shall bring all things to your remembrance. The Spirit shall take of mine and show it unto you. He shall testify of me. He shall glorify me.

And so, when Jesus had retired to his Father's glory, and the heavenly things that had been figured forth in swift succession by the aid of his temporary sojourn in the flesh among the children of men, were passing into swift oblivion, they were arrested, ere it was too late, and placed on full and rich continuous record on this other indelible dial of Christ's biography. And let the promised Spirit only come, and the sun-light of the Spirit shine ('O send forth thy light and thy truth') and, instinct with lively revelations of a living, present Saviour, this dial unerringly reveals Christ's present will, love, and power—his present grace and truth—indeed, his present glory, as of the only begotten of the Father, exactly as his own sojourn on the earth did; when he spake as never man spake, and went about doing good; when the Word made flesh tabernacled amongst us, and disciples saw his glory.

Even so is he with us alway: his biography living by his presence; his presence finding expression in his biography.

4

FURTHER ILLUSTRATION

Why should it be deemed a thing incredible that Jesus lives with us in his biography, that his biography perpetuates his life on earth?

'Even in their ashes live their wonted fires.' So hath the poet sung. And many, doubtless, are the lovely fancies of the poets, doomed to be fancies only; and many the yearnings of humanity, forth-reaching after the good, and beautiful, and true, yet ever doomed to fall short of the goal; till these fancies are redeemed from dreaminess, and find realization, and these yearnings their true point of support, in the humanity of that second man, who is the Lord from heaven. The finest strings of the poetic lyre have a tone of melancholy in them, and the purest longings of the human bosom an element of sighing. For the sad blight of 'vanity' has passed upon us, and withered all flesh and all the glory of man into emptiness and mournful transiency. 'Behold thou hast made my days as an hand-breadth, and mine age is as nothing before thee: verily every man at his best estate is altogether vanity. Surely every man walketh in a vain show' (Ps. 39: 5–6).

But the earnest expectation of the creature waits for deliverance from this doom. The whole creation groans and travails together, longing for the glorious attribute of permanence.

Shall there be no permanence, then, in the very life on earth of the Deliverer himself? Alas! if it, too, must be abandoned to the transiency from which he came, in the name of the Lord, to save us.

Would you endure to have it said of your Lord's life on earth, that it was an hand-breadth, and a vain show? That he came forth like a flower, and was cut down; that he fled away also as a shadow, and continued not? That his days were consumed like smoke? That his life was even as a vapour that appeared for a little time, and then vanished away? That he spent his years as a tale that is told?

A thrill of indignation, and a tear of exulting joy, repel the dishonouring notion.

No. Peter may exclaim in his grand antithesis, 'All flesh is grass, and all the glory of man as the flower of grass; the grass withereth, and the flower thereof fadeth away. But the word of the Lord endureth for ever.' Yet surely we know on which side of these contrasted categories to range the life of the Word made flesh—himself the resurrection and the life. And Moses, complaining of human fragility, may sing thus mournfully, 'Thou turnest man to destruction; and sayest, Return, ye children of men. Thou carriest them away as with a flood; they are as a sleep: in the morning they are like grass which groweth up. In the morning it flourisheth, and groweth up; in the evening it is cut down, and withereth. We spend our years as a tale that is told.' But shall terms like these apply to the life of that very Lord to whom Moses utters his complaint; and that in terms of adoration such as these: 'Lord, thou hast been our dwelling-place in all generations. A thousand years in thy sight are but as yesterday'?

Oh! it is a dishonouring depreciation of the sayings and doings of the eternal Son of God on the earth, to fancy that their import and their efficacy have died away, as do the sayings and the doings of men. I take up the biography of Jesus—so different from all other biographies, in that never any but he hath said to me, 'Lo! I am with you alway, even to the end of the world'—and I turn, let us say, to the record of that woman who pleaded with him so marvellously for her little daughter (Matt. 15: 22), or of that other woman who touched in faith the hem of his garment (Mark 5: 25). Have I the same unquenchable desire as these my fellow-sinners? Have I a case like theirs? Have I a longing heart like theirs? Have I a pleading cry to raise; a trembling experiment to try, like theirs? And would my Lord's word and will and work for them suit my case and save me, as it so exactly suited theirs, and so graciously saved them?

Ah! then let me come and stand with them before him. It is no illusion of the fancy when I try to do so. It is no ideal scene I conjure, up, and no ideal part I essay to enact in it. It is no mere effort of imagination. It is not a mere accommodation of the passage. It is not a mere pious improvement of the incident. No. I have here the biography of Jesus, and what he willed, and said, and did to them; and, lighting it all up with perpetual life and power, I have the promise, 'Lo! I am with you alway, even unto the end of the world.' I may seem, therefore, to stand afar off from the company surrounding Jesus—adown the course of time full eighteen hundred years and more. But that word of Christ, which gave life and salvation, hope and healing to them—like a ray of light springing forth as from a central source, yet (unlike material light) undiminished by the distance—comes streaming onward in the might of the eternal Spirit through all time, down even to me this day, unimpeded and undecaying in its passage. And, as that unchanging ray, in meeting anywhere in all its course a medium similar to what it first struck upon, is reflected, or refracted, or gives forth its tints, or imparts its efficacy, precisely as it did at first; so, let me only take up—as in a far-off circle, yet having the self-same centre, though with eighteen centuries between—an attitude of spirit as in the very line or sympathy of these broken-hearted suppliants, or (say) of that poor leper who cried, 'Lord, if thou wilt, thou canst make me clean'; and then, onward to me, over all that lapse of centuries, unaltered and undecaying, fresh and gracious, and omnipotent and faithful, as when spoken first, there travels, till it reaches me, the majestic word of mercy, 'I will; be thou clean.'

For really, with the story of the leper's cure in my hands, and the sore consciousness of the leper's disease in my heart;

with the leper's misery and feelings and attitude and prayer my own; his Lord, also, mine; up from the page of the biography I have only to look to him of whom it testifies, and to hear him saying, Lo! I am with you also alway; and why should I not by faith take home the Lord's word as spoken, now also, and to me—immediately and presently to me: 'I will; be *thou* clean'?

O stricken one, whom your sins have stricken, and who cannot look the Lord in the face, yet yearns to be allowed to wash his feet with your tears, behind his back, permitted but unseen! Come to the house of Simon the Pharisee. Jesus is there. Lo! Jesus is here as he was there; here now, as he was there then; Jesus, the same; the same considerate, loving, forgiving Saviour; considerate and tender even to your feelings and your shame. For, see how he shields you, how he commends you, how he forgives you: 'Woman, thy sins are forgiven thee. Thy faith hath saved thee: go in peace.' Yes! go in peace; in love, also. And prove your great Defender true when he says to all around you: 'Her sins which are many are forgiven'—evidently forgiven—'for she loveth much,' (Luke 7: 36–50).

O hardened one, whom your sins have hardened; living still without the Christ; living still under all the Father's wrath; loving still your various lusts and pleasures! Come to the Mount of Olives. Jesus is there. Lo! Jesus is here also alway, as he was there then. Jesus, the same; the same yesterday, to-day, and for ever; the same weeping Saviour. Come, and see his tears flowing fast for you. Come, and hear his sorrowing heart breaking open its griefs over your perdition. And substitute, in silent terror, your own lost name for the name of lost Jerusalem: 'O Jerusalem, Jerusalem, how often would I have gathered thy children together, even as a hen gathereth her chickens under her wings, and ye would not! Behold, your house is left unto you desolate' (Matt. 23: 37–8).

O anxious one, searching the word in your study, calling on the Lord beneath your fig-tree! Come forth, O Nathanael, at Philip's call; come forth and meet the Master. For, behold, already he speaks of you to those that are around his person, and commends you to his followers' love as 'an Israelite indeed, in whom is no guile.' Do you ask, 'Whence knowest thou me?' By token of your broken-hearted prayers he knows you, and owns you as his own. For hark! 'Before that Philip called thee, when thou wast under the fig-tree, I saw thee.' He has known your soul in adversity, he has considered your trouble, and has not shut you up into the hand of the enemy. The eyes of the Lord are on the righteous; his ears are open to their cry. Will you not say to him: 'Rabbi, thou art the Son of God, thou art the King of Israel'? And will it not be yours to see heaven opened, and the angels of God ascending and descending on the Son of man—heaven and earth knit together in peace, and good-will, and glory in the highest, by his mediation? (John 1: 45-51).

Are you overmastered by some strong corruption—strong as a devil that will not resign his power over you? Come to this excited group as they stand in wonder round the Lord and the twelve. Come, and say, if as yet you can say nothing better, 'Lord, if thou canst do anything, help me.' For hear what Jesus says: 'If thou canst believe, all things are possible to him that believeth.' And, under strong pressure on the right hand and on the left—pressed by the anguish your corruption works for you, and your terror lest it finally undermine and make void your salvation; pressed, also, and quickened by the glorious proffer of deliverance and victory most full and sure, if only now in the day of visitation you can believe—will you not cry out with tears, 'Lord, I believe, help thou mine unbelief'? Oh! then, you shall never fall a prey to the power of your adversary. Mighty and resistless is your Lord's voice unto him: 'I command thee that thou come out of him.' And though the devil tear you, and leave you as it were dead, your soul shall be saved in the day of the Lord; you shall enter into the kingdom, be it so as by fire.

Are you quite at sea in your many fears and sorrows? Are you embarked on a troubled ocean of cares and trials? Has the Master constrained you to get into the ship and go to the other side, over against Bethsaida? And the evening being come down, and the ship in the midst of the sea, and the wind contrary, is the Master alone on the land? Are you apt to grudge that he is landed in safety, peace, and glory; as if he had forgotten his appointment of a dangerous and stormy voyage for you? Ah! he is looking on. He sees you toiling and rowing. And now, when your fear is at its height, and your danger imminent, about the fourth watch of the night he comes unto you, treading on the waves, and mastering all the tempest. Hark, his voice! For, lo! even thus also, as on Galilee's lake, he is with you alway. 'Be of good cheer: it is I; be not afraid.'

Are you weeping bitterly over your miserable fall—your base denial of your Lord? Or have you gone back in dull despondency to your nets again? (John 21: 13). Your first love forsaken, your steadfastness mournfully fallen from, scarcely do you dare to hope for liberty of heart to say again with truth, 'I love the Lord?' Have you ceased to feel your wonted interest in his cause and kingdom? Is your heart relapsed to your worldly cares and worldly interests, and centred chiefly now on them? Ah! and are you toiling at your task and finding nothing; spending money for what is not bread, and labour for that which does not satisfy? Indeed, having tasted truer joy, how can you ever again on Galilee's shores find happiness without the Lord and his love? Suppose that in the sad wreck that has occurred, no sign of love in your heart to Jesus now remains; and conscious of the past and all its sin, you are ashamed to whisper even to yourself, 'I love the Lord.' That miserable fall stifles even the question, Do I love the Lord or no?

Questioning your own heart may bring no response of grace. But the Lord himself draws near to ask. Behold he comes after you. He finds you at your weary task. He takes you as he finds you—weary, toiling, restless, dissatisfied; making nothing of it; no candle of the Lord shining on your head; no joy of the Lord your strength. Just as you are he takes you in hand to deal with you again. And he comes, the same as ever; the same gracious Lord, unchanged, the same yesterday, to-day, and for ever. Behold! he calls you by name: 'Simon, son of Jonas!'

Look up into his face, and read whether he has come in wrath or love. That face!—burning tears ran down there for sinners; sinners such as you; for the very chief of sinners; for 'Jerusalem sinners'; for men that hated him, and spat on him, and scourged him, and slew him, and sealed and watched his grave, that he might be buried out of sight and out of mind—that they might be troubled with him no more for ever. Great drops of blood, too, flowed down there, down to the ground, where he lay in weakness, with supplications, and strong crying, and tears, bearing the guilt of sinners whom he loved. The heart-melting look of grief, rebuke, astonishment, unquenchable affection, shone there, and melted the heart of him that denied him. Look up into that face of Jesus, the same yesterday, to-day, and for ever; the same to you as to Simon Peter on the shore of Galilee's lake. He is returned from the cross of woe; he is returned from the cold embraces of the grave. He is the heir, too, of all things; he is the Lord of glory. From his grave he has come, and from his glory he is tarrying, to seek and find you; to say, 'Simon, son of Jonas, lovest thou me?'

By his very voice to Peter—a voice not yet dead, living and abiding for ever, living in the power of the Spirit, living on the page of the blessed biography, with you alway to the end of the world; thus truly, lovingly, with present power and love, seeking your love, yearning for it, ready to be gratified by it, ready to rejoice in it, very gracious and ready to own your sincerity, far readier than you are yourself—thus does Jesus say unto you, even now, 'Simon, son of Jonas, lovest thou me?'

Questioning yourself could bring out no clear response. But shall Jesus fare no better when he takes up the question? In the absence of your loving Lord, it may be you could not firmly, clearly, distinctly, with any consciousness of truth, assert, 'I love the Lord.' To your own inquiry, to a fellow-creature's question, it may be that you are wisely silent. Doubts and hesitancies, greatly strengthened by your fall, oppress you. And for the very truth's sake you may refuse to answer the question as you would desire to do.

But listen to the gracious words that proceed from his mouth. It is love's own question. And love itself—infinite and incarnate; a consuming fire, as of the God-head's glory, yet a gentle flame, as in a brother's bosom—is dealing with you, anxious for your love, wooing your love. Shall it not win your love?

Ah! does not that love of his to you, which his very question proves; which has anticipated and been beforehand with your love; which says, 'Ye have not chosen me, but I have chosen you'; that love of which Paul has said, 'The love of Christ constraineth us'; and John has said, 'We love him because he first loved us'; does not such love of his to you enable, decide, constrain you to answer—as between the omniscient Saviour and your own moved and melted heart (your heart broken open, won over, gained for ever)—'Lord; thou knowest all things; thou knowest that I love thee'?

Parent! anxious for the little ones whom God has graciously given to you? Do you not know to whom to bring them? Or do you say, Oh that I knew where I might find him? Lo! Jesus is with us always, even as in the days of his flesh. Realize him, by faith, as with you still, exactly as in his blessed record (Mark 9: 13–16). Bring these little ones unto him. And as you bring them, does he not defend you against all, even disciples, if they rebuke you? Does he not take your children in his arms, put his hands upon them, and bless them?

Sister! mourning a departed brother. Come to the grave of Lazarus. Jesus is there. Jesus is here as he was there; at your brother's grave: Jesus, the same yesterday, to-day, and for ever. 'Thy brother,' he tells you, 'shall rise again,' (John 11).

Gentle one! covetous to learn the words of Jesus; to hear his voice; to learn of him who is meek and lowly. Come to Bethany, and sit with Mary at his feet. For, lo! he is here as there, alway, even to the end of the world (Luke 10: 38–42).

Blind one! sitting by the wayside, not seeing your signs, not seeing your path. Hark! 'Lo I am with you alway.' And hark! again, 'Jesus of Nazareth passeth by.' Brother, it is no figure of speech; no pious fancy; no sacred dream; no accommodation of Scripture; no spiritualizing device. It is true. Jesus passes by. Seize your opportunity. 'Son of David, have mercy on me.' Rise, then, for he calls you. Hear his gracious question: 'What wilt thou that I should do unto thee?' Can you not reply: 'Lord, that I may receive my sight. Open mine eyes that I may behold wonders out of thy law'? And, 'The Lord giveth sight unto the blind, and raiseth up the bowed down.'

Are you coming to the table of the Lord, covetous to be a guest with the King of glory? Would you really sup with him; not in a figure, but in very truth; as truly as the eleven on that night on which he was betrayed?—so that it shall in truth be said concerning you, 'They have been with Jesus'; also, 'They have seen God, and did eat and drink with him.' Is this at any time our marvellous ambition and desire? Oh, give me the biography and the presence of the King. Give me the blessed words: 'And he took bread, and gave thanks, and brake it, and gave unto them, saying, This is my body, which is given for you. Likewise also the cup after supper, saying, This cup is the new testament in my blood, which is shed for you.' And give me, in conjunction with this, the promise, 'Lo! I am with you alway.' Let me truly, and in faith, conjoin these words and that presence. Let the words be instinct with the presence; and let the presence, and its intended aspect or action towards me at the table, find expression in the words. Oh! have I not my Lord himself giving me, from his own hand, his body and his blood—even till he come again, when I shall see him as he is?

Are you often weary in a weary world; weary of your body of sin and death; weary of your many infirmities; weary of your little progress; forced to look now for your only satisfaction to the heavenly rest that remaineth? Oh! the blessedness of having in the meantime the presence and biography of your Lord. Come often, when weary and troubled and lonely in spirit; come and meet the Lord even now in these galleries, where the King still goes with his followers. And as faith casts out the element of time since his first coming, let it cast out also the interval until his second. 'Let not your heart be troubled: ye believe in God, believe also in me. In my Father's house are many mansions: if it were not so, I would have told you. I go to prepare a place for you. And if I go and prepare a place for you, I will come again, and receive you unto myself; that where I am, there ye may be also.' Let faith destroy that interval. Let faith make no account of it, rising above its separating influence; rising above time and space, and asserting its high prerogative to see the things that are unseen—to embrace already the future and eternal. Let faith hear Jesus saying: 'Behold! I come quickly.' And let faith and hope reply: 'Amen. Even so, come, Lord Jesus.'

Until then, there is the promise: 'Lo! *I am with you* alway, even to the end of the world.' After that there is this other hope: 'So shall *we* be for ever with the Lord.'

5

AN INFERENCE:

THE INSPIRATION OF THE GOSPELS

The principle expounded yields an irresistible argument for the inspiration of the four Gospels of Emmanuel's biographers. For if he designed by his Spirit to use these records on the scheme that has been unfolded, then the idea of human imperfection mingling with them is simply intolerable.

I can endure there being spots on the sun. I can even imagine that a record of the Saviour's life—a biography of Jesus intended to be dealt with on no grander scheme, and to serve no use, nobler in kind, than any other religious memoir—might not necessarily have any claim to be counted absolutely faultless. I can conceive that a delineation of the character of Jesus, were it simply to hold a place in literature similar to that held by other pictures or portraitures of the good and great (similar in kind, however much more lofty in elevation or more important in degree) might in that case not be divinely perfect and infallible.

But if this very specific—this singular, matchless and unique—use is to be made of it, namely that the Saviour in all ages means to fill it with himself—looking forth from it, from generation to generation, upon the sons of men, in his very countenance and person, so that he commits himself to us for ever as being exactly what the word declares him to be—then

I demand its absolute infallibility, in order that my Lord be in nothing misrepresented to me. I demand that it be a mirror on which no staining breath of human imperfection has been permitted to pass; that it be a picture without spot, or blemish, or any such thing. For now the question of its perfection implicates my Lord's perfection. His spotlessness is in peril if its infallibility is challenged.

Yes! You can tolerate the thought of spots on the sun. You can endure the idea of imperfection, if there be such, in 'the light' that 'God commanded to shine out of darkness.' But can you tolerate the thought of spot, or blemish, or imperfection, or any such thing, in 'the light of the knowledge of the glory of God in the face of Jesus Christ'? (2 Cor. 4: 6).

You cannot. And you know that his glory is the glory as of the only begotten of the Father, full of grace and truth; the brightness of the Father's glory, and the express image of his person.

But what is all this glory and perfection to you, all lodged, unspotted and unblemished, in the person of the Word made flesh, if the revelation of that eternal Word in the written word be less than as unblemished and infallible?—if the written word be less the express image of the Son, than he is the express image of the Father? In vain, to you, is the infallible glory of God in the face of Jesus Christ, if the face of Jesus Christ be, in the living picture of the record, misrepresented to you; if 'the light of the glorious gospel of Christ, who is the image of God' (2 Cor. 4: 4) fail to bring out that image of God with a perfection quite infallible and divine.

I believe that when Jesus said to Philip, 'He that hath seen me hath seen the Father,' it was the express image of the Father that Philip saw. And I believe that this blessed revelation was not designed for Philip only, and those to whom Jesus then addressed himself—not 'for these alone,' but that (like the prayer of intercession that followed) it is the heritage, 'not of these alone, but of them also which shall believe on me through their word' (John 17: 20). But if Jesus looks forth upon me now from 'their word' by his Spirit, the Spirit lighting up that very word as it has been written, and Jesus thereby looking forth exactly, to the very life, as that written word (if

I may so express it) permits him; then, my Beloved—fairer than the sons of men, chiefest among ten thousand—is to me altogether lovely and the express image of the Father *only* if this word be *exactly* what the Spirit of Christ would have—written as holy men of God were moved by the Spirit—an inspired record and perfect.

Doubtless, an imperfect picture or biography of Christ might not be altogether useless. We are far from saying that it would. Far, indeed, are we from imagining that those unfriendly to plenary inspiration—unhappily believing in imperfections in the evangelists—find the four Gospels of little service to their souls; though the glorious, unique use of them which we have attempted to vindicate must of necessity be hidden from their view. We earnestly wish that on this most momentous theme they were not only almost, but altogether such as we are, excepting those bonds of our remaining darkness and depravity, which keep us back from more fully entering into the marvellous arrangement which God has made for enabling us to tabernacle always when we will with the King in these galleries of his presence. Yet we are far from thinking that no benefit can be derived from perusal of the Gospels where the present view of their specific use is not admitted. We can easily conceive of the Lord blessing them to humble souls who may unfortunately believe them to be imperfect. But far more than that; we can conceive the Lord not disdaining to acknowledge or use them—on this we would, of course, speak with great caution—even though they had not been infallible or perfect records.

But whatever use, in dealing with his people, Jesus might make of an imperfect biography of himself—calling our attention to it, commending it to our perusal, as, in so far, an approximate likeness of himself; far better than complete silence about him, a complete absence of all testimony or tradition as to the sayings and doings of his wondrous life upon the earth—one thing at least is clear. In coming to make any use of it whatever, with whatsoever explanations, cautions, or admissions, he would (we must so express it) stand outside and apart from the picture itself.

That he should enter into it, identify himself with it, invest himself with it, make it vital with his living power and vocal with his own personal voice, make it from age to age the dwelling-place of his presence, the definition, the circumspection and the expression of his gracious presence, committing himself (thoroughly, contentedly and cordially committing himself) to all generations to be judged of as he appears there—this I cannot believe, unless the biography answers his own great idea of what his own biography should be.

It must be perfect; even in all the perfection that Christ himself can give to it; indeed, in all the perfection he can claim for himself. It must be an image, as perfect in its kind in written words of Jesus—as Jesus is the perfect image in human flesh of the eternal Father.

The coalescence of the presence and the biography demands it.

No, more than that, it must be an *auto*biography. Jesus himself must be the author of it, by his Spirit.

6

THE GOSPELS—THE GALLERIES OF THE KING

If the principle explained in the preceding chapters be valid, then, according to our spirituality of mind and in proportion to the vigour and activity of our faith, the narratives of the Evangelists are to us the Galleries of the King, replete and lighted up with living and presently subsisting revelations of our Lord.

For our mental position and our privilege in reading these narratives are, in that case, entirely different—different not in degree merely, but in nature or kind—from what we experience in reading other histories. We do not reproduce the incidents to our mind's eye by a mere effort of imagination, or represent our Lord to ourselves. He presents himself to us—a very specific and quite unique phenomenon, if I may say so. Not by an effort of fancy or conception put forth by us, but as a very reality (spiritual, indeed, but not on that account less glorious—surely, rather, more so) as a very reality achieved by him, we are present with our Lord; he with us by his Spirit and word; we with him by responsive faith—responsive to the word and Spirit—in every scene which the word still mirrors and the Spirit fills with the Saviour's presence.

Does not God in very deed still dwell with men upon the earth? And is it not Emmanuel who does so—God with us? Is it not the Word made flesh that tabernacles among us that we may behold his glory, the glory as of the only-begotten of the Father, full of grace and truth? And has he not ascended far above all heavens—not in order to evacuate his name, Emmanuel, but 'to fill all things with himself'? (Eph. 4: 10). And shall he not fill his own Gospels with his presence—these galleries of the King with his glory? Shall they not have—one might almost say—a preferential claim? Assuredly. Anointed with the oil of gladness above his fellows, and sharing with everyone of them that unction, even his own Spirit, by whom he fulfils the promise, 'Lo! I am with you alway,' the King may be found at all times in these 'ivory palaces' where his 'garments smell of myrrh, and aloes, and cassia.' And it is your privilege to be with him there, O fair 'queen in gold of Ophir.' You shall 'be brought unto him in raiment of needle-work.' You shall 'enter into the King's palace' (Ps. 45: 7–15).

Let me have faith's key to these galleries, these ivory palaces of the King; and what living scenes of grace and glory may I not witness! What voices of majesty, authority, and love may I not hear! What opportunities of beholding the beauty of the Lord and inquiring in his temple may I not enjoy!

I may join with Jewish shepherd and with Gentile sage, as they worship at Bethlehem's manger. And though the scene is hidden from my eyes of flesh, that is the solitary deprivation that I suffer. The eye of faith perceives the 'sign'—'the babe in swaddling bands'—the sign of 'glory in the highest, peace on earth,' of 'good tidings of great joy which shall be to all people.' Therefore, a spectator with all saints, through faith, at Bethlehem, I sing there, with all saints, the glorious doxology and birthday song of welcome—'Unto us a child is born; unto us a son is given' (Isa. 9: 6). And being present by faith, I can hear voices there, which those who were present only by sense could not hear. I can hear the Father, 'when he bringeth in the first-begotten into the world, saying, And let all the angels of God worship him' (Heb. 1: 6). And I can hear the Son himself, 'when he cometh into the world, saying, sacrifice and offering thou wouldest not, but a body hast thou prepared me: Lo, I come to do thy will, O my God' (Heb. 5: 5). And I can hear the Spirit saying, 'Thou, Bethlehem Ephratah, though thou be little among the thousands of Judah, yet out of thee shall he

The Gospels

come forth unto me that is to be ruler in Israel; whose goings forth have been from of old, from everlasting' (Micah 5: 2). So that the beautiful language of Calvin is truly verified, 'Thus Bethlehem, where the child was born, will be to us a door by which we may enter into the presence of the eternal God.' By the same key of faith (that opens—and no man can shut) I can join with Simeon, 'just and devout, waiting for the consolation of Israel'; and in these records, made galleries of the Lord's presence by the Spirit, I can come by the same Spirit by whom Jesus dwells in them—the same Spirit also by whom Simeon came into the temple. And I can take God's holy child Jesus—free gift to me—not, indeed, in the arms of my flesh (the flesh puts me more than eighteen centuries away; it is the flesh alone that does so) but in the arms of my faith. And, blessing God in the rest to which my overflowing heart returns, and feeling that to me now to live is Christ and to die is gain, I can say—'Lord, now lettest thou thy servant depart in peace; for mine eyes have seen thy salvation which thou hast prepared *before the face of all people*' (Luke 2: 25–31).

I can be with Jesus also, along with Joseph and Mary, in the temple; when, having sought him sorrowing, they found him among the doctors, hearing them and asking them questions. And not with the ears of flesh (that only is denied me) but with the inward ear of faith, whose 'hearing cometh by the word of God,' I listen to his first recorded words of loving sonship, laborious service, loyal confession—'Wist ye not that I must be about my Father's business?' (Luke 2: 46–9).

I can be with him at Jordan, when he 'cometh to be baptized of John.' I can hear him asserting his felt responsibility 'to fulfil all righteousness.' I can see him baptized of water in symbolic indication of his union with his church. And I can hear the Father testifying by the Spirit with his spirit, and testifying to all that have an ear to hear, that even in the persons of his guilty people, and as the head of his church, he is still 'his beloved Son in whom he is well pleased'—fountain of acceptance and sonship to them (Matt. 3: 13–17).

Thereafter I can be with him in the wilderness by faith—a privilege which none possessed by sense. And not merely in the way of external spectatorship, but by faith's peculiar and profound appreciation—indeed, appropriation and fellowship—I enter into all that the great transaction imports; having learned—as baptized into him, even as at Jordan he was baptized into me—to accompany him in all his temptations and experience, as mine, and as endured for me, and to carry him with me through mine as his (Matt. 4: 1).

By the record and the Spirit; by the presence and the history; I find him in the synagogue of Nazareth, where he had been brought up (Luke 4: 16). And the Spirit is upon him still. And still he reads from the book. And still the word is in his mouth, as truly now as then. And O! assuredly he tells me—'*This day* is this Scripture fulfilled in your ears; The Spirit of the Lord God is upon me, because he hath anointed me to preach the gospel to the poor; he hath sent me to heal the broken-hearted, to preach deliverance to the captives, and recovering of sight to the blind; to set at liberty them that are bruised, to preach the acceptable year of the Lord.' It is to me that he is preaching. And I wonder at 'the gracious words that proceed out of his mouth.' I am 'astonished at his doctrine, for his word is with power.' For the covenant of his Father with him is true; his Father's Spirit that is upon him, and his words that are in his mouth, have not departed out of his mouth to 'this day'; even as they shall not depart, from henceforth and for ever (Isa. 59: 21). So that in the synagogue of Nazareth he proclaims his gospel to me—to me 'this day'—by his word and Spirit.

Thus also I can join the multitudes whom he taught from the 'mountain'; and I hear him speaking his Beatitudes and 'doctrine' with 'authority'—authority to this day undiminished—'and not as the scribes' (Matt. 5, 6, 7.).

The mountain also of his transfigured glory, I am not debarred from (Matt. 17: 8). Neither do I need to 'make tabernacles' to enjoy the presence of the glorious Lord. The very record, when the Spirit is given, is a tabernacle replenished with his glory. And is it not 'good for us to be here '?

That 'large upper room' also; why may I not keep the feast there with Jesus, and hear all the words of consolation—the fourteenth of John, and the words of intercourse with his children and with his Father that follow—coming fresh from the lips of the present Lord?

And ah! the cross of Calvary! May I not join him there, even as if now his soul were in departing, and there commit mine along with his, unto the Father; he bearing all my sin, I enjoying all his well-pleasingness in the Father's sight, a sacrifice to God for a sweet-smelling savour? Yes, 'I am crucified with Christ' (Gal. 2: 20).

If I see the blessed body of my Lord taken down from the cross and wrapped in linen, have I not a right to be there, and to protest that 'I am become dead to the law by the body of Christ'? (Luke 23: 53; Rom. 7: 4)—to protest, in the like manner, when I see it 'laid in a sepulchre that was hewn in stone, wherein never man before was laid,' that his grave shall be held as a vicarious grave; and that 'I am buried with him by baptism into death; that like as he was raised from the dead by the glory of the Father, so I also should walk in newness of life'? (Rom. 6: 4).

And so, finally, when he is risen, have I no right to be there to meet him; and to claim that, as I 'am become dead to the law by the body of Christ,' it is in order that I may be 'married to him that is now raised from the dead,' even' my Lord and my God'? True, I cannot hold him by the power of sense, and according to the flesh. But even in that, I am only sharing in the prohibition laid on Mary—'Touch me not, for I am not yet ascended.' 'Though we had known Christ after the flesh, yet now henceforth' it would be ours to 'know him so no more' (2 Cor. 5: 16); but to accompany him to Bethany, to receive his parting blessing, to return to our post and wait for the Spirit; and then—'Lo! he is with us alway.'

So may 'the King' be 'held in the galleries' (S. of S. 7: 5). And such are some of the glorious and living transactions which are evermore transpiring there.

In short, the Lord's revelation of himself in the days of his flesh, in all its essential features and details, is, by the gospel history which lives and abides for ever, projected on the plane of every generation as it passes. And when the Spirit is given to take of the things of Christ and show them unto us, the projection starts forth, to the eye of faith, with the stereoscopic,[1] statuesque fulness and solidity of actual reality. More than that, Jesus—by his Spirit adjoining himself to his own representation of himself in his biography, looking out from that true-to-life picture, with his own living countenance of majesty and love, and speaking with his own never-dying word—is truly with us.

Moreover, it is in this light most clearly 'expedient for us that he should have gone away.' His presence by the Spirit is better than his presence in the body; as in many respects, so in this, evidently; that, present in the body, he could manifest himself, as in the Galleries, one by one only; successively; his presence in one causing his absence in all the others. Present by his Spirit, he can manifest himself simultaneously in them all.

So that, perplexed with guilt, you shall find him on the cross; with temptation, in the wilderness. Seeking a testimony of your union with him and your sonship, you shall find him at the stream of Jordan. Longing to hear his gracious words, you shall find him in the synagogue of Nazareth. On the day of the melancholy last earthly duty, you shall find him weeping at the grave of Lazarus—weeping also with you. On the blessed Sabbath-day of high communion, you shall find him in the 'large upper chamber'—his banqueting house, where his banner over you is love.

The 'ivory palaces' are all open to you, O daughter of the King. And you may see 'the goings of the King' in them all (Ps. 45: 8; Ps. 68: 24).

---

[1] Would it be carrying a passing illustration too far to say that, as the beautiful stereoscopic effect—the life-like aspect of the scene—cannot be reproduced save by two pictures slightly varied by the slight alteration of the viewpoint; so the entire absence of variation—a tame exactitude and uniformity—in the Evangelists, while gaining nothing in respect of evidence, would have gone far to sacrifice the charming stereoscopic beauty and statuesque *relevo* above referred to?

PART TWO

SPECIAL INSTANCES EXAMINED

7

THE GALLERIES OF THE KING VISITED

But it is desirable that we should visit some of these galleries more deliberately, and see whether the King is really there. In other words, we propose to test the validity of the principle—the living coalescence of the presence and the history—in one or two very special instances. Let us consider, then—

I. The baptism, and its perpetual testimony.
II. The temptation, and its perpetual triumph.
III. The synagogue, and its perpetual sermon.
IV. The cross, and its perpetual sacrifice.

It must be understood, however, that it is not intended to expound (in the ordinary sense of the term) the different passages in the gospel history to which our attention will thus be directed. The object in view is to examine them with special reference to this single element or attribute of perpetuity; to investigate their susceptibility of being filled through all ages with the presence and glory of the Lord—proving, I trust, that this is a precious principle of exposition, worthy to be kept in view in all devotional use of the Gospels.

I. THE BAPTISM, AND ITS PERPETUAL TESTIMONY

'Then cometh Jesus from Galilee to Jordan unto John to be baptized of him. But John forbad him, saying, I have need to be baptized of thee, and comest thou to me? And Jesus answering, said unto him, Suffer it to be so now; for thus it becometh us to fulfil all righteousness. Then he suffered him. And Jesus, when he was baptized, went up straightway out of the water: and, lo, the heavens were opened unto him, and he saw the Spirit of God descending like a dove, and lighting upon him: and lo a voice from heaven, saying, This is my beloved Son, in whom I am well pleased' (Matt. 3: 13–17).

'By one Spirit are we all baptized into one body' (1 Cor. 12: 13).

Our Lord gave the promise, 'Lo, I am with you alway,' in connection with the command, 'Go ye, therefore, and teach all nations, baptizing them.' It will not be unsuitable, therefore—when testing, somewhat rigorously and in detail, a few eminent cases in which, by fulfilling this promise, he enshrines and reveals his presence to our faith in the gospel history—if we begin with the record of his own baptism.

If, then, Christ is present with us, looking out on us from this portion of the history, he commends himself specifically to our present regard and acceptance, as our baptized and living head, here and now in the enjoyment of his Father's testimony.

Let us, then, in the first place, consider the import of Christ's baptism—his baptism both of water and of the Spirit—and, secondly, his Father's certificate or testimony to his sonship and well-pleasingness in his sight:—our leading object, of course, being to bring out the validity and value of his perpetual presence, as here and thus revealed to us.

Our Lord's Baptism

Consider our Lord's baptism. 'Then cometh Jesus from Galilee to Jordan unto John, to be baptized of him.' 'And Jesus, when he was baptized, went up straightway out of the water; and lo, the heavens were opened unto him, and he saw the Spirit of God descending like a dove, and lighting on him.' Thus the baptism of water and the descent of the Spirit successively solicit our attention.

The Baptism of Water

And what is the specific import of that ordinance as administered to Christ, as solicited and received by him?

Let it be observed that the fundamental idea—the ground thought—in 'the doctrine of baptisms' (Heb. 4: 2) is that of engrafting, or, more generally, of uniting. This is manifest from the language of Paul—really the key to the doctrine of baptisms in 1 Cor. 12: 12–13[1]—'For as the body is one, and hath many members, and all the members of that one body, being many, are one body; so also is Christ. For by one Spirit are we all baptized into one body, whether we be Jews or Gentiles, whether we be bond or free; and have been all made to drink into one Spirit.' The members are many, but the body one. And it is baptism—not symbolical, of course, but real, and of the Spirit—it is baptism that makes many members one.

Hence, penetrating to the original and deepest idea of the sacrament, the Westminster divines say:

---

[1] The same thing is obvious from an induction of Paul's other allusions to baptism—such as those in Rom. 6: 3; Gal. 3: 27; Col. 2: 12; and 1 Cor. 10: 2. The last of these passages is very explicit. 'They were all baptized into (εἰς) Moses in the cloud and in the sea.' Their experience was such, in reference to the cloud and the sea, as to commit them inevitably to the leadership of Moses. It welded them into one compact mass or body, under Moses. It shut them up into Moses. It bound them up inextricably with his enterprise and with him. It left them no alternative. It made them one with him. It engrafted—baptized—them into Moses.

> Baptism is a sacrament, wherein the washing with water in the name of the Father, and of the Son, and of the Holy Ghost, doth signify and seal our ingrafting into Christ, and partaking of the benefits of the covenant of grace, and our engagement to be the Lord's.

Such is the import of baptism with water as administered to us. And what is thus signified and sealed by baptism with water, the baptism of the Spirit actually achieves. 'We are baptized by one Spirit into one body.'

What, then, is baptism with water, when Jesus Christ, the head of the church which is his body, solicits and receives its administration? What does it signify and seal in his case? What is the leading thought in the doctrine of baptisms—what the chief design of the sacrament of baptism—when the doctrine is illustrated in his person, when the sacrament is administered to him?

If the doctrine is not to be varied, and the sacrament is not to be evacuated of its specific meaning, and if moreover the corelative interest which the head and the members must be supposed to have in the one same ordinance of God is to be preserved exact and entire, what can the sacrament of baptism be in Christ's own case but a sign and seal of his engrafting of the church unto himself, and communicating to her the benefits of the new covenant, and his engagement to be hers—her Lord and covenant-head?

By his request for baptism with water, Jesus did, therefore, present himself as the head of the church, which is his body. He formally and expressly announced—He signified and sealed—his adoption into himself of all his elect ones; his assumption—not merely of their flesh or nature into his person, as by his birth—but his assumption of their persons into his body in covenant unity, to be represented in him before the Father and to be one with him in the eye of that law which he came to magnify and make honourable.

This engrafting of the church into one body with himself justifies and explains his acceptance of the work given him to do. On no other ground would it be right or natural that he should stand in the place of his people, bearing their responsibilities, himself their sacrifice for sin, their everlasting righteousness. He is their sacrifice, because he is their substitute and representative. And he is their representative, because he is their head. He represents them most rightfully, because he is one with them most profoundly. And being one with them most profoundly, their obligations accrue to him, and are incumbent on him, while his services are accepted in the eye of the law in their name, and his righteousness is most directly and rightfully available to them.

But if his acceptance of the church into one body with himself explains and justifies his acceptance of the work given him to do, it equally explains and justifies his request for the administration of the ordinance of baptism to himself, prior to his public entrance on that work. In the consciousness of his everlasting covenant oneness with the church as his body, in virtue of which it behoves him to bring in, on her behalf, an everlasting righteousness, he solicits the divine symbol and confirmation—the instituted sign and seal—of the union. In virtue of that union, 'by one man's obedience many are to be made righteous.' And therefore the objection of the Baptist, which would refuse him the sacramental pledge of his oneness with his people, he sets aside by the singularly pointed and beautiful reply: 'Suffer it to be so now; for thus it behoveth us to fulfil all righteousness.'

'Then he suffered him.' And Emmanuel is baptized as the head of the body; formally announced and sealed—mediator between God and man.

Is it any wonder if—'lo! the heavens are opened'? For now he is become the attested antitype of that ladder which Jacob saw (Gen. 28: 10–22), and of which he himself testified to Nathanael, saying, 'Verily, verily, I say unto you, Hereafter ye shall see heaven open, and the angels of God ascending and descending upon the Son of man' (John 1: 51). Baptized into oneness with the church as his body, he is now the medium of communication between heaven and earth.

Ah! I may have read this record of the Lord's baptism without the Lord's presence. But if, while I now read, the Saviour fulfils the promise, 'Lo! I am with you,' then, Lo! the heavens are opened unto me, even as was performed to Jacob and promised to Nathanael. In these Galleries of the King,

I hail and hold the King, as Nathanael did—'Rabbi, thou art the Son of God, thou art the King of Israel' (John 1: 49). And of these Galleries, I exclaim as Jacob did: 'Surely the Lord is in this place, and I knew it not; this is none other but the house of God, and this is the gate of heaven' (Gen. 28: 16–17).

Baptism of the Spirit

But, in this instance, not only do the angels of God ascend and descend upon the Son of man; 'The Spirit of God descended like a dove, and lighted on him' (v. 16).

What object or design can we read in this simultaneous baptism of the Spirit? He had been anointed of the Holy Ghost from the first. From the first he had received the Spirit, not by measure. Why, then, should the Spirit specially descend upon him now? What does this descent of the Spirit indicate? And what does it accomplish?

Let it be remembered that by his baptism with water at the hands of John, Jesus of Nazareth has now taken up a new position; a position, at least, not professedly and publicly taken up by him, until now. He has formally and explicitly embraced, or accepted, or confessed before men, the position and relations which the covenant of his Father had from everlasting assigned to him. By objective and external ordinance, he has welcomed and proclaimed, he has signified and sealed the engrafting into himself of all whom the Father has given to him; with his own consequent and voluntary assumption of the place belonging to their public legal head and representative before the universe, and especially before his Father's law. The Spirit—his already without measure, but acting according to the Father's promise and his own sovereign will on his human nature, and dealing with that nature as it was able to bear, and as varying circumstances and the changing exigencies of Christ's position required—descended now, in symbol, in token and pledge that now and henceforth he would act additionally on the man Christ Jesus, qualifying and sustaining him now more directly and especially for all that, as head of the body, he had been appointed in the everlasting covenant to do and to suffer and to enjoy. And how beautifully is the symbol chosen! The dove; bringing, as it were, the olive branch of peace, and announcing peace as the fruit of the Son's headship and mediation—peace, notwithstanding the sin and wrath with which the blessed Son now loads himself in adopting the persons of sinners into one body with himself.

Can we doubt, then, that the specific grace and operation of the Spirit, at this epoch and henceforth, on the man Christ Jesus, must correspond exactly to the specific design of the sacrament that has just been administered? And so, while baptism is the outward and objective seal, the Spirit is the subjective and inward seal, of that union with himself into which Jesus has formally announced that he embraces all the objects of his redeeming love.

Acting in this glorious function, as the inward and adequate seal of Christ's oneness with his people, how would the good Spirit enlarge his mind and heart to embrace in conscious and special love each and all of that countless band! Identified with them henceforth in point of law, he is henceforth to carry their interests as his own, in virtue of love. That union which, by the baptism of water, has been visibly sealed as irrefragable in objective law, the baptism of the Spirit shall inwardly seal and make irrevocable in subjective love, self-sacrificing love, such as many waters shall not quench, and the floods shall not drown. 'By one Spirit' is even Christ also, the head, 'baptized into one body' with his members.

Whatsoever therefore is now requisite or suitable in him that shall be acknowledged as the last Adam, head of the redeemed of God, First-born among many brethren, standing in the room and at the head of all, that the Holy Ghost shall now work gloriously by his grace in the man that is Jehovah's fellow, and redeemer of the sons of men. Far-reaching wisdom, and understanding, and insight into the Father's eternal counsel with himself the eternal Son (Isa. 11: 2), shall now dwell in his human intellect. Sympathy profound with the Father's electing love shall now beat true and tender in his human heart. Compassion for the countless perishing ones, and adoring desire for his Father's glory in their salvation, shall now qualify him to preach the gospel to the poor, to heal the broken hearted (Isa. 61: 1; Luke 4: 18). Patience unmurmuring; perseverance, in the face of hell's floods of opposition; mercy, in the teeth of men's own malice and rejection of him; longings for his cross, and straitenings till his baptism of blood be accomplished (Luke 12: 50); all these graces, and all others needed in his office, now publicly assumed and entered on, will the Holy Spirit of his baptism unfailingly, and unto the uttermost, operate in Jesus, the head and mediator of his church.

For when Jesus is baptized into confessed and legal union with us, as our head and mediator, the Spirit descends and rests upon him, to be unto him the Spirit of his office, and to qualify and uphold his holy humanity for all that, in it, the only-begotten of the Father shall achieve. So is he baptized of the Spirit.

He is baptized both of water and of the Spirit.

The Father's Testimony

Consider now the Father's testimony. 'And, lo, a voice from heaven, saying, This is my beloved Son, in whom I am well pleased.'

His headship has now been signified and sealed. Shall the privileges of his sonship be now placed in abeyance, or its evidence obscured? Having acknowledged himself, and been sealed in the sacrament of baptism and by the Spirit, as our head, shall the Father hesitate henceforth to own him as his Son?

This is not a question superfluous and unnecessary. For while the sonship is eternal—a necessary relation in the Godhead, and not a result of the messiahship—it is well to consider the relation in which the messiahship and the sonship stand to one another. And the baptism at Jordan assists in the investigation.

Clearly, Christ's assumption of the messiahship did not necessarily, or apart from sovereign covenant appointment, implicate or involve his sonship. A divine person he must evidently be. His godhead is manifestly necessary for his messiahship. To speak reverently, the resources of his godhead cannot be dispensed with, when he would become the head and Saviour of his body.

But is the same thing as obvious concerning his sonship? Might he not, as second person in the Godhead, accept this covenant relation without introducing into it, or being in any way understood to implicate or involve in it, his relationships, privileges and resources as the Son?

The heir of the British throne, for instance, might accept an office and fitly discharge all the duties it entails, without committing on that office (without indeed finding any scope in it for) the prerogatives and powers, the resources or interests, that may belong to him as Prince of Wales. Let the humble comparison—where all comparisons must necessarily be very humble—be followed out. Might not the Word have been made flesh without his sonship being brought forward, or specially revealed, or attested, or drawn upon, or made to yield any aids of grace, love and glory in the work given him to do?

We know indeed that the Word was made flesh and dwelt among us, even so as that we beheld his glory most peculiarly as the glory of the only-begotten of the Father. But this is of special sovereign appointment and grace. And all Scripture shows that, in the infinite riches of the grace of God, the sonship of the eternal Word has been, in all the strength and depth of its relation and resources, involved into the office and work of the messiahship?[1]

[1] This, I believe, will go far to explain the passages which seem, *prima facie*, to ground the sonship on the messiahship. They do not grant sonship to Messiah, in the sense of admitting, or acknowledging, or announcing, a new relation. They grant, or admit, or acknowledge—they vindicate or proclaim—his Sonship, prior and eternal, as committed or embarked on his office and work as messiah; so that, in his office and work, he shall, on the one hand, be acceptable to the Father, *as the Father*, the signatures and traces of the sonship shining gloriously on all that messiah proffers and presents unto the Father in his people's name; and so that, in his office and work, also, he shall, on the other hand, be precious and profitable to the aliens, exactly meeting their case *as such*, laying open his sonship to their perception and participation—in so much that it shall be impossible to see him without seeing God peculiarly as the Father (John 14: 9), and impossible to receive him without thereby receiving the adoption of sons (John 1: 12; Gal. 4: 4-5). But this leads out into a great theme, worthy of a volume for itself.

Hence, at various stages of that work, the sonship is specially, and, one might almost say, solicitously attested. The eternal sonship of the mediator is again and again made to shine out, vindicated into all its own light and honour, forth from behind all obscuring veils, and up from beneath all depressing burdens.

Thus, for instance, at his birth. When he assumed the likeness of sinful flesh, being made of a woman, made of no reputation, being found in fashion as a man and in the form of a servant, it was not merely declared from heaven that he who appeared in this lowly estate was God, but the special glory of his divine sonship was asserted. His sonship is not pretermitted, disallowed, held in abeyance, or obscured, in his incarnation. The annunciation to the Virgin contains this express clause: 'That holy thing that shall be born of thee shall be called the Son of God' (Luke 1: 35). Without prejudice to his being the Son of God, he becomes the Son of man. His messiahship, as Son of man, shall be replete with all his fulness of grace and truth; all his unsearchable riches of love and interest, of acceptability and prevailing advocacy with the Father; all his glory, as the only-begotten of the Father. This is expressly testified concerning him at his birth.

But he is one with us, not only by his birth, not only in respect of a common nature, but by baptism, or engrafting, into one body with us also. Perhaps union so close as this may cloud the evidence, or conceal the glory, or place in abeyance for a time the claims and powers of, his sonship. Identified as he now is with countless myriads of the guilty, how can we

---

Why has the subject of adoption—so rich and fertile in fine thought and feeling, so susceptible also of beautiful theological treatment—been so little investigated and illustrated? It belongs to the category of *relative* grace, and forms the sweet complement and sparkling crown of justification by faith. On justification by faith we have abundant and most precious authorship, for around that doctrine and privilege the great battle of controversy as to relative grace has raged. But the conquerors seem to have paused, exhausted or contented with the victory. Ought it not rather to commend the subject of adoption, that it may be treated apart from controversy? It is certain, however, that a good treatise on adoption—such as should at once do justice to the fine theology of the question, and to the precious import of the privilege—is a desideratum.

The Galleries of the King Visited

expect that the Father should be forward to own him as a Son? To acknowledge his sonship at such a time would seem quite equivalent to extending it—extending it to all whom he has baptized and united into himself.

For the Christ now, after his baptism, must be regarded as including more than the Christ at the incarnation. He must be understood and acknowledged now—and especially if acknowleged in immediate connection with, and obvious reference to, his baptism—as not merely the individual Jesus in his own single person as the head, but as the whole body mystical. For now it may be said, 'As the body is one, and hath many members, and all the members of that one body, being many, are one body; so also is Christ' (1 Cor. 12: 12). Clearly it is so now, formally and confessedly, by the baptism of the living head. Into his one body the members are all baptized by the Spirit, and into union with them all in one has the head himself been baptized. The whole body, therefore, is recognized by the Spirit, and sealed by baptism, as one in Christ.

But the infinitely gracious design of the Father is exactly to extend this sonship to all the body, in so far as, in the nature of things, it can be extended. He means to testify that 'he hath predestinated us unto the adoption of children by Jesus Christ to himself, according to the good pleasure of his will, to the praise of the glory of his grace, wherein he hath made us accepted in the Beloved' (Eph. 1: 5, 6). He means emphatically to tell us that, 'as many as receive him, to them will he give power to become the sons of God' (John 1: 12). He means to give us full assurance that the eternal sonship, loaded, and, in a sense, obscured as it must be by the burden the Son hath now taken upon himself in our guilty persons, with all our sin and curse—abides still, in his sight, a relationship of such delight, love and infinite well-pleasingness as outweighs all the displeasing efficacy of that sin that now lies upon him. And when he who is now baptized of water and of the Spirit shall have been baptized—and he will henceforth be straitened till that other baptism be accomplished—even with his own atoning blood, an offering and a sacrifice of a sweet-smelling savour for sinners, then (says the Father) the love wherewith

I have loved him shall be in them also (John 17: 26). For now that he is baptized into acknowledged union with them, sealing that union with my own Spirit, I now also, with express reference to that oneness thus attested, bear witness that 'This is my beloved Son, in whom I am well pleased.'

But if this testimony declares the acceptance and sonship in the eternal Son of all that are baptized into him, then the baptism of Christ is of presently subsisting value to us. Moreover the testimony lives and abides for ever; a heavenly formula—an everlasting oracle—from age to age inaugurating all the sons of the adoption.

Be invited, then, to meet the King in these galleries, to meet the living head in his baptism at Jordan, and to hear and receive his Father's testimony.

Meet The Living Head

Lo! Jesus is with you as receiving baptism—baptism both of water and of the Spirit. Meet with him and embrace him in the very character which, present with you in this portion of the gospel history, he sustains. Behold him baptizing, engrafting you into himself; and be you baptized and engrafted into him. His presence with you, as looking out on you here in the permanence of this glorious transaction, must surely make it easy for you to do this.

Shall the living head now stand before you as in the act of engrafting sinful men into himself, although he thereby entails upon himself the wrath of God due to their iniquities—the obligation of fulfilling all righteousness on their behalf, even through the baptism of the bloody tree, and through the prison of the darksome grave? And will not you be baptized of the Spirit into him, when you thereby become a beloved son, well-pleasing to the Father in his only-begotten; and lo! the heavens are opened to receive you? If you see him, by baptism into you, taking your place and sin and curse of alienation deep and bitter, will not you, by baptism into him, take his place and righteousness and blessing of sonship inalienable and everlasting?

Call to mind your baptism. Call to mind his. His was true and real. Let yours be equally so. By his, he meant union with you. By yours, embrace, and protest as true, union with him. Let his baptism be the foundation of yours. Rest your baptism upon his. Graft your baptism into his. Let his baptism into you be, as it were, alike and at once the root and reason, the model and motive, of your baptism into him. Be baptized because he was baptized. Be baptized as he was baptized. Be baptized in prosecution and in full attainment of the end for which he was baptized. Be baptized in living concert with him. Be baptized into one body with him.

Lo! he is with you now, expressly as baptized into you, that you, so receiving him, may be baptized of the Spirit into him.

Hear and Receive His Father's Testimony

And mark, secondly, how when thus baptized into him, and being hidden in him, you may hear the ever-living testimony sounding still, even as the baptized head is present still. For your baptism now entitles you to the Father's testimony. And the Spirit conveys it. For the Spirit himself beareth witness with our spirit, that we are the children of God; being joint-sons and joint-heirs with Christ' (Rom. 8: 16–17).

See how, in another passage (Gal. 3: 26–8), Paul ranges into such orderly series and connection these three things:—the sonship; the baptism; the oneness. There is first the sonship—'We are all the children of God by faith in Jesus Christ' (v. 26). But this is grounded on true baptism—baptism or engrafting by the Spirit—'For as many as have been baptized into Christ have put on Christ' (v. 27). And such baptism effects an indissoluble oneness of Christ and his members, and therefore of the members among themselves: 'There is neither Jew nor Greek, there is neither bond nor free, there is neither male nor female; for ye are all one in Christ Jesus' (v. 28).

This oneness you enjoy when baptized into Christ and abiding in him; and therefore, also, this sonship. And the perpetual testimony of the sonship you need not want, if you only abide in Christ as present with you—truly baptized into you, and you into him.

For when you thus dwell in him, the Father cannot seal and attest him without thereby sealing and attesting you. The Father cannot separate between you and him. This were to disavow his Son's baptism, which instead he sealed by the descent of the Spirit, and accepted as a most fit occasion for testifying his sonship. You rejoice in that baptism of your living head. You receive him as baptized into union with his own body. You are greatly facilitated in your reception of him by his presentation of himself to you in this very attitude and transaction of his baptism. Lo! he is with you as on Jordan's banks. And you receive him, and flee into him, and are baptized into him, and abide in him; and you cannot be rightly dealt with except as in him. Neither by yourself nor by the Father can you be truly regarded, except as in Christ, the living head.

But listen! The Father testifies of the Son. He speaks of that living head exactly as the head, exactly as baptized into indissoluble union with you—a baptism that has greatly prevailed to win you over into union with him. The Father speaks of him, now that he is identified with you, bound up with you by baptism, and you with him, as having one interest with him, as having one Spirit with him, as having one mind with him, as being one living organism with him, as having—shall we say?—one ear with him. And when, therefore, that Father testifies of him, now and in these circumstances, is he not testifying of you, and saying in your ear what he said in his; testifying of you all that he testified of him; pointing unto you, as he cannot help doing now if he point unto the Son, for now you are *in him*—and saying therefore truly concerning *you*—'This is my beloved son, in whom I am well pleased'?

Surely this is the ever-living testimony of your sonship, even as it is of his.

In these galleries of the King, then, in this glorious hall of the ivory palaces, we recognize the great Charter-room of our

The Galleries of the King Visited

Adoption; the scene also of our own marriage-union in the Spirit to the eternal Son, our living head. It is here, O fair Queen, that you are first virtually saluted by your lovely and so acceptable title, 'the King's daughter.' And 'hearken, O daughter, and consider, and incline thine ear; forget also thine own people and thy father's house; so shall the King greatly desire thy beauty: for he is thy Lord, and worship thou him' (Ps. 45: 10).

Hearken also, O church of the living God, how, in this Chapel of the Baptism—this Royal Hall of the Adoption—your King testifies of the multitudes of your children; and how he tells you, 'I will say unto the north, Give up; and to the south, Keep not back; bring my sons from far, and my daughters from the ends of the earth' (Isa. 43: 6). And he will make their gathering to you both swift and safe. 'Thy children shall make haste; thy destroyers and they that made thee waste shall go forth of thee' (Isa. 49: 17). And an animating sight it is to see them come, swift and multitudinous, none daring to hinder or to make them afraid. Contemplate that scene, O daughter, by faith and hope. 'Lift up thine eyes round about and behold: all these gather themselves together and come unto thee. As I live, saith the Lord, thou shalt surely clothe thee with them all, as with an ornament, and bind them on thee, as a bride doeth' (v. 18).

A goodly band—a countless throng—of adopted ones shall join you here, O Queen. 'And with gladness and rejoicing shall they be brought; they shall enter into the King's palace. Instead of thy fathers shall be thy children, whom thou mayest make princes in all the earth' (Ps. 45: 15–16); indeed, royal priests unto God. For truly the Father so accepts them; as sons and priests in the high priest and eternal Son himself. And even like Christ, and as being in Christ, none of them glorifies himself to be made a priest; but he who says unto him, 'Thou art my Son, to-day have I begotten thee' (Heb. 5: 5). For does he not say this, in Christ, to every the chiefest prodigal among them all; when, moved of the Spirit, he doth arise and come unto the Father, through the Son; even as no man can come unto the Father but by him? Does not the Father own that baptism of the Spirit which has made the prodigal one with his only-begotten? Does he not welcome him with the very love and welcome wherewith he greets that only-begotten one himself? Does not his sweet paternal voice, continually living by the Spirit of the Lord in this gospel history, break in upon the now spiritual ear of such an one, in deepest tenderness and love? And may not such an one hear, as the testimony of his own adoption, the blessed oracle—'This is my beloved son: in him I am well pleased'?

Blessed is the one who has been with the Beloved here.

Yet temptation awaits you—'if thou be the son of God.'

Let us proceed, therefore, in these Galleries, to the Citadel, where the Son, and the sonship, and the sons, are assailed—in vain.

II. THE TEMPTATION,
AND ITS PERPETUAL TRIUMPH

'Then was Jesus led up of the Spirit into the wilderness, to be tempted of the devil. And when he had fasted forty days and forty nights, he was afterward an hungered. And when the tempter came to him, he said, If thou be the Son of God, command that these stones be made bread. But he answered and said, It is written, Man shall not live by bread alone, but by every word that proceedeth out of the mouth of God. Then the devil taketh him up into the holy city, and setteth him on a pinnacle of the temple, and saith unto him, If thou be the Son of God, cast thyself down: for it is written, he shall give his angels charge concerning thee; and in their hands they shall bear thee up, lest at any time thou dash thy foot against a stone. Jesus said unto him, It is written again, Thou shalt not tempt the Lord thy God. Again, the devil taketh him up into an exceeding high mountain, and sheweth him all the kingdoms of the world, and the glory of them; and saith unto him, All these things will I give thee, if thou wilt fall down and worship me. Then saith Jesus unto him, Get thee hence, Satan: for it is written, Thou shalt worship the Lord thy God, and him only shalt thou serve. Then the devil leaveth him, and, behold, angels came and ministered unto him' (Matt. 4: 1–11).

The Galleries of the King Visited

'Ye are they which have continued with me in my temptations: and I appoint unto you a kingdom, as my Father hath appointed unto me' (Luke 22: 28–9).

Here is the citadel, or fortress. It is the King's impregnable trilateral. And its three sides are loaded evermore with the ordnance of the mediatorial kingdom, all in full force and play, in ceaseless action, pouring down their deadly fire continually upon the foe whom they have so often ploughed and scarred already. And lo! the King is known for a refuge here. For he is alway here, even to the end of the world. His two-edged sword, proceeding from his mouth, flashes here continually in the eyes of the enemy. Here he breaks the arrows of the bow, the shield, the sword, and the battle; himself more glorious and excellent than the mountains of prey (Ps. 76: 3–4).

Here, the sons of the adoption, baptized and engrafted into the eternal Son, must do battle, in conjunction with him and under him, in defence of their sonship; as here he defended his. Nor is the issue of the battle which is really waged here in doubt. Every combatant who dwells and abides here by faith shall be more than conqueror. 'And he that overcometh shall inherit all things; and I will be his God, and he shall be my son' (Rev. 21: 7). His assaulted sonship shall be perfectly protected here, and at last publicly acknowledged—saith the Lord. For thus do all the faithful serve themselves heirs to the promise; having realized in themselves the description; 'Ye are they that have continued with me in my temptations. And I appoint unto you the kingdom which my Father hath appointed unto me.' And lo! he is here, in his temptations, that we may continue with him in them.

Yes; we have Christ's presence in this portion of the gospel history very eminently: the presence of the captain of salvation in this entrenched camp, where our lot is cast and our cause is safe, in the wilderness.

For the history does not here record a wholly past event. It reveals an abiding state of things, a battle still 'continuing.' This conflict is prolonged through the whole history of the church; through the whole, still current, campaign that opened with the proclamation of a war unparalleled—'I will put enmity between thee and the woman, and between thy seed and her seed; it shall bruise thy head, and thou shalt bruise his heel' (Gen. 3: 15).

And if the war still rages round the camp, is the King not here himself? And if he be, is he present any otherwise than as revealing himself in the history? Truly he is looking out from the battlements of his fortress still. 'He standeth behind our wall, he looketh forth at the windows, showing himself through the lattice' (S. of S. 2: 9). Tried faith, assaulted by the enemy, finds her living head present in his history here at this epoch very specially. And faith shall clear herself from all complicity with fancy or fanaticism when she boldly maintains that—Lo! he is here, defending the camp and repelling the foe, as of old.

For, in the first place, the assault is carried on by the enemy only because he knows that Christ is here—and it is the same assault prolonged. In the second place, the defence is possible, and is carried on, by the church, only because she knows that Christ is here—and it is the same defence prolonged. And, in the third place, the issue is the same, because Christ is with us now exactly as in the wilderness then; prolonging his action and victory perpetually.

The Identity of the Assault

The assault is carried on by the enemy because he knows that Christ is here; and it is the same assault prolonged.

For, against what is it specifically that the enemy, with such persevering subtlety, directs his attack?

It is our Lord's sonship. 'If thou be the Son of God, command that these stones be made bread' (v. 3). 'If thou be the Son of God, cast thyself down' (v. 6). And if the Lord hath said unto thee—'Thou art my Son, this day have I begotten thee: Ask of me, and I will give thee the heathen for thine inheritance, and the uttermost parts of the earth for thy possession'; it looks little like it, if thou hast not even 'thy daily bread'; for how then should 'thy kingdom come'? No; accept the 'kingdoms of the world and the glory of them' from me (v. 8–9).

The Galleries of the King Visited

All the three shafts of his quiver are aimed against the sonship.

But it is not the sonship absolutely considered that Satan assails. It is the sonship as testified at Jordan. It is not the sonship of Christ considered in his own private person merely. It is his sonship in his public character, as representative, head and elder brother, of all the sons of the adoption.

It is the baptized Christ whose sonship Satan assails; even as it is the baptized Christ whose sonship the Father has testified. By his baptism into union with you, the Son hath laid his sonship open as a fountain of adoption to you. And the Father's approbation has been indicated. '*Immediately* the Spirit driveth him into the wilderness. And he was there in the wilderness forty days tempted of Satan' (Mark 1: 12–13). Is it possible to doubt that the temptation is the counterpart to the baptism, and that in the temptation the sonship is assaulted, exactly in the very relations and in the very light in which it is brought out in the baptism?

It is for your sake that Christ's sonship is assailed. It is because he has been baptized into you; sealed of the Spirit and witnessed of the Father, as the Son, beloved and well-pleasing, notwithstanding his union with you; you thereby a son, well-pleasing and beloved. For this reason is the sonship the object of attack. It is assailed because the Son shares it with you. It is the common sonship which is assailed.

Satan, doubtless, is shrewd enough and subtle enough to know that the eternal sonship, absolutely considered, as a relation simply of the eternal Word in the Godhead, is infinitely beyond his reach. His sonship, as apart from you, he would never think of assaulting.

Satan, also, is shrewd enough and subtle enough to know that any sonship of yours, absolutely considered, such as might be held to be involved in your relation simply as a creature to your creator, is infinitely beneath his contempt. Such sonship of yours, as apart from Christ, he would never trouble himself to assault.

But sonship in Christ, as laid open to you; and sonship in you, as enjoyed in Christ; that he will assault. For the sonship of sinners is not now, apparently, so utterly beneath his contempt, when grafted on the sonship of the eternal Son. Nor is the sonship of the eternal Son now, apparently, so utterly beyond his power, when loaded as it is with the destiny of sinners. If the Son is baptized into sinners, and sinners are baptized into the Son; may not the sin so peril the sonship that a triumph may be neither, on the one hand, impossible, nor, on the other, worthless?

It is the baptism—it is the oneness—which induces Satan to assail the sonship. And the battle is absolutely one, whether the sonship is assailed in Christ or in you.

The enemy never thought of tempting Christ concerning his sonship, till Christ was baptized into you and acknowledged as a Son, well-pleasing, even though united to you. And he never thought of tempting you concerning any sonship of yours, till you were baptized into Christ, and acknowledged as a son, well-pleasing, because united unto him. It is the oneness that causes the battle. And surely the battle is one.

Now mark how by reason of the baptism—Christ's into you, yours into him—the sonship, alike in him and in you, presents itself in circumstances that seem to render an assault upon it feasible to the foe. For it comes forward on the field in circumstances most disadvantageous, if not dangerous.

It cannot but be so, when sonship is in any conjunction with sin. Immediately, on such conjunction, the sonship though not overthrown is concealed. Its fulness of grace and truth, its impregnable, inviolable security, its splendours of convincing evidence, its unsearchable riches of privilege, its incorruptible and undefiled inheritance that fadeth not away—all retire out of view and remain concealed. They may all abide most sure and full—in the spiritual kingdom that transcends time and sense. But on the platform of temporal interests and things palpable to sense and reason the evidence of the sonship has vanished. And not only so. All that on that platform might seem relevant to the question gives an adverse testimony. The Son would appear to be treated as an outcast. Apparently he is disowned.

This is—temptation. It is the essence—it is the great and all-embracing case—of temptation. To be a son of God, verily and irrefragably; and yet to have no evidence of it within the sphere of sense and time and reason; but everything in these categories rather contradicting your claim—this is your probation of God while here; this is what Satan malignantly manages against you.

Into this very position the eternal Son was pleased to enter, when he brought his divine person and eternal sonship into our service; and was baptized into union with us, most sinful aliens. His sonship remained. The descending Spirit sealed it, and testified with his spirit that he was the Son of God. Indeed, the Spirit led him into the wilderness to be tempted. And 'as many as are led by the Spirit of God, they are the sons of God': a truth holding good pre-eminently of him who is the first-born among many brethren, the Son in his own eternal right. And the Father bore witness of him as the Son—'This is my beloved Son, in whom I am well pleased.'

His sonship remained. And the Spirit sealed it. And the Father witnessed of it. But in the region of the things that are seen and temporal, all proof of it vanished.

Hence, Satan's hope. And hence, the style of his assault.

1. What! The Son of God? And no bread for thy hungry body? Thy Father, who placed his son Adam amidst plenty and in the garden of delights, when thou needest bread, gives thee a stone? And yet he can turn these stones into sons—sons to Abraham! Is this dealing with thee as if thou wert a Son? But Adam, then, was sinless; and thou hast cast in thy lot with the fallen sons of fallen Adam. And thy sonship thou hast perilled for them. Behold! then, what ruin hath happened to it. Thy Father treats thee as an outcast now. Not in words, but in strongly-speaking deeds—in systematic dealings—he disowns thy sonship now.

2. What! The Son of God? And yet despised and rejected of men? Above all, rejected of the sacred people? Can the Son of God not compel their astonishment, veneration, and acceptance? Cast thyself down from this pinnacle of the temple into the holy city. Thy Father's angels will charge themselves with thy safety and rejoice to see thy glory. Shall they not be a life-guard—a body-guard of

honour—to the son of the King of kings? And the people shall impatiently make thee a king.
3. What! The Son of God? And no inheritance? No kingdom in the world? No glory? And yet the oracle said, 'Thou art my Son; this day have I begotten thee' (Ps. 2: 7). And it promised thee an inheritance for the asking, 'Ask of me, and I will give thee the heathen for thine inheritance, and the uttermost parts of the earth for thy possession' (v. 8). And behold! Thou hast not where to lay thy head: nor any kingdom of any kind here, save what thou mayest consent to receive from me? Such havoc has thy baptism of lost aliens into thyself made of thy sonship, and thine inheritance as the Son!

But—In the *first* place, my sonship appertains to a realm or world far above that of sense and time; a realm whose verities neither bread nor stones can prove nor disprove. I will seek the evidences of my sonship in the kingdom to which it belongs; where the evidence, all-sufficient, is—my Father's word. 'Man liveth not by bread only, but by every word that proceedeth out of the mouth of God.'

Nor, *secondly*, because I claim to live as the Son of God in a realm transcending earth and reason, will I therefore burst all laws and bonds and limits imposed on those who sojourn here below. Dwelling with men, in this lower realm—the Son of God from the higher world—all this world's constitution and arrangements appointed of my Father will I dutifully observe. I will not cast myself down. 'I will not tempt the Lord my God.'

And, *thirdly*, though I look for a kingdom in this very realm of sense and time, it is no such kingdom as the god of this world could give. It can accrue to me, and be acceptable to me, only by the powers of the unseen, spiritual, eternal realm—the kingdom of heaven—sanctifying the kingdoms of this world, and embracing the realm of the sensible into the realm of the spiritual and heavenly and holy. 'Get thee behind me, Satan.'

I content myself with the proof of my sonship which the heavenly realm affords. I content myself with the appointed subjection to the laws and limits which my presence in this lower realm imposes. I content myself with waiting for the time when the higher realm, with its holy powers, shall penetrate and pervade the lower, and heaven shall sanctify for me a kingdom on the earth. Meantime my sonship and my inheritance are safe. 'Get thee behind me, Satan.'

Now, it is not merely the same sonship that is assailed in you. The circumstances in which it is assailed, the grounds of the assailant's hope and the style of the assault are the same.

Baptized, or engrafted, by faith into Christ, you are a son of God in his eternal Son. And the whole evidence of your sonship is spiritual. It consists, subjectively, in the seal and witness of the Spirit; and, objectively, in the word and call of the Father. When baptized into Christ, you have the same evidence of your sonship, as he had of his when baptized into you. On the one hand, 'Because ye are sons God hath sent forth the Spirit of his Son into your heart, crying, Abba, Father'—'testifying also with your spirit that you are a son of God' (Gal. 4: 6; Rom. 8: 16). On the other hand, 'Behold what manner of love the Father hath bestowed upon us that you should be called the sons of God' (1 John 3: 1). Inwardly, you have the Spirit's seal; and outwardly, the Father's word. These are the evidences of your sonship when united to Christ—as they were of his, when united to you.

But clearly in your case, as in his, they are spiritual; they do not belong to the realm of the material and temporal. And being spiritual, they are hidden; often hidden from yourself; being seen only by faith: and your faith is not always strong and clear. But whether hidden from you, through unbelief, or not, they are always hidden from sense. You are entitled to maintain your sonship; indeed, to maintain it with all boldness, as a present and a sure prerogative in Christ—'Now are we the sons of God' (1 John 3: 2). We 'are' the sons of God. We are his sons, even 'now.'

But you must grant that 'it doth not yet appear what you shall be' (v. 2). A sure and present prerogative, it is far from being an obvious one. It is by no means 'apparent.' The realm of the visible and earthly furnishes no proof of it whatever.

Rather, all that transpires with you there might seem to go against the truth of it.

Yes! if I am united to the Son, and sealed by the Spirit, and acknowledged by the Father, I must admit that my sonship is nevertheless not apparent; nor can I point to any tokens or badges of it discernible to the eye of sense. Though I claim to be a son of God, I must admit, that, all things considered, to the carnal mind it does not look like it. I have no visible fairest robe upon me—to point to as my Father's gift, and compel the world's acknowledgment. I have no material garments for beauty and for comeliness, no crown of glory sitting on my brow, no palm of victory waving in my hand.

High is the rank and lofty the renown implied in being sons to the King of kings and Lord of hosts. When the world demands some proof of our claim, it might be expected that we should be able to point to some grand and faith-compelling demonstration. But no. 'It doth not yet appear.' Frankly must we own that no perceptible priestly robes of primogeniture, whiter than the snow, adorn us; and no fair mitre made after any pattern shown in the mount, to certify that we are priests. No throne, no sceptre, no regalia have we—in proof that Christ has loved us and made us kings. And no Mahanaim of the Lord, no visible angelic hosts, encompass us on either hand proclaiming, 'Thus shall it be done to the man whom the king delighteth to honour.' Nor do the forests clap their hands at our approach, nor the mountains and the hills break forth into singing, in welcome to the sons and heirs of the King of glory.

Rather, the whole creation groans because our sonship is hidden, waiting for the manifestation of it (Rom. 8: 19). There is a shameful cross lying heavy on our shoulder, rather than a graceful diadem shining on our head. No palm of victory is ours, but the trembling and the toil of battle. Diseases grapple with our frame, having no respect to our adoption. And manifold afflictions fall on us—even more than on other men (Ps. 73)—and the sighings thereof clash rudely on the ear of sense with our high claim to be the family and seed-royal of heaven. And death at last confronts us, and makes it far more manifest that we are victims of the loathsome grave, than sons of God and immortality: as if we must say unto corruption—not to God—Thou art my Father; and to the worm, Thou art my sister; rather than the Son of God call us his brethren. Verily our sonship is concealed. 'Our life is hid.'

But 'our life is hid with Christ in God.' Our sonship is concealed, with the only-begotten himself, in the bosom of the Father. Hence it is, to Satan, an object of assault, as Christ's was. Or rather, it is assailed in us, exactly as in him. We continue with him in his temptations and in all our afflictions he is afflicted. It must be so. For the sons of the adoption and the eternal Son are mutually baptized into each other, sealed by the same Spirit of peace, and attested in the one utterance of the Father. And the common sonship, alike circumstanced in him and in them, sustains the one same reiterated or prolonged assault.

Mark the sameness of the assault as sustained by you. And mark the sameness of the enemy's threefold stroke as he aims to pierce or cleave your shield of faith.

For, your sonship—your filial life of faith—as a sonship concealed, as a hidden life, presents itself in these three aspects: It is a life of sonship whose security is perfect; its seclusion profound; it manifestation or disclosure postponed. In each of these, its three great conditions, the enemy assails it. He assails this great trilateral on all sides.

1. This sonship of yours, this filial life in the favour of God, the tempter would have you doubt its security. He hints that it is in the utmost peril. He points to your poverty; your infirmity; your ignominious lot; your heavy cross; your utter want of sensible evidence of any such prerogative, and the strong presumptive—*prima facie*—evidence against it. And with subtle malice, tempting you outside the spiritual sphere, in which your life is safe, and your evidence of sonship all sufficient, he proposes carnal methods to secure its safety, as if it appertained to this present transitory world—'Command these stones that they be made bread.'

No; you reply, in the eternal Son—or he in you. Its safety is not endangered. For it is a sonship to be realized in faith (John 1: 12, Gal. 3: 26)—a life that I must live by faith. And faith cometh by hearing, and hearing by the Word of God—'Man shall not live by bread only, but by every word that proceedeth out of the mouth of God.'

2. Well; but if it be so secure as this, you need not keep it so secluded. Bring it forth in its glory from its quiet, unpretending retreat. If its safety is so perfect, and its evidence so sufficient, in the supernatural realm that transcends space and time—why be in bondage to the laws of space and time? Surely you can make free with them—son of the great King, as you profess to be. Cast yourself down from this height. Alight, as on the up-bearing wings of the angelic hosts, on Jerusalem's thronging streets, or in the crowded court of worshippers below. And compel from them, by such a token, their credence of your sonship to God.

No; you reply, in the eternal Son—or he in you. The unbroken seclusion of my filial life shall not thus be invaded. The Lord shall hide me in the secret of his presence. He shall cover me with his feathers, and under his wings will I trust. I will not tempt the Lord my God.

3. But see how long your inheritance is delayed, how drearily the manifestation of your sonship is postponed. Why should you scruple to anticipate—to force out—a demonstration, to hasten the revelation of your glory? Assume the dominion promised you as a son, as the heir of all things. Cut short the weary painful route, in which alone—by patience and obedience and suffering and shame and death—does the crown seem likely to be reached or the promised glory unveiled. Accept at my hand, by a trifling concession, the kingdoms of the world and the glory of them. Receive your satisfying portion from me. For hope deferred makes your heart sick.

No; you reply, in the eternal Son—or he in you. My hope maketh not ashamed; my hope is an anchor of my soul sure and steadfast, entering into that within the veil where the glory is. And if I hope for that I see not, then do I with patience wait for it. In God's own time the 'manifestation' of his sons and their glory shall come; and the whole creation, now groaning in sympathy with their affliction during the concealment of their sonship, 'shall be delivered from the bondage of corruption into the liberty of the glory of the sons of God' (Rom. 8: 21). My soul, wait thou only upon God; for my expectation is from him. How long, O enemy, wilt thou imagine mischief against me. Thou only consultest to cast me down from mine excellency; thou delightest in lies (Ps. 62). 'Get thee behind me, Satan.'

Thus in union with Christ—Christ present with you in this portion of the gospel history, in this entrenched camp in the wilderness—you are assaulted, *first*, as to the security of your sonship. But it is safe. And you abide in peace, not faithless, but believing, living by your Father's word (that word which has already said to the eternal Son in you, and to you in him)—'This is my beloved Son; I am well pleased in him.' The seclusion of your sonship, *secondly*, is sought to be invaded, and you are tempted to bring it out in collision with the conditions under which in this world you are placed. But you maintain its secrecy notwithstanding. You cultivate an unseen fellowship with God. You abide under the shadow of the Almighty. The manifestation of your sonship, *thirdly*, you are tempted to anticipate. But you oppose the suggestion with your patience. You have continued with the Son in his temptations, and he hath appointed unto you, in communion with himself, the kingdom which the Father hath appointed unto him. You can refuse, therefore, to be indebted to the enemy for anything whatever. You will endure no proposed compromise with him. You defy him. And you discard him. 'Get thee behind me, Satan.'

In every point of view, then, is not the assault on you exactly a prolongation of the assault on Christ? And is it not prolonged just because, lo! Christ is with you in this entrenched camp in the wilderness, this impregnable citadel of the King's Galleries? It is, in fact, the presence of the King that draws down upon you his adversary's wrath—'As it is written, *for thy sake* we are killed all the day long.' Nevertheless, 'in all these things we are more than conquerors,' also, *'through him that loved us'* (Rom. 8: 36–7).

The Identity of the Defence

For not the assault only, the defence also is the same. And it is not the mere general scope and drift of the defence that is similar, analogous, or coincident. The instrumentality wielded then and now is identical. So also is the power wielding it. The armour is the same: so also is the source of strength and skill. For the instrumentality or armour is—the word. The power or source of skill and strength is—the Spirit.

It is of the essence of Christ's position in this conflict that he has humbled himself to be dependent wholly on the Word and Spirit of God for his defence in this battle.

Consider, again, what his position is. He has just completed a very solemn transaction. He has received the administration of a holy sacrament, in which he has ostensibly and professedly taken up the position of surety and representative and head of the fallen children whom the Father hath given him. He has become to them a second Adam. He has been baptized into one body with them. And the Spirit has descended as the seal of the union. And the word of the Father proclaims his approbation of it; vindicating the sonship and righteousness of the Son, as not imperilled by the guilt and alienation of those with whom he is now identified. For the Father has respect to that baptism of blood which will clear all that guilt away, and will admit the guilty into the fellowship of Christ's well-pleasing righteousness, and the aliens into the privilege of his sonship. Baptized into his new position, Christ is furnished with the Spirit and Word of God—the sealing, strengthening Spirit, the approving, comforting word.

Immediately his destiny is one of temptation. And by the Spirit and Word of God he meets it.

Yes: immediately temptation is his lot. The narrative points out an immediate succession in the circumstances. The third chapter closes with the story of the baptism; and the fourth opens with the record of the temptation in terms that imply no interval between—'Then was Jesus led up of the Spirit

The Galleries of the King Visited

into the wilderness to be tempted of the devil.' With Luke, the same connection was clearly in view—'And Jesus being full of the Holy Ghost returned from Jordan, and was led by the Spirit into the wilderness' (Luke 4: 1). And Mark is more emphatic on this point than any of the other evangelists; for having narrated the incident of the baptism in terms similar to theirs, he adds—'And immediately the Spirit driveth him into the wilderness' (Mark 1: 12).

There is no delay. There can be no reprieve. Immediately when Jesus has signified and sealed his union with those who fell from pristine holiness through temptation—temptation becomes his own personal lot.

For his union with them is real—intensely real. It is a union in which he is to master by experience all the circumstances of their lot, personal sin alone excepted. If they fell through temptation, he is to stand—to stand steadfast and victorious—amidst temptation's utmost power. The same tempter, also, to whom the first Adam succumbed is to fail with the second; all his force and wiles being allowed their utmost scope, in order that they may be baffled and confounded. And as Messiah's chosen ones can, in any circumstances, enter heaven only through temptations that shall follow them up to the celestial gates—as if a band of soldiers fought their way, hand to hand, through the narrow streets of a hostile city, exposed to a galling fire from every roof and loopholed wall on either hand—the Captain of Salvation, bringing many sons unto glory, himself takes the lead, presenting his own person to the chiefest brunt of the enemy's fire; and, although he is Emmanuel, God with us, he is to use no other armour and wield no other strength than the meanest true soldier in his ranks can equally call his own. He is no true captain of salvation, 'made perfect through suffering,' successfully meeting the exigencies of the case, righteously and triumphantly conveying the many sons unto glory, unless he subjects himself to these conditions. He is himself to be led of the Spirit, and he is to wield the word, which is the Spirit's sword. He is to have no other resources.

Nevertheless there is a subtle illusion concerning either the person or the position of Christ, as the God-man, apt to creep into the mind, and fitted to cloud the evidence of the great truth that in all things, in this conflict, he was made like unto his brethren, sin only excepted. We call to mind his godhead;[1] and we are apt to fancy that, by reason of his godhead, nothing could be difficult or arduous to his humanity.

This illusion, I believe, takes two forms—a grosser and a more refined. In the former, it resolves itself into a vague but fundamental misconception of what is implied in the incarnation of the eternal Word. The idea, if forced into something like definiteness, would be found to be very much this; namely, that the omniscience of the Godhead was immediately pouring ceaseless and inevitable streams of light and knowledge into Christ's human mind; and the omnipotence, streams of strength into his human frame. This is, of course, to maintain the unity of the mediator's person, at the expense of destroying the distinction of the two natures. But the distinction of the natures is as perfect as the unity of the person, in so much that, while the man Christ Jesus is the eternal Son of God, whatsoever light or power, or wisdom or strength, or grace or glory from the Godhead (only source of all good) shall be ministered by the Spirit from moment to moment to the human nature of the second Adam (the Lord from heaven) is as much a matter for the divine will to determine, as in the case of the first Adam, or anyone of all his children.

The illusion, however, takes a more refined form, and resolves itself into a misconception, not of the incarnation, but of the humiliation that followed thereon. For that dependence of the humanity on the will of godhead, of which we have just spoken, is essential. It holds in Christ's estate of glory, as well as in his estate of abasement. In his exalted and enthroned humanity, Jesus Christ is glorified now with the glory which he had with the Father before the world was. His humanity,

---

[1] See the last paragraph of Dr. M'Lagan's celebrated sermon in Marcus Dods on the Incarnation: 'Oh! but in him was Godhead—and he had the promise of the Father that he should not fail nor be discouraged until his mighty task were completed. And is not Godhead also your refuge and your strength, a very present help in the time of trouble? Does not the Holy Spirit dwell also in you?'

however, is still dependent on godhead—as every creature of God must be. But he is not now in the form of a servant. God has highly exalted him, and given him a name that is above every name, that at the name of Jesus every knee should bow.

It was not so in the days of his flesh. Having made himself of no reputation, and taken on him the form of a servant, and being found in fashion as a man, he humbled himself (Phil. 2: 7-8). By the consentient will of Father, Son, and Holy Spirit, the Son (of course remaining God) presents himself in fashion as a man and in the form of a servant; and thereby—so far as his obedience unto death is concerned—He places in abeyance for a time and by covenant agreement, his right to draw on the resources of his own godhead, any otherwise than as a man—an obedient servant and a believing son—may do.

Unquestionably herein is the essence of his humiliation. The fundamental idea of his humiliation is not apprehended, unless this be understood.

Strength, therefore, was needed by the human nature of our Lord, as truly as by human nature in any other numerical instance, in any circumstances of conflict and temptation. But, as the incarnation of the eternal Word—the fact that the man Christ Jesus was God—did not render him as man independent of the will and help of God, so in his humiliation—the necessary consequence of his baptism, or rather of the oneness with guilty men which his baptism sealed—the actual will of God concerning him was that his strength should come to *him*, only as it comes unto his people. He, like them, shall have to say: 'God is my refuge and my strength, a very present help in every time of trouble.' And He, like them, shall receive his supplies from godhead—his own godhead—only through the Spirit, to whom the consenting Trinity commit the actual executive and achievement of all their work and will.

In a word, faith in God—that faith which is wrought by the agency of the Spirit and which grasps the truth of the word—was not dispensed with, or unnecessary, in Christ's case, because he himself was God—the God-man. For although the man Christ Jesus is God—the second person of the Godhead—it was not in his own person that he trusted. 'He trusted in God.' It was turned to his reproach (Matt. 27: 43). But it was true. And we will glory in it.

It was true. He so thoroughly became our brother, as to say, in the *first* place—'I will declare thy name unto my brethren, in the midst of the church will I sing praise unto thee'—and in the *second* place—'I will put my trust in him.' Therefore is he entitled to say, in the *third* place (clearly placing himself, in this respect, on the same footing, or in the same category, with his children)—'Behold I and the children whom thou hast given me' (Heb. 2: 12–13).

Thus putting his trust in God, the man Christ Jesus— the second person of the Godhead humbling himself in human flesh—did not draw directly on his own divine resources:—'He who was rich for our sakes became poor.' But suffering his humanity to feel all its own insufficiency as a weak, dependent creature, he drew all his strength from God, through the Spirit, by faith in the word of promise—as every believing soul must do. Thus he tasted intensely all our sinless infirmities. He passed through all our sinless experience of frailty, insufficiency, anxiety, arduous exertion, and vigilance; watching unto prayer; being in an agony. And as he did not—contrary to his covenanted humiliation even unto death—retreat into his prerogatives as God, to shield him from the full brunt and pain of all that fell to his lot as the second man: so his experience of our actual woes was not evasive and ideal and apparent merely, but most deep and real and true.

No: examine again in this very light these depths of Satan's devices. For, consistently with the views already given of these assaults, this also is evident concerning them; that, in the first, the enemy tempts our Lord to leave this position; and, in the last, he taunts him with keeping it.

He first of all tempts him to do what would violate the law of his humiliation; to cease acting simply as man; to give over that quiet trust in God which man should evermore cherish, when God's living word has spoken. He tries to seduce him outside the limits of his probation as God's righteous servant. He would provoke him to return or retreat into the privileges

The Galleries of the King Visited

or prerogatives of godhead: 'Command these stones that they be made bread.'

How forcible—how infinitely well-aimed, in this light—is the very first word of the reply; 'man'—'man shall not live by bread only, but by every word that proceedeth out of the mouth of God.' Jesus remains in the position suitable to him as man. Whatever man, when God has commanded, is bound to do; whatever man, when God has promised, is entitled to expect—*that* he will do most humbly, and *that* he will expect with confidence. As man—claiming, here at least, no higher prerogative-in all things like unto the brethren—as man simply, he will fear the Lord and hope in his word. For it is the law of man's duty and the charter of man's hope, that—'Man shall not live by bread only, but by every word that proceedeth out of the mouth of God.'

And his remaining in his believing duty as man was at once his safety and his victory. Exactly by refusing to transgress the laws and limits of his humiliation he triumphed. By exalting himself—be it said with profoundest reverence—He would have been abased. By remaining in his humiliation he conquered. 'He that humbleth himself shall be exalted.' It is verified unto the uttermost in Jesus.

Viewed, also, in the same light, Satan's closing effort acquires a deeper significance. Failing to draw Christ away from his position as man, he taunts him with keeping it; and points out to him what he would insinuate as a necessary issue. You refuse to act as the Son of God—according to your absolute prerogatives and powers, as such. You cling to your ostensible position as the Son of Man. Man's estate, at all hazards, you are resolved to avow and abide by. You will not be induced to abandon it. Then be it so. But think what man's position is. He is a worshipper of me. He holds of me. Ever since I gained dominion over him, he has held of me as his liege lord. You seek the kingdoms of the world. As man, you do so. I will give them to you; man as you are, and are determined to remain. Only, man's acknowledgment of my sovereignty you must render—'All these will I give unto thee, if thou wilt fall down and worship me'—'Get thee behind me,

Satan: it is written, thou shalt worship the Lord thy God, and him only shalt thou serve.'

Yes! he would remain in man's position; partaker of man's nature, standing in man's place, but in nothing partaker of his depravity. In all things made like unto his brethren, sin only excepted. Tempted in all points like as we are, yet without sin.

Whatever (on the one hand) his assumption of man's nature as a creature and man's place as a sinner may bring upon him, he will not in cowardice, unbelief, and breach of covenant retreat into his powers as God to shield him from. But (on the other hand) when the taunt or hint is thrown out, that, if he is to make man's position his, he must make it wholly his, and yield to the sovereignty of man's successful tempter, as naturally all men do; this he rejects with a holiness worthy of God, standing in the room of sinners, yet holy, harmless, undefiled, and separate from sinners; a sin-bearer, holy as his Father in heaven is holy, 'made sin for us,' yet remaining righteous; more than that, 'made sin for us,' and thereby 'the Lord our Righteousness.'

It appears, then, that there is an exact identity between those powers and privileges for *defence* in this conflict to which the eternal Son of God restricted himself, and those which are assigned to the sons of the adoption—and that this very identity the enemy, with profoundest subtlety, directed his efforts to subvert. But he was unsuccessful.

Let this be most carefully observed. Our living head and captain of salvation restricted and confined himself in his conflict with Satan to the word and Spirit of the Lord. Omniscient, he did not betake himself to the depths of his omniscience to find the adequate thought or truth divine wherewith to foil the serpent's subtlety. He found it in the written word. The depths of his omniscience are inaccessible to you: the written 'word is nigh thee.' Omnipotent, in like manner he did not draw on the stores of his omnipotence for power to foil the great dragon's strength. He found it in the might of the promised Spirit. And while he has not promised to make you omnipotent, he has said, in reference to his Spirit that dwells in you—'my grace is sufficient for thee; my strength is made perfect in weakness.' It is a blessed truth that in Christ's conflict, exactly as it must be in yours, the word was his only sword, and by the Spirit's strength only did he wield it.

Armed with the word, and animated by the Spirit, the Son of God went forward to his temptations—as man. His purpose was not to show what absolute godhead—omnipotence and omniscience—could achieve, but what the Spirit and word of God could do for man. Thus he accepted the conflict in which the probation of his messiahship was to open. To destroy the works of the devil (beginning, as they did, with the successful temptation of the 'first man') 'the second man' began by enduring all that temptation could inflict.

Such is the parallel. Is it necessary to point out the circumstances, so favourable to the first Adam, who nevertheless fell; and the altered circumstances, so altogether adverse, amidst which the last Adam nevertheless triumphed? Surrounded by the sweet amenities and overflowing sufficiency of Eden, the head of the covenant of works fell—tempted with the fruit he so little needed. Surrounded by the horrors of the wilderness, without food for forty days, and now an hungered, the head of the covenant of grace refused to grasp in unbelief—though immediately at his disposal as God—the food which, as man, he needed so deeply. With the new-created animals around him, in placid peace, each obedient to his gentle sway; himself, under God, the lord of them all, absolute disposer of them by divine right; alike able and entitled, therefore, as their king, to slay[1] with instant death any serpent of them all, beneath whose glittering form or glozing tongue treason to heaven's high king might lurk—the first man fell. The second man was 'in the wilderness forty days, tempted of Satan, and was with the *wild beasts*.'

> *Surrounded by the sweet amenities and overflowing sufficiency of Eden, the head of the covenant of works fell—tempted with the fruit he so little needed. Surrounded by the horrors of the wilderness, without food for forty days, and now an hungered, the head of the covenant of grace refused...the food which, as man, he needed so deeply.*

Surely he very nobly redressed the evil of his prototype ('figure of him that was to come') and he took from Satan all his boast. As man—resigning all resources in the conflict but those which are now open to man; resigning all advantages which the first man abundantly enjoyed; hampered, moreover, and loaded with all the disadvantages which the first man's fall entailed—the second man, trusting to the word and Spirit of God, passed through an ordeal in which the terms and conditions could not have been more hazardous to himself, nor more favourable to his foe. And he passed through that ordeal with triumph.

Is he not with us now—in our wilderness ordeal—as in the gospel history, carrying on the defence still? And the resources he wields in it—and you wield in it, in him, your head—are the same. 'Abide in him, and he in you.' He wields the Spirit's sword—and he wields it in the Spirit's strength. Still the two-edged sword goes out of his mouth—'It is written'—'It is written.' And still it goes forth with the mighty power of the Spirit; until again, the ever-living triumph crowns the ever-living and unchanged defence; and 'the devil leaveth' both you and your Lord.

The Identity of the Victory

The victory, with its reward and its refreshings, is the same—its *ultimate* reward and its *immediate* refreshings.

The identity of the reward is clearly shown—'Ye are they that have continued with me in my temptations; and I appoint unto you the kingdom which my Father hath appointed unto me.' And how specific and exact is the reversal of the picture, when you contrast the conflict and the prize! Take the first and the last stages of the battle, and the first and last

---

1 'As often as they beheld anyone of the animals that was in the world, they ought to have been reminded both of the supreme authority, and of the singular goodness, of God; but on the contrary, when they saw the serpent an apostate from his Creator, not only did they neglect to punish it, but, in violation of all lawful order, they subjected and devoted themselves to it, as participators in the same apostasy. What can be imagined more dishonourable than this extreme depravity?'—Calvin on Genesis.

The Galleries of the King Visited

portions of the conqueror's reward (as these are ranged, for instance, in the series of promises to 'him that overcometh' set forth in the seven epistles to the churches) and notice the beautiful antithesis between the first of each, and between the last of each.

First you have—not as Adam, a plenteous, peaceful Eden, but—the wilderness, and dire necessity there. Such is the opening scene in the drama of temptation. Mark its exact reversal in the beginning of the triumph. 'To him that overcometh will I give to eat of the tree of life, which is in the midst of the paradise of God' (Rev. 2: 7).

And as to the closing scene—you have an offer from Satan of royal gifts (kingdoms and glory) to be held in allegiance to him. Such is his final effort to destroy you. Mark the exact adaptation of the closing promise of reward. 'To him that overcometh will I grant to sit with me on my throne, even as I also overcame, and am set down with my Father on his throne' (Rev. 3: 21).

But who shall speak of the glory to be revealed?

Rather let us consider the refreshings that may be obtained in the meantime. These are twofold:—an increase of comfort, and an increase of usefulness. And they may be seen identically both in Christ and in his people.

Increase of Comfort

The successful conflict is followed by an increase of comfort. 'The devil leaveth him, and, behold, angels came and ministered unto him' (Matt. 4: 11)—a double consolation.

The Devil Leaves Him

The devil leaves him. A breathing time is graciously granted him. The paroxysm passes off. The strain of the hot encounter is, for a time, relaxed. It is only for a season, indeed. The prince of this world will come again. Still, as a season even, as an interval—as a respite or reprieve—it is valuable. The weary soldier has time to breathe freely; time to refresh his weary spirit; time to re-arrange his garment and his armour, not being ignorant of the fray.

This is the experience of the Captain of salvation, and of his soldiers too—especially the more tried and intelligent of their number; I mean, spiritually and experimentally intelligent in the Christian warfare. They know how that special times of hot conflict are assigned them; when Satan seems inflated with desire and expectation to destroy them; as if he said, 'God hath forsaken him: persecute and take him: for there is none to deliver him' (Ps. 71: 11)—times when they cannot but exclaim with David, 'Lord, how are they increased that trouble me'—'the enemy hath thrust sore at me, that I might fall' (Ps. 3: 1; 118: 13). But let them retreat into the camp of the King into the fellowship and company of their captain—who is 'their shield, and their glory, and the lifter up of their head'—who also is 'their strength, and their song, and their salvation' (Ps. 3: 3; 118: 14). Let them, by his word and Spirit, stand forth in him, strong in the Lord and in the power of his might. They know that after such fierce trials—identified, by faith, with Christ's temptations, continued in and faithfully fought in Christ's fellowship—a time of special, manifest relief is given them. The devil is compelled to leave them for a season. The Lord commands a calm. The Lord gives his beloved sleep.

Angels Ministered to Him

But it is not merely a negative relief. A positive refreshing is provided. 'Angels came and ministered unto him.'

Such was the privilege of the first-born among many brethren. The brethren are joint-heirs with Christ in all things. And 'are not all the angels ministering spirits, sent forth to minister to them who shall be heirs of salvation?' (Heb. 1: 14).

Ah! who knows how greatly the blessed calm and the sweet refreshings that succeed a time of sore trial—well and bravely met in the word and Spirit of the Lord—may be due to the ministry of angels? May not they be commissioned of the Father to spread a table for you in the presence of your baffled enemies?—to anoint your head with oil?—to fill your cup to overflowing?—and, in very deed, to keep your foot from being dashed against a stone (while you do not for that reason tempt the Lord your God)? You would not think your Father's hand less truly or less sweetly in the consolation, because he wielded in it the instrumentality of angels. Jesus, doubtless, did not think so when the angels strengthened him. Nor will you. Neither will you put your trust in angels, but in the Lord alone. 'The angel of the Lord encampeth round about them that fear him, and delivereth them. O taste and see that the Lord is good: blessed is the man that trusteth in him' (Ps. 34: 7–8).

Such is the increase of comfort. Evil angels retire. And the blessed principalities of light hover round—as if to congratulate, and to cheer you. Assuredly they come to strengthen you.

Increase of Usefulness

There is also an increase of *usefulness*.

This is very strikingly illustrated. 'And Jesus returned in the power of the Spirit into Galilee: and there went out a fame of him through all the region round about. And he taught in their synagogues, being glorified of all' (Luke 4: 14–15).

Again it is in the Spirit that Jesus is strong—'in the power of the Spirit.' And clearly the Spirit rests upon him, not more abundantly (for the Father from the first did not give the Spirit to him by measure) but as operating, according to his good pleasure, with additional rewarding power and approbation on the man that had foiled the foe. And so, in the power of the Spirit, it is clearly with the tramp of a conqueror's foot-fall that Jesus returns from the wilderness to Galilee. Nor is the tone of his teaching destitute of traces of his victory. He is glorified of all in their synagogues. Nor can the people comprehend what firm voice of power and wisdom is this. And his fame goes forth throughout the land.

What a prospect this holds out to those who have communion with their Lord in the office of instructing others! To such, successfully endured temptation will prove the occasion of fresh acquisitions of power, imparting a tone of superhuman independence to the ministry which they have received of the Lord to fulfil it (Col. 4: 17).

But whatever your ministry or service or appointed labours may be, you cannot in any conflict abide in your living head and come off a conqueror, without being warranted most fully to expect, in your experience, even as in his, an increase of strength and usefulness. For your confidence in the word and Spirit will be increased. You will live by the word (Matt. 4: 4) a life of greater energy. You will depend on the Spirit for larger measures of strength. The word will dwell in you more richly. And the power of the Spirit will rest on you more abundantly.

Therefore, if after a well-fought battle, the devil, for a time, leaves you; and if angels, as it were (or rather, as it really is, for so has the Father said) come and minister to you, if the Lord grants a breathing time and a banqueting time, too, do not dwell too long upon it. Do not drain your well-filled cup. Up again, refreshed for duty! Up to your ministry once more, whatever that ministry may be. Come out from your wilderness-temptations, from your secret chamber of grief, from your secret banquet-room of joy—back into Galilee again, back again to the scene of your labours. And come 'in the power of the Spirit.'

It will be so. You will thus return—if you have shared the assault, the defence, the victory and the refreshings, of your Lord's very conflict; if you have experienced his presence in the battle, as here in the gospel history. For then he returns with you from the field—still as in this gospel history—just as he returned into Galilee. Yes, he returns with you. For lo! he is present with you still. Lo! he is with you alway. 'His presence shall go with you, and he will give you rest' (Exod. 33: 14).

III. THE SYNAGOGUE, AND ITS PERPETUAL SERMON

'And he came to Nazareth, where he had been brought up: and, as his custom was, he went into the synagogue on the sabbath-day, and stood up for to read. And there was delivered unto him the book of the prophet Esaias: and when he had opened the book, he found the place where it was written, The Spirit of the Lord is upon me, because he hath anointed me to preach the gospel to the poor; he hath sent me to heal the broken-hearted, to preach deliverance to the captives, and recovering of sight to the blind, to set at liberty them that are bruised, to preach the acceptable year of the Lord. And he closed the book, and he gave it again to the minister, and sat down. And the eyes of all them that were in the synagogue were fastened on him. And he began to say unto them, This day is this scripture fulfilled in your ears. And all bare him witness, and wondered at the gracious words which proceeded out of his mouth' (Luke 4: 16–22).

'He whom God hath sent speaketh the words of God: for God giveth not the Spirit by measure unto him' (John 3: 34).

Will the Lord enshrine his presence here? Will he live over again—will he continually live—this part of his biography amongst us?

Eminently and manifestly he will. The whole case is singularly fitted to bring out very clearly the evidence of what we have already attempted so variously to illustrate.

We behold our Lord in the synagogue of Nazareth exercising his prophetic office. And while all the sensible and temporary circumstantials of the case have vanished, all the essentials survive to this hour.

Take the scene in Nazareth on that Sabbath-day as a manifestation of the presence of the only-begotten of the Father, full of grace and truth. Separate the temporary from the permanent—and you will find that you have separated the accessory from the essential, leaving all that was essential permanently present in the church below still.

For, what are the essentials?

There is the word. 'He stood up for to read.'

And it is the word of the Lord he is to read. 'There was delivered unto him the book of the prophet Esaias.' And he accepts the opportunity thus afforded him of honouring the word. 'He opened the book and found the place where it was written.' That which is 'written' is his theme as a prophet, even as that which is 'written' has already been his sword as a king. And what he reads from the word has reference to his own preaching of the word—his preaching the gospel to the poor, his preaching deliverance to the captives and recovering of sight to the blind, his preaching the acceptable year of the Lord. It is all of the word, the Scripture. And how does he comment upon the word now read? 'This day is *this Scripture* fulfilled in your ears.'

As to instrumentality, as to theme or topic or *material* in his teaching, the word is the essential.

As to efficiency; or spiritual agency reaching the heart, enlightening the mind, making wise the simple—what is the essential, in this view?

Mark the first utterance of the oracle—'The Spirit.' 'The Spirit of the Lord is upon me because he hath anointed me to preach the gospel to the poor.' He places this in the foreground. He points to this as his great qualification. On this he hazards all his expectation of success in his office. The Spirit of the Lord is upon him.

Here is his own 'epistle of commendation'; recommendatory of him as able to fulfil the duty of his office—'For, he whom God hath sent speaketh the words of God: for God giveth not the Spirit by measure unto him' (John 3: 34). Here, also, is his hope of having many living epistles of commendation written in the hearts of his people, 'known and read of all men: manifestly declared to be the epistle of Christ,' because 'written with the Spirit of the living God' (2 Cor. 3: 1-3). The whole efficiency is of the Spirit. As to spiritual efficiency or agency, the Spirit is the essential.

When, therefore, 'all that heard him bare him witness, and wondered at the gracious words that proceeded out of his mouth' (v. 22)—when 'they were astonished at his doctrine; for his word was with power' (v. 32)—the entire essential of the gracious words and powerful doctrine was of the Scripture;

and the entire essential of the grace and power was of the Spirit.

That is to say, Christ executed the office of a prophet, that day, in Nazareth, in revealing to men by his word and Spirit the will of God for their salvation. The features of his visible countenance and the pulsations of the air from his audible voice did not enter into the matter at all. So that his bodily presence (or, as it ought rather to be called, the bodily manifestation of his presence) may have vanished, but his presence is with us in our sanctuaries now, essentially and exactly as in the synagogue of Nazareth then.

A thousand times shall faith assert this claim and every time she will deny that there is any trace of illusion or fancy or fanaticism in her assertion of it. She will evermore produce the tangible, unchanging, rigid rule of the word, whereby all fanaticism is excluded. And she will trust to the guiding light of the promised Spirit, who can neither err nor mislead. And knowing that her prophet is the Christ because the Spirit of the Lord rests on him for ever, and knowing that the word also lives and abides for ever, she will maintain that she enjoys her Lord's presence in all essentials as fully as the spectators in the synagogue of Nazareth—and far more fully than those who were spectators merely.

Are we to be in such bondage—so deliriously intoxicated and enslaved—to the senses of this vile body, as to maintain that whatever has vanished from the eyes of our flesh is lost to us? Are we to subordinate and to subject thus shamefully the things that are unseen and eternal to the conditions of space and time and the body of our humiliation? And are we never to be satisfied that 'the King eternal, immortal and invisible' is near, unless he submit a proof that shall be cognizable to those eyes and hands which have soon to be hidden in the grave? 'Thomas; because thou hast seen me thou hast believed: blessed are they which have not seen me, and yet have believed.'

With adoring reverence let a supposition be made. (With adoring reverence—for we 'beseech thee,' O Emmanuel, 'shew us thy glory'; till like Elijah we wrap our face in our mantle (1 Kings 19: 13), till like Moses we make haste, and bow our head toward the earth, and worship (Exod. 34: 8).)

One thing have you desired of the Lord; that will you seek after; that you may dwell in the house of the Lord all the days of your life, to behold the beauty of the Lord, and to inquire in his temple.

Let it be supposed, then, that, on the first day of the week, when you are assembled to worship God in the Spirit in the name of Christ, the blessed Christ who is with you from the first, if even two or three have truly met in his name, suddenly reveals his presence to the eyes of your flesh; and he who alway walks, unseen, among the seven golden candlesticks, appears unto you, standing in the midst—as he appeared unto the disciples on the evening of his own resurrection-day (John 20: 19), saying 'Peace be unto you.' He does not interrupt your worship. He takes the conduct of it. He will make known his Father's name unto his brethren; in the midst of the congregation will he sing praise unto him (Ps. 22: 22; Heb. 2: 12). He stands up to read. And there is delivered to him the book of the prophet Esaias. And when he has opened the book he finds the place where it is written: 'The Spirit of the Lord God is upon me.' And he reads it with the 'still small voice.' And as he reads, you wrap your face in your mantle. For the word is with power, and with the demonstration of the Spirit. And while he penetrates your heart with his Spirit, he turns all your thought to the word, saying, 'This day is this Scripture fulfilled in your ears.'

Would this be the presence of your Lord?

But suppose that having thus seen the Lord, you cannot but wrap your face in your mantle; that you smite upon your breast and cannot so much as lift up your eyes unto him; or that some veil or curtain descends and hides the divine reader from your view, while still the gracious words proceed from his mouth.

Have you not your Lord's presence still?

But suppose again that, ceasing to use his own voice, he gives the book unto the minister and sits down; leaving your pastor to minister the word, himself continuing to minister to you the Spirit (continuing, that is, to give you the word and Spirit still) while he himself, hidden from your view and now silent, still sits in your assembly:—

Have you not your Lord's presence still?

The Galleries of the King Visited

And now an ambassador for Christ, as though God did beseech you by him, prays you in Christ's stead—'Be ye reconciled to God.' And the word is the matter of his commission; even the word of reconciliation which Christ has thus committed to him. And the Spirit is the agent in commending it, in his own light, to you. And the prophet of the church—his countenance unseen by you, his literal voice unheard by you—is present in the body. Of what advantage to you is his bodily presence? It is by his word and Spirit that he is advantageously, really, profoundly present with you. Let him ascend to his Father and your Father, to his God and your God.

Have you not your Lord's presence still?

Yes—'Where two or three are gathered together in my name, there am I in the midst of them.' 'They have seen thy goings, O God; even the goings of my God, my King, in the sanctuary.'

Even though Jesus were with you in the sanctuary bodily, he would bring no new revelation: he would read from 'the book.' He would speak of 'this Scripture, this day fulfilled in your ears.' And he would cast no spell of amazement upon your soul from his visible person or audible voice: he would seek no such poor triumph over his audience—no such factitious influence upon their mind. He would hazard all the effect of his word on the demonstration of the Spirit. His own word and your soul he would leave in the hand of the Spirit. By the word he would send forth his truth. And by the Spirit he would send forth his light. 'O send forth thy light and thy truth.'

But does the bodily manifestation of his presence at all enter into the essence of this great transaction? No, verily. And, therefore, verily and essentially you have Christ's presence in your sanctuary, even as in the synagogue of Nazareth.

O send out thy light and thy truth; let them lead me, let them bring me unto thy holy hill, and to thy tabernacles. Then will I go unto the altar of God, unto God my exceeding joy. O God, thou art my God; early will I seek thee: my soul thirsteth for thee, my flesh longeth for thee in a dry and thirsty land, where no water is; to see thy power and thy glory—even the light of the knowledge of the glory of God in the face of Jesus Christ—so that I have seen thee in the sanctuary.

If we have the word and the Spirit of Christ, we have the presence of Christ in the sanctuary.

But it is clear that this train of thought lands us on the verge of a very great enlargement or (to use the language of geometry) extension of our theorem. The coalescence of the *presence* and the *history* is merely a limited case, though no doubt the most interesting case, of a wider and grander principle—the coalescence of the *Spirit* and the *word* in general.

This is a coalescence or conjunction set before us in Scripture in many interesting lights. In one view, and most practically, it constitutes in fact God's covenant, established with the mediator, and, in him, with the church his seed, and all her seed or children—'As for me, this is my covenant with them, saith the Lord; my Spirit that is upon thee, and my words which I have put in thy mouth, shall not depart out of thy mouth, nor out of the mouth of thy seed, nor out of the mouth of thy seed's seed, saith the Lord, from henceforth even for ever' (Isa. 59: 21). Practically this is God's whole covenant; for all the purchase and provisions of the covenant are stored up, and conveyed to us, in the word; and it is the Spirit who takes of that purchase and those provisions—which are just the things of Christ—and shows them to us (John 16: 14). And, it is because of the covenant taking this form and taking effect in this manner in the church, that the church is called upon in the very next utterance:—'Arise, shine; for thy light hath come, and the glory of the Lord hath arisen upon thee' (Isa. 51: 1). The word and Spirit of the Lord are the light and the glory of the church.

Because of this coalescence of the word and Spirit, long before he came in the flesh, was Wisdom's presence in the world; indeed, 'in the streets; in the chief places of concourse: in the openings of the gates—saying, Turn ye at my reproof: behold I will pour out my Spirit unto you, I will make known my words unto you' (Prov. 1: 20-24). And when, in the fulness of time, he is made of a woman, and speaks with human lips—'he whom God hath sent speaketh the words of God, because God giveth not the Spirit by measure unto him' (John 3: 33).

The Galleries of the King Visited

How intimate is this conjunction—testified as it is by John concerning Christ in the days of his flesh, as true of him then; by Solomon, as true even in his days; and by Isaiah, as true—'from henceforth even for ever.' In the language of one[1] whose eloquence and subtlety of thought are oftentimes as marvellous as his massiveness and grandeur:

> the Lord hath so knit together the certainty of his Word and his Spirit, that our minds are duly imbued with reverence for the Word, when the Spirit, shining upon it, enables us there to behold the face of God; and, on the other hand, we embrace the Spirit with no danger of delusion when we recognise him in his image, that is, in his Word.

It would be out of place to enter on any of the manifold trains of fine and fertile thought opened up by a theme so rich as that of—the word and Spirit. But we may repeat and extend a question which occurred at an earlier stage of our inquiries. In reference to the coalescence of the presence and the history we were led to ask—does any other history or biography possess an advantage so marvellous as that he whom it commemorates should adjoin himself to the record and take possession of the mind of him who reads the record? And the analogous question, of course, arises—does any other work of authorship possess an advantage similar to God's word generally, when God's Spirit dwells in him who humbly reads the word and shines upon it with the light of God? Is it enough to say that this really is *equivalent* to the presence of the Lord? Ought it not rather to be confidently affirmed that this is the Lord's presence—most intimately, most profoundly, most intensely—far more so than the presence of any fellow-creature can be with us?

I give you, let us say, my written word. I send a most carefully written letter to you. I have watched and laboured every sentence of it, to secure the utmost possible simplicity and accuracy; and to make my meaning not only most intelligible, but, as far as possible, unavoidably and unmistakeably plain.

---

1 Calvin: *Institutes*, Book I, chap. ix, 3.

You give my carefully written word an equally careful perusal. You watch and labour to understand every sentence of it; to take up my very meaning with perfect accuracy; to avoid fathering on me any thought which I did not mean—or failing to apprehend any thought which I did mean—to convey.

And yet, with all this, is it infallibly certain that we shall understand each other? Or, more precisely; is there any provision in this arrangement for securing that you shall infallibly understand me? There is not.

But suppose that, with my written word, I could convey, into your mind or spirit, my mind or spirit; and that my spirit had such command over your spirit as to secure that the action of your intellect and heart in reading my letter should fit in exactly, and harmonize, with the action of mine in writing it. Then, though we might be separated by the diameter of the globe, or, though one of us should be in heaven above and the other on the earth below, I am present with you by my word and spirit; and very real and intimate and intense is our communion—more so, by far, than if we were merely face to face in the flesh.

Is it necessary to point out that this is the very arrangement which actually subsists under Christ's present method of instructing you, while he is in heaven above and you are here upon the earth; very beautifully illustrated (indeed literally ex-exemplified) by his letters to the churches? 'These things saith he'—so do these epistles open: they are the word of Christ. 'Let him that hath an ear hear what the Spirit saith unto the churches'—so do these epistles close: the Spirit of Christ is in them, and with them. It is the very arrangement which we have supposed; only freed, as between you and your God, from all the imperfections to which even this arrangement, as between you and a fellow-creature, would be subject? So that you shall even infallibly be put in possession of the Lord's meaning. You shall assuredly 'have the mind of Christ.' And Christ's most intimate presence shall be with you—not to the eyes of your flesh, but to the now heaven-bright eyes of your spirit.

But we must resume and extend a former inference also.

The Galleries of the King Visited

The Inspiration of the Scriptures

If the presence of Christ in the gospel history inevitably infers the inspiration of the four Gospels, the analogous presence of the Spirit in the Scriptures generally, infers, by similar necessity, the inspiration of the entire Scriptures too. On the presupposition that the Spirit enshrines himself in the word, even as Christ in the memoir, the whole word must be as perfect and infallible as that special portion of it. With the perfection of that portion, Christ's perfection is imperilled, if Christ livingly conjoins himself with it, and looks out from it, in all ages, upon the sons of men, as in a living picture there. But if the Spirit in like manner cleaves to the word, by a divinely guaranteed connection 'from henceforth even for ever'; then the infallibility of the spirit is so identified with the infallibility of the word that a threat to one is a threat to both.

Many, doubtless, of those who deny the plenary inspiration (or perfection) of the word may not think they suffer any loss when made to see that the imperfection or fallibility of the word cuts the tie of living union between the word and Spirit. For they will probably not value nor feel interested in asserting and defending that union, as the friends of plenary inspiration do. Nevertheless it is of some consequence to set it clearly forth that the relation in which the Holy Spirit can stand to Holy Scripture, and the kind of use which he can possibly make of it in his dealings with men, must be wholly—specifically and fundamentally and wholly—altered, if it is not literally his own word.

Even supposing the Scriptures were not inspired of the Holy Ghost, as we contend, to such specific and peculiar effect as renders them his word—his published works, just as Butler's *Analogy* and Calvin's *Institutes* and Augustine's *Civitas Dei* are published works of Butler and Calvin and Augustine; supposing the Scriptures were merely good and holy writings, as those of Augustine and Calvin and Butler are—holier, it may be, and better far, than the best of these, yet in the same category with them; written by good men, as these were, with the same kind of help and influence from heaven—doubtless in larger measure yet the same in kind; in such a case we do not say that the Holy Ghost would refuse to stand in any relation to them whatever, or utterly refuse in any way to use them. We do not, by any means, say so. We do not say so, just because we do not say that he refuses utterly to use the works of Augustine and Calvin and Butler—or withholds his blessing from the use of them. But we contend that in this case, the relation in which he must stand to the Scriptures, and the use which he will make of them, must be the same in kind—in no respect specific or peculiar or unique, but the very same in kind—as when the works of these human authors are concerned.

But is that the relation in which, seeking *certainty* in the things that belong to my eternal peace, I am content to see the Spirit standing to the Scriptures; or the use which I am content to hope he will make of them in instructing my never-dying soul? Let that relation be supposed as intimate and excellent as possible, in the nature of the case; and that use as great and constant; yet the Spirit can in no respect identify himself with these writings. He must stand outside and apart from them. He cannot enter into them; and make them his own. For his own they are not. And it would dishonour and degrade the Holy Spirit to adopt them as his own, and become responsible for their errors and imperfections. It simply cannot be. He may make some use of them; but not such as making them his own would imply. He may use them. He may work by means of them on my mind, as he may do me good by the works of Augustine or Calvin or Butler. But mark the specific, awful issue—the Spirit of God is silent.

Yes! There is eternal silence in the church on this scheme, so far as any voice of the Spirit, any voice divine, is concerned. He may work. But he does not speak. The plastic movements of his hand may be upon my heart. But he does not speak to me. He and I have no intelligent communion. My God is silent to me.

And will my Father never speak to me? Will he persist in giving me my daily bread amidst this awful silence? I protest that I cannot eat it. Will he offer to make the published works

The Galleries of the King Visited

of mere men useful to me—including among them these writings of Moses and the Prophets and the Apostles—while he himself is still awfully and ominously silent? I protest that I cannot hear them, for my heart is breaking for the longing that it has to hear my Father's voice.

Yes! And he is not silent to me. 'The mighty God even the Lord hath spoken.' To speak—is pre-eminently his. 'I am he that doth speak: behold, it is I.' And 'the Spirit speaketh expressly.' And 'let him that hath an ear hear what the Spirit saith unto the churches.'

For the Spirit enters into his own word. He expresses himself by means of it. He can do so without compromise of his own mind, or constraint upon his own thoughts or feelings, because it is his own word. It expresses what the Spirit of Christ doth 'signify' (1 Pet. 1: 11). It does full justice to his meaning. He will not disown it, therefore. And it will not dishonour him. He and his own utterances—the Spirit and the word—are wholly consentient. Their living coalescence, therefore, is possible. And it is guaranteed. Their division is, in fact, inconceivable. And the word is thus quick and powerful by the Spirit. The Spirit is intelligible by the word.

Without the Spirit, the word is dead. Without the word, the Spirit is dumb. The one a dead letter: the other a dumb power. Like the ivory palaces, if the King never entered them, the cold, drear, death-damp of centuries in all their noble halls—so would the word be to me, if the Spirit were not there. O let the Spirit and glory of the Lord fill the house. Like when the Spirit dumbly brooded on the face of the waters (they could yearn after no acquaintance with his mind and heart)—so would the Spirit's work be on me, if he disowned and set aside his word. O let him count me his intelligent companion. Let him explain himself, and speak with voice articulate, intelligible. Let him not deal with me as with matter, inert and dead. Let him deal with me as 'a living soul'; for he himself is 'a quickening Spirit.'

Let the Spirit give life to the letter of the word. Let the word

> *Without the Spirit, the word is dead. Without the word, the Spirit is dumb. The one a dead letter: the other a dumb power.*

give expression to the mind of the Spirit. And so has the Lord arranged.

But the whole arrangement, with its glory, so unique and perfect, must vanish, if the true and proper inspiration of Holy Scripture be abandoned.

The same inference follows from pursuing the train of thought in a slightly altered direction.

There is delivered unto Jesus in the synagogue of Nazareth—and, lo! he is with us alway—the book of the prophet Esaias. Diligently mark how he reads. And to strengthen—while it will also rigorously test—the case as I now want to try to put it, let a careful induction be made of all the instances in which Jesus quotes, and comments upon, the Scriptures.

Compare his comments and his quotations.

His comments. These are his own words. He is entirely responsible for them. If you believe his godhead, these words, being his, are inspired, infallible, divine. The hearers wondered at the gracious words that proceeded out of his mouth. They were astonished at the doctrine, for it was with power. He spake as one having authority. When he closed the book, and said—'This day is this Scripture fulfilled in your ears'—these words were infallible truth. 'He whom God hath sent speaketh the words of God.' His comments were divine.

Were his quotations any less so? I confidently ask any intelligent reader of the Scriptures, is there the very slightest reason to think that the extract on which he founds his gracious words and astonishingly powerful doctrine—words and doctrine undeniably infallible and divine, as coming from the lips of God manifest in the flesh—is any less gracious or powerful or truly divine, than those utterances of the Son of God to which the extract gave occasion? You believe that your Lord's gracious words in the synagogue of Nazareth were infallible—divine; that, as he spake them, his hearers heard the Word of God, directly from the lips of the eternal Word himself. But I protest that I can as easily conceive of that divine speaker in the synagogue going back on his address, towards its close, professedly to remedy some error he had made in the course of it, as I can conceive him indicating the very slightest dissent from any portion whatever of those Scriptures from which he had so reverently read. It is impossible that an unbiassed reader can avoid seeing that he deals with the quotations as having the same authority with his own comments. When he closes the book, and is now about to speak of himself—*ex se ipso*—the audience are not about to hear anything more truly divine, more truly infallible, than that which had been read to them. 'This day is this Scripture fulfilled in your ears.' For the blessed reader conjoins himself livingly with 'this Scripture'—enshrines himself in it, exactly as we say he enshrines himself in the gospel history. He is giving these Nazarenes his presence, as looking out upon them from this living picture of the Evangelic prophet; and he finds a voice for himself in 'this Scripture' which obviously is as truly his own voice and divine, as it is his own voice that utters afterwards the gracious words and the powerful doctrine that astonish them.

Yes! I cannot believe that the light of the world—the very truth—would have dealt with these Scriptures as he thus dealt, had he not meant explicitly and entirely to homologate them; asserting for them the same divine and unchallengeable authority which he claimed for his own utterances in expounding them.

Return for a moment to the supposition which we asked you, with adoring reverence, to entertain. Let the Lord Jesus be visibly present in your sanctuary on the Sabbath-day. And he stands up to read.

Would you endure the thought of 'delivering unto him' for this purpose any 'book' that you do not believe to be plenarily inspired, perfect, infallible—his own? For your own sake, would you not crave to hear him speak what, coming from his mouth must be divine, rather than hear him read what you believed to be good, perhaps, but human and imperfect. For your own edification, would you not infinitely rather say— 'Speak, Lord, for thy servant heareth?' And as to its bearing on him, and his honour, would you not feel that you were infinitely degrading your Lord and seeking to bring him into bondage to an imperfect standard, if you asked him to express his mind, or teach his truth to you, by the instrumentality of any 'book' that you could not call entirely his own?

As he reads and quotes from his own Scriptures, mark how free he is. He does not use them as if they hampered him; as if he were adjusting himself to a foreign element; as if he were inserting his thoughts into forms of expression imperfect and unsatisfactory; as if he were feeling the infinite difference between the 'words which man's wisdom teacheth' and the 'words which the Holy Ghost teacheth.' Most clearly his mind is at home in the words of Holy Scripture, in its own element, finding in them expression most adequate, exact and thorough. Holy Scripture is evidently, to his eye, clear and very pure, as his own thoughts are pure and unbedimmed. It is bright, to his view, as his own intellect is bright. It is as holy, true, and good; as perfect; full of grace and truth. It is not only the revelation of himself; it is his own revelation of himself. He can thoroughly dwell in it. He can shine out from it—in no respect misrepresented.

But if these Scriptures are good and from God not in any more specific sense (though it may be in far higher degree) than the works of Butler and Augustine and Calvin; then the whole tone and tenor of my Lord's dealings with them, if 'delivered unto him for to read,' must inevitably, to my mind, be essentially and wholly different. In that case, were he bodily present in our sanctuaries now, I can conceive him pointing out—indeed, I cannot conceive how he could possibly avoid pointing out—that Moses (it may be) had misapprehended somewhat the exact pattern shown to him in the mount; that Isaiah had not quite correctly brought out what the Spirit of Christ which was in him intended to signify; that John had in a slight measure failed to indicate the specific thought in some of those profound discourses of his Master which he had undertaken to report; and that Paul, when he wrote his First Epistle to the Thessalonians, had manifestly been mistaken in expecting to survive till the Lord's second coming (1 Thess. 3: 15)—as those who twitter against the inspiration of the Scriptures try to show—though afterwards he came to see into the future more correctly (2 Thess. 2: 1–3).[1]

---

[1] For a passing, but abundantly sufficient answer to this piece of Broad School folly, see Chapter 11. Here it is enough to remark, that if Paul was wrong,

The Galleries of the King Visited

And really if such a service remains to be rendered to the church concerning the Scriptures—even to reveal infallibly where they can, and where they cannot, be trusted—and if the Lord's bodily presence in the midst of us be indispensable to our obtaining this satisfaction, it will be very hard for poor and needy souls to believe that they do not suffer an incalculable and irreparable loss by their Lord's ascension to his glory. On such a footing I boldly challenge any thoughtful man to prove that it was 'expedient for him to go away.'

But can you really conceive of the great teacher, were he with us in the body, thus continually correcting the text-book, and adjusting it to his own views continually?

Expressly to avoid incongruity between the lecture and the text-book, teachers of science and philosophy very generally compose text-books of their own. They do so even although multitudinous and able expositions of their theme may be already extant. They have their own modes of conceiving their subject; peculiar lights in which they take pleasure in presenting it; their own favourite forms of expression; their own particular arrangement. They do not choose a book concerning which they feel it needful, now and then, to stop and point out where the demonstration might have been improved, or abbreviated; made more symmetrical, more general and comprehensive, or perhaps even more conclusive. Especially if the teacher has himself made eminent contributions and discoveries in the branch of philosophy and science which he expounds. He is, in such a case, peculiarly and most reasonably jealous of his own contributions to his own department being committed to writing by some confessedly incompetent stranger, and then appointed to be used by himself as his class-book! He resents the insult.

And yet he knows that in entering on his discoveries, however grand they may be, he did so, as already in possession of a great legacy of experiment and of observation, of wisdom and of knowledge, that had for ages been accumulating in the hands and by the discoveries of others.

intellectually, in his first Epistle, he was still further wrong, morally, in his second. For instead of saying, 'Let no man deceive you' (2 Thess. 2: 3), he was in that case bound as a man of honour to apologise, and to say rather, 'I deeply regret that I deceived you!'

With reverence let the application be made. In Christ are 'hid all the treasures of wisdom and knowledge.' All discoveries in the divine science of salvation are his own. He had no predecessor. He has no colleague or coadjutor. He is the only revealer. 'No man hath seen God at any time; the only-begotten which is in the bosom of the Father he hath declared him.' And he claims the great text-book as entirely his own. He teaches his own discoveries by his own most holy word.

Christ executes the office of a prophet in revealing to us by his word and Spirit the will of God for our salvation. As truly as the Spirit is his, so truly is the word. It is verbally, plenarily, wholly his. It is inspired, infallible, divine.

Supposing it were not so; were the eternal Word to manifest himself as bodily present with us on earth, would it be presumptuous, would it be unwise on our part, would it be unacceptable or offensive to him, if from every broken heart and earnest soul there arose the cry unanimous, even 'as the sound of many waters'—O Christ! thou art the Wonderful, the Counsellor; thy children crave a light unto their feet, a lamp unto their path; a Scripture infallible—such as 'cannot be broken'?

Would not such a prayer be good?

But I protest that it forms part of my adoration of Christ to believe that he has anticipated us concerning every warrantable and good desire; that the holy and the wise wishes of his church can never transcend—but must always find themselves within, and falling short of—the pre-arrangements which he has made in the counsels of eternal love for meeting all her exigencies; and that the particular desire supposed—being obviously good, and flowing, as it necessarily must, from the mournful contemplation of an uninspired and imperfect Scripture—would argue a capacity in the church to desire, without blameworthiness, what God had not arranged to give, and would therefore rob him of the glory of that great name under which I rejoice to adore him—'Able to do exceeding abundantly above all that we can ask or think' (Eph. 3: 20).

IV: THE CROSS, AND ITS PERPETUAL SACRIFICE

'It is finished' (John 19: 16-30).

'Christ, through the eternal Spirit, offered himself without spot to God' (Heb. 9: 14).

'Lo, in the midst of the throne, stood a Lamb as it had been slain' (Rev. 6: 6).

'I am crucified with Christ' (Gal. 2: 20).

Our thesis must now pass through its most rigorous ordeal.

Is it possible that Christ can enshrine his presence in this portion of the gospel history; that the Prince of life can livingly adjoin himself to the record of his very death; so that he who is glorified and made most blessed for ever shall still look forth upon us from the shameful, cursed cross of Calvary? Is it not a mere illusion of the fancy to expect that Emmanuel should do what might even seem to approach the singular paradox of—living his own death among us continually? Must not the principle we have had in view break down at last? Can it stand the test of the Cross?

We trust to show that, instead of breaking down, it shines out here in its conclusive evidence and fullest glory; revealing the face of 'Jesus Christ and him crucified.'

Were the death of Christ, indeed, to be regarded, in the first place, as the passive endurance of a penalty merely: or, in the second place, as nothing more than an event or incident in our Lord's history; in that view, of course, past and gone, more than eighteen centuries ago: or, in the third place, as an expedient in the divine government (as some say), paving the way for something more ultimate and therefore more important, so that the cross, having served its purpose, falls very much out of sight—it would, in any of these cases, be difficult indeed to maintain that Christ should revive the record of it continually by conjoining his living presence with the gospel history here.

But the sacrifice of Christ is not an endurance merely; it is an offering. It is not an event—not eventual or incidental—merely; it is substantive. It is not an expedient; it is a substitution. And in all these points of view, the one sacrifice of the cross, offered once for all, is *perpetual*. It abides continually. And it is revealed unto us, exactly by the living Christ enshrining his presence in the history of it. We have then no dead record of something that is over and gone. We have a living revelation of the present and perpetual sacrifice. So that, before our eyes is Jesus Christ set forth, manifestly crucified among us (Gal. 3: 1).

Let us consider the sacrifice in these three points of view.

And we shall be satisfied of its perpetuity, as seen—first, in its offering through the eternal Spirit; secondly, in its enthronement, substantively, in the heavenly glory; and thirdly, in its appropriation by faith in all ages.

Some of the grandest aspects of the Cross will thus successively claim our attention.

The Perpetuity of the Sacrifice Seen in Its Offering Through the Eternal Spirit

'Christ, through the eternal Spirit, offered himself without spot to God' (Heb. 9: 14).

The intervention of the eternal Spirit in the death of Christ is here declared to have achieved a very specific result. It sustained—not merely Christ's holy patience, but—his obedience unto death; his holy and triumphant agency.

For, not only was he a holy, patient sufferer; he was an unsubdued, invincible actor—an agent—in his own death; a positive and active offerer of himself. Not only was he a slain Lamb; an offering; a sacrifice; a piacular and atoning victim. He was an atoning priest—the one only high priest of our profession; not dying out of the priesthood, as the priests of the house of Levi, who were not suffered to continue in their priesthood by reason of death (Heb. 7: 23); but rather dying into the fullest glory, and most intense and crowning activity and efficacious might, of his priesthood, by offering himself a sacrifice to God. And in this—this more than voluntariness (that is too weak a term

The Galleries of the King Visited

by far to indicate this grand and glorious doctrine, for a mere sufferer may suffer voluntarily) in this intense priestly activity, in which he not only suffered voluntarily but offered powerfully, he was sustained of the Holy Spirit.

Now, to see the transcendent triumph which Christ gained in prevailing, through the Spirit, to offer himself—in prevailing to maintain a state of activity and a forth-putting of actual obedience and unsubdued positive dutifulness and power; just consider how Christ's action or agency in his death outlives or outlasts, and triumphs over, all other agency or action concerned in it.

For there is prodigious action going forward in this death of the cross—action multiplied and most intense. Now is the judgment—the crisis—of the world. It is the most marvellous epoch of Christ's universe of time and space. And all agents are gathered together to it, to enact their characteristic parts in chiefest energy of all their powers.

Man Is in Action

Man is in action here:—man, in all capacities and in all relations; church and state; Jew and Gentile; apostate church, in person of the high priest and his clamorous menials; persecuting state, in Herod and Pontius Pilate. 'Herod and Pontius Pilate, with the Gentiles, and the people of Israel, are gathered together, for to do whatsoever God's hand and counsel determined before to be done' (Acts 4: 27–8). Their agency is in the death of Christ. 'Jesus of Nazareth ye have taken, and by wicked hands have crucified and slain' (2: 23). 'They shall look on me whom they have pierced' (Zech. 12: 10).

Satan is in Action

Satan is in action here. He instigated the traitor. He filled the rude multitude with clamorous malice. He goaded the envious priests and scribes to their malignant purpose. He shook the imbecile and feeble Pilate, and bore down his scruples and misgivings. It was early predicted that Satan's hand should be in the cross of Christ. The serpent was to bruise the heel of the promised seed.

The Father's Hand

The Father's hand and agency must be acknowledged in the death of Jesus. Not his eternal counsel and purpose only, fore-ordaining it; but his positive hand and action in it, when the appointed hour is come. For the Father was acting as the Judge, seated on the tribunal, when the substitute and surety stood at his bar for the guilty. It was the Sovereign Lord that made him to be sin for us. The Lord laid on him the iniquities of us all. Hence it pleased the Lord to bruise him. The Father said—'Awake, O sword, against the man that is my fellow; smite the Shepherd.'

View the death of Christ in these three lights or aspects, in reference to these three very different causes or agencies concerned in it, and how variously does it appear! From the side of man, or in respect of man's action, it is a crime—the darkest crime. From the side of Satan, or in respect of Satan's action, it is a blunder (blessed be God)—the deepest blunder. From the side of the Father, or in respect of the Father's action; representing the Godhead and sustaining the honours of the divine majesty, law and government, it is a penalty—the most holy infliction of a penalty most righteous. And it is—crime, blunder, penalty—each in largest possible proportions, because the various action, in respect of which it is all these at once, is action in its intensest energy.

Is there any scope, in such a case, for Christ's own action here at all?

Behold the dying Lamb of God made sin for us! Behold him set upon by man's action—man's hand, filled with instruments of torture and of death; by Satan's action—Satan's hand, filled with shafts and fiery darts deep-poisoned in the worst of hell; by the sword of justice, gleaming in terrific wrath, and wielded flashingly on Emmanuel's soul by a hand almighty, which he has always feared and loved! Is there any possibility of the blessed sufferer enduring through the burning and the shock of this chiefest hour of woe? With terrible concurrence of all powers of hell and earth and heaven against him; Satan, man, God; each in full-strung exercise—all energies of each, infinitely diverse, yet conspiring to act upon him to their uttermost of strength, unto his uttermost of agony and woe—must not the water-flood prevail? Must he not sink beneath the stream? Or, if still he does not murmur, and still he possesses his soul in patience, shall it not be to his everlasting and sufficing glory that, as a lamb before her shearers is dumb, so he openeth not his mouth; a quiet, patient sufferer, now that he can act no more, but must suffer merely? Is it thus?

No: no. This is not half the glory of the cross; nay, not a thousandth part of the gorgeous moral grandeur of the cross of Jesus. His own positive, powerful action is not overborne and in abeyance. He is obedient unto death; and thereby death's conqueror and death's destruction. He is a living, triumphing, glorious agent, even in death; never to the last overborne, but keeping the field and gaining the victory.

Men torture him with that cross; and, with refinements of their cruelty, they act against him to their uttermost. But they do not prevail. Weak and impotent, indeed, against the Prince of life are all the efforts of his human foes. His cross is a chariot of triumph against all that the hand of man can do.

Satan buffets him; the god of this world, permitted in the hour and power of darkness for once to go all his lengths, and do his uttermost. And terrible and strong are his reiterated assaults as, again and again, in the unseen shock of conflict, he leads up his reserves of principalities and powers of darkness; choosing, in fell hate, the hour when his bleeding antagonist is being crucified in weakness, on that sad sore cross where, by his own will, his hands are tied. 'The archers have sorely grieved him, and shot at him, and hated him. But his bow abideth in its strength; and the arms of his hands'—his outstretched, crucified hands—'are strong by the hands of the mighty God of Jacob; from thence is the Shepherd, the Stone of Israel.' And it is not in Satan; nor in all his hosts, brought forth this day on the plain of their decisive battle; to make the crucified Messiah give up the ghost.

And his Father hides his face from him in frowns and darkness; and answers him not a word at the voice of his cry. Or the only answer is another and another stroke of the Father's awakened sword, as it smites at the Father's call; till angels, who, at the Father's call also, had worshipped the first-begotten when brought into the world, have their love to him and their loyalty unto the Father strung to the intensest agony which holy blessed bosoms can feel, as in a sharp endangering trial, while they are ready to burst out into impatience—'O thou sword of the Lord, how long will it be ere thou be quiet? Put up thyself into thy scabbard, rest, be still.'

And will he not, in quiet patience, submit; and fall a victim unresisting?—holy and unmurmuring cessation from the unequal conflict being the uttermost the case can witness now, and *that* a marvel and a glory for evermore.

No: no. Jesus prevails to suffer all the tortures of man, and all the shafts of Satan, and all the strokes of his Father's sword—and, behold! in his hour of chiefest weakness, he is strong to bear them all. His own activity is not overborne, and laid to rest, and in abeyance. He is the livingly active and triumphant Saviour still. Weak man, he sets far aside from him. Baffled Satan, he banishes back to his place of darkness. His Father's wrath, he bears it all; exhausting in his afflicted soul the vials of all his curse.

He has passed through the hour and power of darkness unsubdued. He has borne the wrath. He has broken the strong bond of the curse. He has made an end of sin. He has vanquished Satan. He has spoiled principalities and powers. He has torn the handwriting of indictment that was against his people, and nailed it to the cross.

He has done all these things, in the hour of the extremest weakness to which his mediatorial person, in its utmost possible humiliation, could be reduced. He has done all these things in the most adverse circumstances—with his friends all fled; his enemies allowed their utmost scope; his Father hiding his face and inflicting judicial vengeance; with his body in utmost anguish, and his soul exceeding sorrowful even unto death. But now—with man's puny rage exhausted; with Satan baffled and bound; with death trampled on; and with justice ready to echo his cry, 'It is finished,' and her sword all but turned now to protect his honour and see to it that not a bone of him be broken—with no power in action now that could even seem to constrain him, his own outliving action now becomes conspicuous. And with the cry of triumph on his parched but powerful lips; and his Father's light and love shed abroad again in his faithful heart; and the joy set before him, in the saved souls of men, shining bright to his undimmed eye of faith; and the pleasure of the Lord, as a palm of victory, prospering in his hand; and as a Son, crying, Abba, Father, and committing his Spirit to his Father's hands—even thus the conqueror livingly dies; by his own prevailing act, lays down his life for the sheep, a ransom; offers himself to God, a sacrifice.

Is it not a sacrifice of a sweet smelling savour unto God?

For, on the one hand, irrefragable and transcendent proof is now given of his love to his Father. His own word is now fulfilled—'The prince of this world cometh, and hath nothing in me' (John 14: 30). Jesus has defied and discarded him; baffled him and bruised his head; spoiled him and made a show of him openly, triumphing over him in his cross. And by no power of Satan, but by his own manifest and mighty will, and after Satan's powerlessness has been demonstrated, Christ has given his life for the sheep, so as even the blind 'world might know that he loveth the Father,' and is acting 'as the Father gave him commandment' (v. 31). And will not the Father accept and respond to this proof of his Son's exceeding love to him? Yea; 'therefore doth my Father love me because I lay down my life for my sheep' (John 10: 17). On the other hand, his love to his people now is as little susceptible of doubt as its evidence is capable of increase! Had he passively, and in mere meekness, surrendered in the struggle, I could not tell how far his death was to be explained on the score of love to me on his part, or power over him on the part of the curse or of hell, of the evil world or of all-devouring death. But when I see death and the world and the principalities of hell all foiled, exhausted, bruised, and banished from the field; the curse of the righteous law, also, not exhausting the life and strength of the blessed curse-bearer, but borne as by one who is not weak to succumb but 'mighty to save'—I then see that his death is to be attributed exclusively to his love. I see that he is 'loving the church and giving himself for it' (Eph. 5: 25)—'loving me and giving himself for me' (Gal. 2: 20). I see this, because I see that 'no man taketh his life from him; he layeth it down of himself' (John 10: 18). And I feel that there is as much truth and power as there is tenderness and pathos in the appeal—'I am the good Shepherd; the good Shepherd giveth his life for the sheep' (v. 10).

He offers himself without spot to God, a sacrifice without spot or wrinkle or any such thing (adorned, rather, with all possible moral preciousness—the Branch of the Lord, beautiful and glorious, excellent and comely), bringing in an everlasting righteousness; transcendently magnifying the law in both its great commandments—loving God, confiding in him, adoring him, obeying him, steadfastly confessing him, even amidst his frowns of darkness and in the furnace of his wrath; loving his brethren of mankind, also, while they were worthy of the curse he was bearing for them, and hurrying him to the death which he was dying in their stead!

And to uphold and empower him unto this, the eternal Spirit was his without measure.

By the same eternal Spirit, through whom he livingly offered himself in death a sacrifice to God, Christ can fill the record of his death with his own living presence; and make it no dead record of something altogether past, but a present and living revelation of him who was dead and is alive again, who was even the living one in the instant when he died. In all other instances, death is—life conquered and placed in abeyance. Christ's death is—life conquering and extinguishing death. But for this, there were essential contrariety and incongruity in the idea of his living presence looking out on us from the history of his death. But if in his very death he was livingly offering himself—his profoundest life (for he is the fountain of life) never trenched upon, but through the eternal Spirit, triumphing—if in his very death he was the living one, looking out towards God as the living one, even in his act of dying, may he not from the record of such a death, livingly look out on us?

For the sacrifice so offered up is a perpetual sacrifice. And if he can adjoin himself to any portion of his gospel history, will he not adjoin himself to this rather?—to this pre-eminently, in which his greatest mediatorial work is commemorated; and by which, therefore, the profoundest elements of his mediatorial glory shall be revealed?

Had the death of Christ been a mere passive sufferance, then—apart from the considerations which prove that, in such a case, it could have been no real atonement at all—it is clear that perpetuity could in no important or intelligible sense have been predicated of it. As a passive endurance of pain, it is past and gone. He is made most blessed for evermore. The shame is swept away in floods of glory; and the pain is swallowed up in ever-flowing tides of blessedness.

That this living one, blessed and glorious, could in any real sense, or for any conceivable end, enshrine his presence in the record of a mere passive death of agony and shame—were that what our present argument required us to maintain, well might we abandon the attempt in despair. Anything more inconceivable and incongruous could scarcely be entertained in dreams.

But the death of Jesus was the offering of himself a sacrifice. It was the grandest action, in holiness and love, which his soul had ever put forth. Every active principle in his spotless humanity—actuated, and sustained to the loftiest possible elevation of moral glory by the eternal Spirit—was acting in purest beauty and strongest energy. As a mere endurance the cross would have passed away with the occasion. As a positive mediatorial work it does not pass away; for every principle in the mediator's soul then in action, as he offered up himself without spot to God, passed over with him as his soul entered into paradise, blending, without a break, into the functions of the intercession, and abiding with him now in his resurrection glory. For, in a word, it was his love to the law that was in action while in death he magnified the law and made it honourable. And it has passed with him to his priestly throne. The righteousness of the cross is an everlasting righteousness. 'My righteousness shall be for ever and my salvation from generation to generation.'

It is, indeed, a righteousness not encompassed now with the shame and sorrow, the dark concealing clouds, and the fiery wrath, which on every side environed it upon the tree. It is not now loaded by the sin that weighed so heavily upon it, yet never crushed it. And it is not now in conflict with the death which assailed, yet never staggered it. But, cleared of the obscuring influences of the cross—and liberated from the conflict of the cross—the sacrifice, the righteousness, perfected in the furnace, and refined into the splendours of the highest law-magnifying mediatorial merit, liveth and abideth for ever.

Why may not the living righteousness shine to our faith in the record, or the revelation rather, of its triumph? Why may not the presence of the living Christ look out on us as from the cross of Calvary?

The Perpetuity of the Sacrifice Seen in its Enthronement in the Heavenly Glory

> 'And, lo! in the midst of the throne—stood a Lamb as it had been slain' (Rev. 5: 6).

The sacrifice of Calvary is not a mere event. If it were, perpetuity might be predicated of its issues, but not of itself. It is not a mere event. *It is substantive.* It is not a mere incident in the mediatorial history. It is the mediator.

It is the mediator, considered as the Lamb of God—the slain Lamb. And the living mediator, a Lamb as it had been slain, may enshrine his presence in this portion of the mediatorial or gospel history—most eminently.

In the priesthood of Christ, the priest and sacrifice are one. He was the offerer—'He offered.'—Himself was the sacrifice—'He offered himself.' He is enthroned as the priest. And the Epistle to the Hebrews largely celebrates the enthronement in this light; presenting it, indeed, as the tenor and substance of the grand argument—'Of the things that we have spoken this is the sum: We have such an high priest, who is set on the right hand of the throne of the Majesty in the heavens' (Heb. 8: 1). But Christ is enthroned also as the sacrifice. And

The Galleries of the King Visited

the Revelation of John copiously celebrates the enthronement in this other light—'For I beheld, and, lo, in the midst of the throne—stood a Lamb as it had been slain.'

Now this enthronement of the sacrifice argues its glorious and heavenly perpetuity, or (let us say)—its glory; its heavenliness; and its perpetuity.

Its Glory

The exaltation of the sacrifice to the very throne of God illustrates its transcendent glory.

What is the glory of a sacrifice—an atoning sacrifice? It is its efficacy. It is its power or virtue to propitiate the offended lawgiver and make peace; to expiate sin and make reconciliation for iniquity; to cleanse the offender's conscience from dead works to serve the living God. And this glory belongs transcendently to the sacrifice of Calvary. Else why, as a sacrifice, is it placed in the glory of the throne?

Doubtless this glory—this efficacy—belonged to it in the hour of its offering on the tree. The exaltation of the sacrifice did not contribute any glory which was not inherent in it before. It did justice to the sacrifice, and nothing more than justice. It brought to light the full splendour of moral, spiritual glory embodied in it. It took away the covering of shame. It unveiled the face of Jesus Christ and him crucified. And then the glory which was there shone forth. But until then, the glory had been concealed. 'For he shall grow up before him as a tender plant, and as a root out of a dry ground: he hath no form nor comeliness; and when we shall see him, there is no beauty that we should desire him' (Isa. 53: 2).

Verily the glory was veiled. He was crucified in weakness, in anguish, and in shame.

The sacrifice transpired on a mean, degraded platform—this earth, cursed for man's sake. It was transacted, also, in the presence of a very mean and limited spectatorship; amidst circumstances fitted to revolt every pure and upright mind, the sun in the heavens turning aside the brightness of his face; and there was darkness over all the land until the ninth hour, as if, all the glory being veiled, this inconceivable shame—to the Jews a stumbling-block—should be covered too. A very narrow and transient affair, to sense and reason, as it reproachfully transpired without the camp, was the sacrifice of the slain Lamb on Calvary. A few passing hours of time embraced it. A single little world in space beheld it—and even there, only a handful of the race; and most of them beheld it with contempt. And when, on the shameful altar—that cursed cross—our bleeding paschal lamb expired, he was hurried with indecent haste to the darkness of the tomb, because the Pharisees' Sabbath was at hand.

Might not the arch-enemy—accuser of the brethren—concede to you not a little concerning this sacrifice; admitting its propitiatory nature and powers, but scorning the fascinated, fond enthusiasm with which your faith glories in the cross? No doubt this sacrifice may not, in every point of view, be destitute of worth and efficacy. It may have not a little eminence and value, measured by the small standard of earth and time; set forth on the little platform where it transpired among human things, itself one among the rest; claiming its place among others; passing away even as other events pass away. It may even be conspicuous in history. But it is a poor world in whose history it is embraced. Carry it round among the worlds of light, and you take the shining radiance out of it.

No, the revelation of God teaches us to answer. There is a central home of light—light that is inaccessible and full of glory. The throne of the Lord God Almighty is in it—justice and judgment its habitation—countless myriads adoring at its footstool. No mean platform is there; no narrow, transient state of things. No blinded spectatorship; no voice of malignity; no weapon of offence; no traitor's kiss; no cursed tree. There is nothing there that defiles. The glory is incorruptible and undefiled, and fades not away. And in the untold splendours of its central light—even in the midst of the throne—the King Eternal is worshipped by the wing-veiled choirs of the cherubim.

By his own blood, Jesus entered there. His sacrifice he placed in the seat of heavenly glory most conspicuous, most august—centre of all the adoring worship; in the midst of the throne of the Majesty in the heavens. And it was not out of place. There was no unseemliness; no incongruity; no excess of reward; no superfluous majesty and beauty. The Father's voice, rather, was, as in the oracle of welcome—'Sit thou at my right hand'; while the rapturous and instant cry was from the angels—'Worthy is the Lamb that was slain,' the elders and the ransomed going on to shout—'Thou wast slain for us, and hast redeemed us.'

There is no light in all the universe of God—nay, no light even in him that covers himself with light as with a garment—that can pale the glory of the slain Lamb of Calvary, or take the shining radiance from the sacrifice he offered there. Returned from the grave and ascended up on high, he placed his sacrifice amidst the searching blaze of heaven's divinest glory. And it endured the scrutiny. It outshone it—and became the sweetest light of heaven. For the glory of God doth enlighten it, and the Lamb is the light thereof.'

Its Heavenliness

The enthronement of the sacrifice illustrates its heavenliness. For it is a heavenly sacrifice. And it is seen to be so, when enthroned in heaven, the Lamb in the midst of the throne.

Such a sacrifice became us, even a heavenly one. Such a sacrifice we needed. For it was from heaven we had become aliens. It was from the possibility of being enrolled among the family of heaven we were excluded. Nor could any other than a sacrifice, in its very nature heavenly, redeem for us a seat in the heavenly places.

Now heavenliness is incorruptibility and immortality. So does the Apostle teach, when amplifying and explaining what he means by our bearing 'the image of the heavenly,' even 'the Lord from heaven' (1 Cor. 15: 47–9), he specifies—and comprehends all under—this twofold classification: 'This corruptible shall put on incorruption, and this mortal shall put on immortality' (v. 53). Incorruption and immortality; that will be the image of the heavenly; that will be the heavenliness of them that are heavenly. They are the very attributes of the God of heaven—'the incorruptible God' (Rom. 1: 23)—'who only hath immortality' (1 Tim. 6: 16).

If, therefore, we are to be reconciled to heaven, it must be by a heavenly sacrifice—if redeemed for heaven and a heavenly life, it must be by a heavenly ransom—a sacrifice and ransom that is, in which there must meet the two qualifications of incorruptibility and immortality. The Lamb of God is such a sacrifice. 'For we are not redeemed with corruptible things, as silver and gold; but with the precious blood of Christ as of a lamb without blemish and without spot' (1 Pet. 1: 18). Behold the incorruptibility! Behold, also, the immortality! No mortal lamb is this. 'A lamb without blemish and without spot: who verily was fore-ordained before the foundation of the world' (v. 19).

The efficacy of this sacrifice—indeed, its entire suitableness—depends on its heavenliness. Earthly, or worldly, sacrifices might suffice for the first covenant, which 'had ordinances of divine service' connected with 'a worldly sanctuary' (Heb. 9: 1). There must be a heavenly sacrifice to establish our worship in the heavenly places. Earthly ransoms might redeem an earthly forfeit—or exempt from the penalty of being unclean according to the flesh, and excluded from the earthly tabernacle. And the earthly pattern of the things in heaven might be purified with corruptible and mortal blood. But the heavenly things themselves must be purged with a better sacrifice. For the forerunner was to enter into heaven itself, there to appear in the presence of God for us (Heb. 9: 23–4).

'If he were on earth,' argues Paul, 'he would not be a priest' (Heb. 8: 4). He would not be a legitimate priest at all, if his whole priestly function and ministry were transacted on earth, or even natively, and in the first instance, belonged to earth. There are many such priests—an entire priestly tribe—in Israel. Christ pertained to another tribe, of which no man gave attendance at the altar; the tribe of Judah, of which Moses spake nothing concerning priesthood (7: 13–14). No legitimate, earthly priest, therefore, could he be. The Levites were the earthly priests; their whole office confined to earth, and transacted here below; serving, as they did, unto the example and shadow merely of heavenly things (8: 5). Christ was to serve unto the heavenly things themselves; achieving our reconciliation to heaven; establishing and maintaining our peace with heaven; purchasing for us a throne of victory in heaven. And we have such an high priest, who is set on the right hand of the throne of the majesty in the heavens, a minister of the heavenly sanctuary and mediator of a heavenly covenant—a covenant of incorruptibility and immortality, ordered in all things, and sure.

Nor is it the heavenliness only of the priest that is thus proclaimed—himself originally the Lord from heaven, and now our high priest 'passed into the heavens'—'made higher than the heavens' (4: 14, 7: 26). The heavenliness of the sacrifice is, by implication, testified too. Indeed, its heavenliness is expressly and explicitly attested by its enthronement. For Jesus is enthroned in special recognition of his sacrifice, a Lamb as it had been slain.

They can be no aliens from heaven whose faith rests on this slain Lamb of God. Their citizenship is in heaven. They are raised up to sit with Jesus in heavenly places. They are blessed with all spiritual blessings in heavenly places. Their treasure is in heaven. They are come unto the heavenly Jerusalem. They are partakers of a heavenly calling. They seek a better country, that is an heavenly. But in respect of all these, their implications with heaven, they are dependent on the sacrifice. What then, if the sacrifice itself were not heavenly? But how precious to see it throned in heaven—a Lamb in the midst of the throne!

It was offered on earth. For the scene of sin's offence must be the scene of sin's expiation. And amidst earth's conditions of weakness, and shame, and sorrow, and transiency, the sacrifice was perfected upon the tree. Its heavenliness was veiled most of all in the hour in which, by its exhaustion of the curse and its fulfilment of all righteousness, it rivetted a bond of union between earth and heaven. To carnal eye and reason; it appeared the most earthly and offensive of all earthly things—foolishness to Greeks, to Jews a stumbling-block. Nevertheless, it belonged neither to Greece nor Judea, nor to earth at all. It was heavenly. It was heaven fastening its cords of love to earth; girdling round the earth with mercy and with righteousness, and fastening it to heaven. It was heaven tasting earth's death, to destroy death from off the earth, and open for earth the way to heaven and heavenly life for ever.

Yes! It was a heavenly sacrifice—magnifying a heavenly law—establishing a heavenly covenant—procuring for us a heavenly country—and admitting us, even on earth, to partake by faith in heaven's worship. And, behold, now it is not out of place in heaven itself. It occupies heaven's very throne. It modulates all heaven's history. It is celebrated in heaven's song. It gives its own peculiar lustre, the sweet unrivalled glow and lustre of mediatorial grace and glory, to heaven's light. It casts the rainbow of an everlasting covenant around heaven's judgment seat. It blends the interests of the redeemed below with the activity of heaven above. It makes heaven, in their believing consciousness, their own real home, most germain to their feelings and their faith. And it will bring all the redeemed of the Lord to heaven in the end.

Its Perpetuity

The enthronement of the sacrifice exhibits it as the true continual burnt-offering.

A consciously sinful creature has necessarily some sense of his need of a continual sacrifice. For my guilt is always new, and my sin is always finding me out. My guilt (and my sense of guilt), each of these is a present and real thing. And if you show me no perpetual sacrifice, you throw me back for my relief upon a past thing—something altogether past, and which, to me, with sense of sin present and real, must be utterly unreal and a shadow. If you would expel and annihilate that sense of sin which is present now in my conscience, you must yoke with my present sense of sin a present sacrifice for sin, able by its present and perpetually subsisting powers to meet my present and perpetual need.

Hence the joy with which experienced believers contemplate the death of Christ as the opening of a fountain, never closed (according to promise)—'In that there shall be a fountain opened to the house of David, and to the inhabitants of Jerusalem, for sin and for uncleanness' (Zech. 13: 1). That joy is the broken heart's welcome of the sacrifice, in view of its perpetuity.

Hence, also—so far as any *desideratum*, or crave, in human nature is concerned—the origin of the Mass. It professes to answer a sinner's need and desire for a perpetual and present oblation for sin. And it does so by making the Supper a continual repetition of the sacrifice.

We admit the necessity (rightly understood) of a continual oblation for sin. And we admit that such is the oblation or sacrifice of Christ. Indeed, we especially and enthusiastically contend that it is so. We rejoice continually that, at whatsoever time in all the world's history a sinner comes to seek the great propitiation—or a believer comes at whatsoever time in his own history as a sin-sick soul, contrite and contending with sin—he finds the sacrifice no past, departed, dead, forgotten thing; changed as a vesture; rolled aside as a scroll; but living, perpetual, present, in all its power to calm and cleanse the conscience. Always he finds Christ as Christ crucified; always the Lamb as a slain Lamb, a perpetual, never-ceasing, presently powerful sacrifice.

But we see the sacrifice to be thus continuous and perpetual, because we see no atoning merit in the Supper; no, nor anywhere at all, in heaven above or in the earth beneath, save in the one sacrifice once offered on the tree. And even it we see to be perpetual, because not offered often—not offered twice—but only once, and once for all; because he exclaimed, 'It is finished.' And the perpetuity of this most finished efficaciousness—most finished or perfected, and perfecting also to them that are sanctified—we see borne out by the throne now assigned within the veil in glory to the Lamb that was slain.

Nor do we know whether most to condemn the blasphemy, or the folly, of seeking any other guarantee of its perpetuity.

What! Shall we peril the perpetuity of the sacrifice on the celebration of the supper?—on the dispensation of any ordinance on earth, and in the hands of men? Shall we risk its never-ceasing efficacy on the chances of the preservation in the church on earth of any rite whatever, whose celebration may, nay, must be intermittent, however frequent? Construct a cordon of celebrations of the Lord's

Supper—or any rite in human hands—as accurately as you please; get up, and keep up, as accurately as you can, incessant relays and repetitions of the dispensation; place one cohort of the priests on the day shift—we are driven to humiliating comparisons—and another on the night (as when our poor brothers, the hard-wrought sons of toil, change labour day and night beside the blazing furnace ceaselessly); make such arrangements as would need a worldwide hierarchy bound by iron bands of association such as Rome alone can form or maintain:—and what have you, at the utmost, as your guarantee for the perpetuity of any atoning virtue you may imagine such a rite to carry with it? Nothing but a series of earthly conditions—a succession of things which being seen are temporal (2 Cor. 4: 18), transient, evanescent—passing away with the world and the fashion thereof.

Is it on a footing of such earthliness—of earth's security, which is just earth's insecurity and fallibility—that I am content to rest and risk the perpetuity of that sacrifice, without which, as presently mine, I cannot live; with whose failure for the smallest interstice of time my death and perdition were inevitable?

No, truly. It is not down here below—not in this lower world; not in the church on earth, nor in any of its ordinances, however good and holy—that the basis and ground of the never ceasing efficacy of the great sacrifice is seen to rest. But away, far away from earth's fallible estate; away from earth's shaking, ever-reeling, transient conditions: beyond the realm which the star-light glorifies, and the far-piercing glass or science of the wise so little sounds or fathoms; away beyond all heavens, in the realm of cloudless light, where time passes not by day and by night, but where the things unseen and eternal are, and the throne of the Father of lights—*there*, passed through the heavens and now made higher than the heavens; far above, not merely earth's transient and treacherous estate, but far above all principalities and powers, all thrones and dominions; *there* is the sacrifice, who is the priest also, on his throne—a Lamb as it had been slain—bearing out, in his own hands, in office of eternal priesthood, the never-ceasing virtue of his one peerless, priestly death—the one offering whereby he hath for ever perfected them that are sanctified.

And now, under the perpetuity thus attested of the one only sacrifice of Calvary, under the shield and shining glory of a perpetual heavenly sacrifice—no altar now is reared in the church below, but a table spread; no atonement offered, but a Supper received; no ritual practised to preserve or prolong or prop up a treacherous or transient reconciliation; but a feast upon the sacrifice—in testimony that our reconciliation is eternal; our access always free; our forgiveness accessible at all times to faith; our covenant ordered in all things and sure.

The Perpetuity of the Sacrifice Seen in its Appropriation in all Ages

'I am crucified with Christ' (Gal. 2: 20).

Were the sacrifice of Christ a mere *passive endurance*, perpetuity could in no sense be predicated of it. But Christ actively and triumphantly offered himself, and every living principle of action in his holy soul which went to constitute or to achieve the sacrifice is living now. There is, therefore, no incongruity when the living Christ enshrines his promised presence in the gospel history of his cross.

Were the sacrifice of Christ a mere *historical event*—an incident in the mediatorial history—perpetuity could in no sense be predicated of it. But it is a substantive sacrifice. It is the Lamb of God. And the Lamb is in the midst of the throne as it had been slain. Instead, therefore, of discovering any incongruity in our Lord's presence shining out upon us from the gospel history of his Cross, we see that his refusal so to appear to us—to our faith on earth—were a disparagement of exactly the aspect in which he appears to beatific vision in heaven.

Were the sacrifice of Christ a mere *expedient*, designed to open the way for ulterior beneficial measures towards the sinner, perpetuity could in no sense be predicated of it. Nor would there be any reason to desire its perpetuity. All our attention would be concentrated on those beneficial measures that were to follow it; and the indispensable preliminary, having been right well and satisfactorily gone through and adjusted, might be allowed to fall aside into comparative oblivion. This is not the place to enter, into the theology of so large a question: but we may say, in a word, that this will be found as a general category to cover almost all false views of the nature and design of the sacrifice of Christ. It was not such an expedient—transferring all our reasonable anxieties to the ulterior measures for which it paved the way. It is a *substitution*, carrying all our salvation in it, and demanding to be itself appropriated. Hence its perpetual subsistence is obviously necessary.

The death of Christ is a true and proper substitution. Christ exchanges places with me. Or rather, Christ enters into my place, dwells in it, and makes it his—and that, in order that I may enter into his, and dwell in it, and make it mine.

Mine it was originally. Christ makes it his. But, by making it his, he greatly modifies it—modifies it for me. Gladly may I take the place that is now his, and which is also mine. For, it is indeed mine. I am not out of place. I am in my own place still—my own place more than ever.

But my place, when Christ came to enter into it, was the place of a curse. And entering into it, accordingly, he found his place to be the place of a curse; that is, the cross—'for cursed is everyone that hangeth on a tree' (Gal. 2: 13). His place, when I come to enter into it, is therefore—the cross; and entering into it, I find it to be the place of the blessing—'for Christ hath redeemed us from the curse of the law, being made a curse for us, that the blessing might come upon us' (Gal. 2: 14). In love, he enters into my place, to fulfil all righteousness—condemned in the guilty: by faith I enter into his, to enjoy the righteousness—accepted in the beloved. If he enter into my place, he cannot avoid the cross; for the curse points always to the cross as its only goal and outgoing. If I enter into his place, I can as little shun the cross; for the blessing is found always in the cross, its only shrine and home. He found my curse pointing sternly to the cross as his only place, if he was to stand in my room. I find even his blessing pointing as uncompromisingly and sternly to the cross as my only place too, if I am to stand in his room. It is impossible that I can avoid the cross. With all its humiliation and shame I must make the cross mine—and be crucified with Christ. For if Christ exchange places with me—even me condemned; I must exchange places with Christ, even Christ crucified. So did he himself indicate when he said—'Except a man deny himself, and take up his cross, and follow me, he cannot be my disciple' (Matt. 16: 24).

For, assuredly, he had not in view the meaning which the mere moralist puts upon his words. A very superficial exposition it is of a very profound saying, which would make the cross we are commanded to take up have reference merely to the provocations one meets with in social life—or even any particular adversity, however great, and which, in common phrase, is styled a cross, or a crook in the lot. Besides, it should be remembered that 'a cross,' in this sense, is quite a modern expression. Nor was it the mere moralist's meaning of self-denial—the graceful giving up of little or even great gratifications—that Jesus had in view when he enjoined that a man 'deny himself.' He meant what he said, in all its completeness—and intensity:—'Except a man deny himself'—renounce himself—his own entire standing before God, his own entire character and disposition towards God, even root and branch; getting spiritually into the position in which he may be able truly to say—'Look not upon me; see, O God, our shield'—'It is not I, but the grace of God: it is not I, but Christ liveth in me'; without this, 'he cannot be my disciple.' He must deny himself. But in order so to do, he must, to avoid annihilation, exchange places with some one else. It must be with me. But the cross is the only place for exchanging places. Therefore in denying himself, it must be by taking up his cross and following me. He must make my cross his, and take it up as his own.

Plainly this is the meaning of our Lord. He had been predicting his own cross, and Peter had dissuaded him from enduring it (v. 21-2). Jesus tells him that not only he, his Lord and Master, must endure the cross, despising the shame, but that every disciple must conjoin himself with his crucified Saviour and bear the cross too. Except I embrace Christ's cross, making it my own, entering into it intelligently, appreciatingly, approvingly, appropriatingly—prizing it as a satisfaction to divine justice and a fulfilment of all righteousness (thus condemning myself as worthy of the curse, and seeking no blessing but what comes through the magnifying of the law)—I cannot be Christ's disciple. I must be crucified with Christ. My old man must be crucified with Christ that the body of sin may die. I must be crucified with Christ that I may live—that Christ may live in me. The death, the cross, the sacrifice, must itself be mine.

Manifestly, then, it cannot be a mere event or expedient. It must be something substantive and presently subsisting—if presently and now I have to embrace it.

Were it merely the fruits and consequences of Christ's death that I were called to receive, the cross might be regarded as an historical event or incident, past and over and gone; or as a valuable expedient for securing ulterior advantages. But if the mercy and forgiveness, the reconciliation and the peace, the grace and glory—all the fruits and the advantages—can be mine, only by appropriating the cross, how am I to appropriate an event or an expedient? A politic and advantageous expedient—an important and beneficial event—I may commemorate, but can hardly (in any intelligible sense) appropriate. And it is remarkable that the very ordinance of commemoration—the Holy Supper—is a sacrament in which, by sign and seal, the Lord gives participation in the sacrifice. 'This is my body broken for you; take ye; eat ye. This is the new testament in my blood; drink ye all of it.'

The simple issue is this. The one grand object of appropriation for a sinner is—'the righteousness of God'—as it is written, 'The righteousness of God is revealed from faith to faith' (Rom. 1: 17). And the sacrifice is just the righteousness under a special denomination, or regarded in a special aspect and relation—as related to the penal side of the law. Substantively, the sacrifice is the righteousness. It is the righteousness passing through the furnace and ordeal of the cross—the righteousness coming forth most glorious from the perfecting crisis of its history.

Passing through this crisis it becomes available to me a sinner. Apart from, and as before, this crisis—it is not available. It must be perfected through suffering (Heb. 2: 10). It must be brought nigh to me through suffering. It is through the cross that it is perfected and brought nigh. By the door of the cross the everlasting righteousness is 'brought in.' 'He brought in' by the cross 'an everlasting righteousness' (Dan. 9: 24).

Otherwise it is not brought in. It stands outside—a wall of fire, a furnace of consuming fire, between it and me. But, behold, it comes. It comes to me through the consuming fire. And it is brighter than that very fire that has kindled on it but not consumed it. And the light of it is stronger than the sun as he shines in his strength. And it is of very gentle, gracious aspect too. And it has a sweet and 'still small voice.' For listen! It expostulates with me very tenderly, and very powerfully, and in words of wondrous wisdom, concerning my doubts and fears. This 'righteousness speaketh on this wise; Say not in thine heart, Who shall ascend into heaven? that is to bring Christ down from above'—as if no justifying righteousness had come from heaven to earth at all; 'Or, Say not in thine heart, Who shall descend into the deep? that is to bring Christ up from the dead'—as if the righteousness had failed in its attempt to reach you, and been consumed in the furnace of the cross or imprisoned in the realms of death. 'But what saith it? The word is nigh thee, even in thy mouth and in thy heart; that is, the word of faith which we preach; that if thou shalt confess with thy mouth the Lord Jesus, and shalt believe in thine heart that God hath raised him from the dead, thou shalt be saved. For with the heart man believeth unto righteousness' (Rom. 10: 6–10)—believes with the view, and the effect, of obtaining a righteousness that shall secure justification of life.

Such is the expostulation and appeal of the righteousness, returned from the cross and from the grave, as it courts and entreats my believing appropriation. And truly it is a substantive righteousness which I am entreated to appropriate. It is a living, personal righteousness. In a word, it is Christ. 'For Christ is the end of the law for righteousness to everyone that believeth' (Rom. 10: 4). It is not some suffering endured by him. It is the great sufferer, the great offerer, himself. It is not some event in Christ's history. It is the historical and ever living Christ himself. It is not some expedient preliminary to redemption. It is the Redeemer. It is the Lord our righteousness. It is the slain Lamb—our righteousness shining forth perfected upon the cross.

It is now in heaven. But—'the Word is nigh thee.' And the righteousness shines out upon you from the Word. 'I am not ashamed of the Gospel of Christ,' for this very reason, says the Apostle; even because 'therein is revealed the righteousness of God from faith to faith' (Rom. 1: 16–17). What is this but a proof that—

The Lord our righteousness enshrines his presence very eminently in the closing chapters of the gospel history, unfolding and perpetuating the glory of his Cross?

PART THREE

ADDITIONAL ELUCIDATION

8

CHRIST'S PRESENCE, REAL AND PERSONAL—BY THE SPIRIT

WE have already seen that it is by his Holy Spirit that Jesus fulfils the promise of his real and personal presence with his people. But the subject is worthy of fuller consideration.

At the same time it may give fresher interest to the theme, and somewhat enlarge our view, if—to use the language of the mathematician—we take the theorem in its most general form, instead of dealing merely with a single case. Without confining ourselves, then, to the consideration of the true reality and distinct personality of Christ's presence, let the wider truth engage our attention: namely, that *the Holy Spirit is the author of all reality, and of all personality, in religious life and fellowship.*

THE SPIRIT THE AUTHOR OF ALL— REALITY IN RELIGION

This is a quality or characteristic which, in certain quarters, is in great demand. Semblances and shams, hollownesses and formalisms, are warred against and run down. And the demand is imperious, and almost fanatically urged, for reality, solidity, substance; something tangible; something that may be grasped, and trusted in, and held fast.

So far as it goes, the demand (from whatever quarter) is good. But it is better if it can be really met. And what if old-fashioned spiritual Christianity alone can meet it?

Yes! it is a good demand. You crave reality. You have a longing, yearning, quenchless desire for something real.

You have had enough of thoughts: you seek for things. You have wearied your soul with speculations concerning things divine. You seek the divine things themselves. Long trains of religious ratiocination; full schemes of religious doctrine; the tracking and tracing of the mutual connections of truth with truth; their cross-lights, and side-lights, and harmonies—in all this, perhaps, you are no mean proficient. And considering that the fall—while it has removed all spiritual light from man's mind, and all spiritual love from his heart—has left all the constituting elements of rationality and responsibility, it is not amazing if even the natural man be found capable of great proficiency in reasoning on the statements of divine revelation and constructing well-ordered schemes of doctrine from its contents.

For, let us bear in mind what it is, precisely, that the natural man is disqualified for. 'The natural man receiveth not *the things* of the Spirit of God; for they are foolishness unto him: neither can he know them, because they are spiritually discerned' (1 Cor. 2: 14). They are 'the things' of the Spirit of God which he cannot receive; which he cannot know; which are foolishness to him—very discernible, but not by him; very real in themselves, but not to his apprehension. It is not said that he cannot reason concerning divine *doctrines*; but that he can neither receive nor discern divine *things*.

What is it that 'eye hath not seen, nor ear heard, and that hath not entered into the heart of man'? It is 'the *things* which God hath prepared for them that love him' (1 Cor. 2: 9). What is it that the Spirit searcheth and revealeth? The *deep things* of God (v. 10). What is it that no man knoweth save the Spirit of God, and he to whom the Spirit unveils them?[1] Again, the

---

[1] I cannot refrain from drawing the reader's attention to the following remarkably beautiful passage from *Principal Rollock's Works* (vol. i, p. 385). Rollock was the first Rector of the University of Edinburgh, and the first who introduced the famed Scottish Lecture into the instruction of the pulpit.

things of God. The things of God knoweth no man but the Spirit of God (v. 11). For what end is it that we receive, not the Spirit of the world, but the Spirit which is of God? That we might know the things that are freely given us of God (v. 12). And what is it that the very doctrine—the speech of inspired

> It is indeed a pleasant little work of love to unclothe his sentences of their antique spelling, and present, as we now do, a train of thought as original and expressed in as beautiful language as any that the most elaborate refinement of modern days can produce:
> 'Now, look to the manner of the revealing of these things. The Spirit reveals, because he opens our hearts, and takes away the veil from off our hearts, to let us see them; otherwise, in vain was it to lay them before us. I see another manner of this revelation; and, therefore, look what more the Spirit does. He is not content to take the veil from thy heart; but he takes thy soul by the hand, as it were, and leads it in through the deepness—['the deep things']—of God. He will ravish it out of the body, as it were, and lead it into that light that has no access—['the light that is inaccessible']—and he will say: Lo! there is the mercy; Lo! there is the righteousness; Lo! there is the everlasting life that is spoken of. Seest thou not them all in him? Thus will he point out everything in God. Therefore, no doctrine avails without this Holy Spirit; seeing that he alone takes the veil from off our hearts and leads us in to see the things that are spoken of. There is no perfect doctor but the Spirit of Jesus only. There is no creature—though he were an angel—that can take off the veil from thy heart to let thee see, or open thine ear to let thee hear, perfectly. And therefore, in preaching, depend not on the mouth of men, but on the Spirit of Jesus Christ only.
> 'Yet I shall make the matter more plain, and show how the Spirit will take thee and let thee see the things which are in God. I will use a supposition, which cannot be; yet it will make the matter more clear. I suppose that my spirit or soul entered into thee. If my spirit or my soul be in thee, there would be nothing within me but thou wouldst see it; all my thoughts would be patent to thee. Now to apply this. This is no supposition: God will put his Spirit in us. For if his Spirit be not in us, woe be to us for ever. If God put his Spirit in us, must it not follow of necessity that we must see in God, at least the things that concern our weal and salvation. That Spirit in me—in thee—must reveal to me—to thee—the things that lie in the very deepness of God which concern our weal and salvation. And that man that has the Spirit of God will see the very heart of God and his mind. He will see the remission of his sins in the mind of God; and all, by the benefit of the Spirit of Jesus that dwells in him. So we have a great advantage here; that, by the benefit of the Spirit, we see the things that are in God.'
> The Word, however, must be introduced; else no reason is given for our seeing in God 'at least the things that concern our weal and salvation.' Secret things belong unto God even after he has given us his Spirit (Deut. 29: 29). In his Word we see the things that belong to us. See above (pp. 133–4).

men—envelopes and contains, rendering it imperative that their speech be inspired indeed; for otherwise how should it carry such contents? Again, the answer is, the things of God. 'Which things also we speak not in the words which man's wisdom teacheth'—the divine wine would burst such bottles of man's construction—'but in the words which the Holy Ghost teacheth' (v. 13).

The things of God: the deep things of God: the things of the Spirit of God! Such is the Apostle's language most persistently.

And is such emphatic phraseology not full of meaning?—more especially, when thus so carefully repeated, when thus so continually clung to? Doubtless it is. And it fastens down our attention on the precise nature of that inability which the Apostle then goes on (v. 14) to predicate of the natural man; namely this—that however much, and logically, and with perfect accuracy, you may reason concerning divine *doctrines*, you cannot, without the Spirit, receive nor discern—you can neither grasp nor see—divine *things*.

Take, for example, the doctrine of forgiveness. Who can tell how profoundly you may study it; how acutely you may argue it; how clearly you may teach it; how instructive to others your statement and exposition of it may be? Forgiveness—as a topic of speculation—may be one among the thoughts of your mind; and, in this light, even as a natural man, you may possibly do great justice to the theme. But forgiveness as a privilege—actual and real forgiveness—must be not one of the thoughts of your spirit, but one of the thoughts of God's Spirit; one of those thoughts of peace and not of evil which he knows that he thinks concerning you (Jer. 29: 11); the thoughts of God, not transient and inefficient like your thoughts, but substantial, effectual, eternal; the thoughts of God, which in their self-realizing substantiality are worthy to be called 'the things' of God. Forgiveness to be real must be one of these things of the Spirit of God; and, in that view, without God's Spirit you cannot discern it. As a mere thought, or doctrine, or scheme of thought, in your mind, it is altogether unreal; an abstraction; a shadowy, unsubstantial, airy nothing. Scanned and studied to eternity it would leave you unforgiven still. As

CHRIST'S PRESENCE, REAL AND PERSONAL

one of the things of God—real, and that may be grasped and held fast—you are forgiven when you see it and receive it.

Adoption, in like manner, you may deal with merely as a doctrine, giving it a lodgment among your thoughts. And you may master all its details and bearings. But still it may remain unreal to you. As an actual reality, as an act of God's free grace, a real transaction conferring real privilege and plead able right, it is among the things of God—those things which the natural man does not receive, neither can he know them.

Ah! it is this dealing with divine *doctrines*, to the exclusion of the divine *things* which the faithfulness of God has enshrined in them, that leaves so many with a religion destitute of the element of reality; and destitute, therefore, of power and comfort and refreshment.

But if our religion is to be real, if the real *things* of the Spirit are to be introduced into it, it is the Spirit himself that must introduce them. The Spirit will be the author of this reality.

To see this, let us consider in what the sense or feeling of reality consists—the conviction and assurance of reality or realism, in any field or sphere, whether material or mental; whether of art or science or trade; whether in camp or council; in a word, in any pursuit or interest known to man. Into what must we finally resolve our conviction of reality? To what must we ultimately trace that impression or assurance?

Clearly—metaphysical speculation apart—to a certain correspondence between the object apprehended and the subject apprehending; a certain harmony or mutual suitableness. Between the qualities of matter, for instance, and the senses of the human body by which we perceive these qualities, there is a certain correspondence or adaptation, by reason of which matter becomes to us, necessarily, in our apprehension, no shadowy, abstract, airy semblance, but an actual, existent, real thing. Between the phenomena of sound and the human ear there is a relation which inevitably begets the conviction that the sounds I hear are real; not ideal and imaginary, the echoes of dreamland. If they be musical sounds—the performance on a many stringed instrument of one that can handle it well—they will be real to me only as sounds, and not as music, unless I have a mental sense or faculty, a musical ear or taste, corresponding to their quality as musical; as the literal ear is adapted to their more general character as sounds merely. Why is it that, to the merchant, prices and markets and rumours of markets come home with all the impression of intense reality? It is because there is a corresponding habit and character of mind in such an one. There is a relation and suitableness between the subject mind and the object presented to it, in virtue whereof the impression of reality springs up immediately when subject and object come together.

And it is so in every sphere of knowledge or of contemplation.

If, therefore, the character and glory of God—his authoritative claim to your love—your exceeding sinfulness in refusing it; if the fact of your condemnation—the substitution and righteousness of Christ—his redeeming love and faithfulness; if forgiveness of sin—adoption—the light of God's countenance—the joy of his salvation and the comforts of his spirit; if the beauty of holiness—the goodness of God's law—and the rewards of his favour: if these are to you as yet but shadows and ideas and unrealities, it is because between your spirit and these things of God's Spirit there is no suitableness, no living relation, no true harmony or adaptation or correspondency.

But the Spirit of the Lord can give these things great reality in your estimation and conviction. For he can establish a glorious correspondency. Between these objective or outward 'deep things of God,' on the one hand; and your mind (as the active subject engaged in contemplating and dealing with them) on the other, the Spirit can create a living and blessed harmony. He has these deep things of God in his keeping. They are his own—'the things of the Spirit.' He has your spirit in his keeping also, and at his full and sovereign disposal. He can frame it into the very image and character and glory of God. He can fashion it into the very figure and mould of God's holy law, and give unto it the leading attributes and tone of 'the deep things of God.'

And then, when the character and glory of God are outwardly presented to your mind (itself now formed in that same glorious character); when the authority of God is held up to you in imposing that same holy law which is now within your heart; and sin is held up to you as the transgression of that holy law; and Christ's atoning blood and surety-righteousness, as magnifying that holy law; and forgiveness (with acceptance, even complete justification), as following from that holy law, having been magnified and made honourable; the sovereign love of God, also, as originating all this redemption, and the light of his countenance as following in its train; with the peace that passeth understanding, and the joy that is unspeakable and full of glory, and the hope that maketh not ashamed, and the rest that remaineth—oh! then, because of the exact correspondency between your inner man as formed anew of the Spirit, on the one hand, and these things of the self-same Spirit, on the other, there is in all your soul an impression (not inferential, but direct; not the fruit of reasoning, but intuitional; inevitable also, and ineradicable, as well as immediate) that you are seeing and receiving, that you are discerning; handling, grasping, the things of God; things that are real indeed, even as no things can be more real, indeed, none are so real: 'for the things that are seen are temporal, but the things that are unseen are eternal' (2 Cor. 4: 18).

Yes: the things that are seen are temporal. *They* are the shadows—the transient, the superficial. They perish in the using. They pass away with the fashion of the world. But the things that are unseen—they remain real unto eternity, gloriously solid, substantial and enduring. 'Riches and honour are with me; yea, *durable* riches and righteousness. I cause them that love me to inherit substance.' For 'faith is the *substance* of things hoped for, and the evidence of things not seen.' And the regenerating Spirit, working faith in you, is the author of reality in your religion, introducing into it effectually the substance of 'the things of God.'

You are in a new world now. And it is a real world though spiritual. Indeed, it is peculiarly and intensely real because spiritual; its spirituality, to you, is too obvious for reasoning, because you now are spiritual through the Spirit dwelling in you.

And if any natural man, disputing with you now, should call in question the reality of those things which to you are alike beyond all price and above all proof, and should judge you fanatical because what is still foolishness and fancy to him is solid reality held fast by you—you refuse to reason with him, and you repudiate his judgment. For the spirituality which has brought spiritual things within your discernment, has carried you beyond the discernment or judgment of those that are not spiritual. 'The things of the Spirit of God are spiritually discerned. And he that is spiritual judgeth all things, yet he himself is judged of no man.' The Spirit of God is the judge of all things that are objectively real; and he is the author, subjectively, of all conviction or sense of their reality.

The Spirit the Author of All— Personality in Religion

This is a feature of true religion very plain and obvious; but very apt, nevertheless, to be forgotten. Religion is not a mere sacred seriousness of spirit; it is the conduct of your relationship towards a personal and living God. It is not an absolute and abstract, but a relative and intensely personal, thing. Religion is and must be so, in its most general notion, and in its various adaptations to all ranks of God's rational creatures. It is peculiarly so in its specific and sovereignly instituted adaptations to fallen man.

The religion suitable for fallen man, the religion of redemption and redeeming love, is eminently distinguished, intensely pervaded, by personality.

It does not summon your attention, and demand your submission, to a mere impersonal law, without. And it does not seek to subject you to some mere impersonal influence, within. Objectively, or from without, it brings to bear upon you, personally, the claims of a personal God. And subjectively, or inwardly, it makes your person a living temple of the living God.

Your sin, for instance, it does not represent as disharmony with an abstract law, but as disobedience to a living lawgiver; as ungodliness; as ingratitude and enmity to God; insubordination, disloyalty, rebellion; in a word, as personal offence against God. Your relation, as a sinner, towards

God, it reveals specifically as one of personal controversy and misunderstanding. It unfolds a provision for removing that controversy and establishing a personal friendship—establishing a friendship that shall be the basis of a permanent personal fellowship. The leading arrangement in the provision for achieving this, is the introduction and ministry of a personal mediator, who brings the alienated parties, even the offended lawgiver and his guilty subjects, together again in peace; defending and upholding the endangered honour of the one, and expiating the dishonourable and indefensible transgression of the other. The precise service which this mediator renders to you is that of introducing you personally in peace to a personal God, your Father which is in heaven; of establishing a personal good understanding, a personal reconciliation; and of authorizing and enabling you to conduct thereafter, in his mediatorial name and merit, a personal intercourse and personal walk with God—an intercourse and walk, in which you render unto God the expressions and actings of your personal confidence, love, and duty; while he manifests a gracious personal interest in you, and exercises a watchful, protective, personal oversight over you.

Surely, all throughout this religion, there is an element of personality most intense. You may recognize it in the primary and pristine claim of God which this religion urges: 'Thou shalt have no other gods before me: my son, give me thine heart.' You may hear it sounding mournfully in the complaint and controversy to which the rejection of this claim gives rise: 'I have nourished and brought up children, but they have rebelled against me.' It pervades the inquiries which this religion originates: 'O that I knew where I might find him'; 'Lord, what wilt thou have me to do?' It breathes in the broken-hearted confession which this religion prompts—'Against thee, thee only, have I sinned'; in the blessed invitations it gives—'Come unto me and I will give you rest.' It breathes in the gracious assurances which it administers—'Behold, I, even I, am he that blotteth out your transgressions; your sins and your iniquities I will remember no more'; in the present privileges it confers—'I will come unto you and make my abode with you' and in the final hope and prospect it holds forth—'Behold, I come quickly.' And 'so shall we' personally 'be for ever with the Lord.'

Now, for the actual bringing in of this glorious element of living personality into your religion, you must be indebted entirely to the Holy Spirit. And this will not be difficult to show.

I shall not insist on the fact that to the inspiration of the Holy Ghost we are indebted for that written word in which alone the living, articulate voice of God, as a living, personal God, is heard. And I shall not insist on the other fact, that to the operation of the same Spirit we are indebted for the constitution of Christ's mediatorial person as Emmanuel, the Godman, in whom an infinite yet personal God is manifest in the flesh. In so far as a personal God is brought within the range of our cognizance by the written word, on the one hand, and by the eternal Word incarnate, on the other—all these worketh that one and the self-same Spirit. But these are his operations outwardly, or objectively. It is his inward or subjective work of grace in the hidden life of faith we are now concerned with.

Doubtless then, it will be admitted that all actual personality in your religion must depend on your appreciation by faith, and your apprehension, of the person of Christ. It is in him that you see the personal Father—'He that hath seen me hath seen the Father.' It is through him that you draw nigh, personally, to the Father—'No man cometh unto the Father but by me.' It is by him, and as at his hand, that you surrender yourself in all confidence unto the Father, proffering to him your whole person and love and service—'By him let us offer the sacrifice of praise continually'—indeed, 'our bodies, also a living sacrifice, holy and acceptable, which is our reasonable service.' By him it is that all the Father's personal law-claims against you have been satisfied; and by him that all the Father's personal love-gifts to you are bestowed. Through him you have personal fellowship, and a personal walk, with God. All the vital personality of your religion has its centre and its source in the person of Jesus.

But then, can the person of Jesus be actually realized without the ministry, the indwelling, the operation, of the Spirit?

The person of the Father is inaccessible and undiscovered, save in the Son—God manifest in the flesh. But the person of the Son is accessible to us only by the Spirit. Your thoughts about the person of Christ may be the most impersonal of all things, and will never, of themselves, beget a living personal religion, or personal relation to the Saviour. It is not thoughts about his person, but his very person, that you need. And is he not away in heaven? Personally, is he not removed away from us, as far as the heavens are higher than the earth? While his human body is in glory, is not the person of the mediator as inaccessible—as far beyond our reach and cognizance—as the person of the Father himself?

It must be so—save for the Spirit. And this was the great lesson an ascending Saviour sought to teach. You remember how he laboured to comfort the eleven. And this was the hinge and point of the consolation.

For, call to mind the exact, specific grief under which their hearts were now ready to give way. What was that grief? It was the sad anticipation that their personal intercourse with Jesus was about to close. True, a personal relation of love and gratitude and confidence had been established. He had instated himself in their hearts as the object of an affection which they believed would be undying. And after he had withdrawn from them, deeply would they cherish the recollection of the gracious words that had proceeded out of his mouth, and the many passages of touching love that had characterized his going out and in with them. The hope, also, of meeting him again in the kingdom of the Father, would be the solace of their remaining weary days; and often would the half-querulous, plaintive question of loving hope deferred break from their widowed hearts—'Why tarry the wheels of the chariot of my Lord?' And between the recollections of the blessed past, and the anticipations of the more blessed future, would they strive to bear up in the weary widowed interval.

For in what other light could they regard that interval than as one of utter widowhood? The blessed fellowship that had been the light of their life suspended; the living interchange of sentiment and of affection with their beloved interrupted; memory, indeed, in action to bring back the past, and hope to forecast the future; but with the present a blank, by the removal of their Lord and Brother, their 'All in all'; access to his person, and personal intercourse with him, now impossible! Is it any wonder that 'sorrow hath filled their hearts'? (John 16: 6).

And what kind of consolation does Jesus minister? What is its drift and tenor?

Does he strive to reconcile them to the want of personal intercourse with him? They were regarding this interval as one of bereavement and saddest separation; as one of fellowship suspended and intercourse impossible. Does Jesus admit this representation and advise them to be of good cheer notwithstanding?

We utterly mistake the whole purport and drift of his consoling words if we think so. He does not admit this representation. He repudiates it. He abundantly, and one might say, elaborately, exposes it as a misrepresentation. He denies that his personal fellowship with them will be suspended. He expressly asserts that he will not leave them orphans; he will come unto them: that he will come and make his abode with them: that in the keeping of his commandments they shall find him manifesting himself unto them: that, a little while and they shall see him, just *because* he goeth to the Father; that he shall see them again and their heart shall rejoice; and finally, that though apparently he leaves them behind him in the world, they shall nevertheless be in *him*—and, therefore, he in them (John 15: 6)—more intensely, and so to speak, more specifically and more effectually in him than *in the world*; insomuch that while 'in the world they shall have tribulation, yet in him they shall have peace'—as in their real and true and peaceful—their fire-proof and war-proof—home (John 14: 18–19, 21, 23; 16: 16, 22–3).

And the achievement of all this—the continuance of his presence and personal fellowship even after his ascension, or rather because of his ascension—He devolves upon the Spirit of truth which is the Comforter. 'It is expedient for you that I go away: for if I go not away the Comforter will not come unto you; but if I depart I will send him unto you' (16: 7). And when he is come, 'he shall not speak of himself.' He shall not call your attention to himself as if to make up for my absence and for suspended fellowship with me—thereby acknowledging my absence and completing it by the substitution of himself. He shall not turn away your hearts and minds from me, depriving you of your recollections of me, and substituting instead fellowship with himself. It shall not be so. I do not promise you the Comforter as a substitute for my presence, but exactly as securing and retaining my presence with you. For his whole work shall be to 'testify of me' (15: 26), and to 'glorify me' (16: 14). It shall be all of me. 'He shall take of mine and shew it unto you' (v. 15). And thus, in 'a little while'—even when I shall have ascended to my Father and your Father, being by the right hand of God exalted, and receiving of the Father the promise of the Holy Ghost to shed forth on you abundantly—'in a little while ye shall see me, because I go to the Father' (v. 16). I do not depart to deprive you of my presence, and to cut you off from my personal fellowship; but to confer—in large measure, with permanency more uninterrupted, with intimacy more profound and vivid—the very privilege you are afraid to lose. For all that the Father has is mine; and the Spirit shall take of mine and show it unto you. So that my Father and I will make our abode with you, even as you have read in the Scriptures—'Thou hast ascended on high, thou hast led captivity captive; thou hast received gifts for men; yea for the rebellious also'—not that the Lord's presence might be removed, but—'that the Lord God might dwell among them' (Ps. 68: 18).

By my Spirit I will be with you still. By my Spirit I will be in you henceforth. And surely, by my Spirit I may be with you truly and indeed.

For he is my Spirit. In the glorious Godhead, I and my Spirit are of one substance, power and eternity; and in my divine eternal love to you, my Spirit, with me, is of one mind and will. In me as your elder brother, also, he dwells without measure; and if you trust a brother's love and sympathy as you have found them in your friend of Nazareth, do not forget that it was my Spirit who created and sustained those fraternal fellow feelings and affections in my heart. Oh! then, will you not account that I am with you—I personally with you personally—when I send you my Spirit; and when, coming, loyal to me and understanding you, he refrains from speaking of himself, and takes exclusively of mine and shows it unto you? I may be hidden for a time from the eyes of your flesh: but I will be more brightly disclosed, by the Spirit, to the eyes of your understanding. My hand of flesh may not again grasp yours till the heavens be no more: but the arms of my love shall embrace you more sensibly than now, and the arms of your faith hold me more steadfastly—through the Spirit. Your humble homes may witness no more the kindly entrance of him whom man despises, whom the nation abhors: but he whom the Father shall have glorified shall dwell within your hearts, formed in you, 'the hope of glory.' When the world shall have scattered you, and separated you from one another, they shall be unable to separate you from me. When they shall isolate you, John!—on the lonely isle, and you, Peter!—in the silent dungeon, and your personal fellowship with each other is impossible, your personal fellowship with me shall subsist inviolate. By the Spirit I shall be 'the inmate of your heart and the companion of your life.' Dungeons and exile shall not suspend our intercourse; for my Spirit dwells in you and shall be in you—aye and until you are for ever with the Lord, until I come again and receive you to myself that where I am there you may be also.

Surely, the religion of this ascended mediator is one of intensest personality; a religion of personal relations, affections and fellowships. But it is the Spirit on whom the actual realizing of this depends. It is the Spirit that originates—that maintains and ministers—this personal knowledge of the Son and of the Father in him; this personal meeting with the Son, and, in him, with the Father; this personal interchange of love and mutual interest. The person of Christ is the source of personality in your religion. But the person of Christ is unknown and inaccessible to those that have not the Spirit. It is as good as if it were not, to those that are still dead in sin. Your religion will be truly personal only if you have the Spirit.

Let us close this chapter with a few words of application or appeal on the two sides of our present theme.

Christ's Presence, Real and Personal

Would You Have a Real Religion?

Would you have a real religion?—a religion, not of airy shadow and mere thoughts; not of pious dreams and sacred theories; not of cold creeds and abstract speculative reasonings; but a religion, real, in which your soul shall rest as on a solid rock; or (to change the figure) in which your soul shall feed as on a solid and substantial repast; or, again, in which your soul shall clothe herself with armour as real as the warrior's mail; or, once more (without a figure) in which you shall find justifying righteousness as real as your sin and grounds of hope in your death as valid as your too real grounds of fear?

You need a religion such as this. Your present state in this world, and your prospects beyond it, render such a religion indispensible. Your sin is real. Temptation is real. Difficulty, perplexity, affliction, sorrow, are real—all too palpably and painfully real. And, O how real is death!—death as it comes whether to yours or to you! And then, behind all—yon great white throne!

Oh! you need a plea as real as the sin to be forgiven, and as the sentence of death to be reversed. You need a pardon as real as that throne before which you will have to plead it.

I beseech you by the mercies of God that you content yourself with nothing less than a religion of realities. Do not dream about theories and thoughts, however accurate and good. But grasp the solid things of the Spirit of God, the things which are freely given you of God; and which (as coming from him) are no empty phantoms truly, but the undeceiving and exhaustless realities which he has prepared for them that love him. Ah! seek a real atoning sacrifice and a real forgiveness of sin thereby—a real justifying righteousness and real acceptance therein—a real title to heaven and a real preparation for it. Nor need you fear to miss them if you seek them. 'For the Lord God is a sun and shield; the Lord will give grace and glory; no good thing will he withhold from those that walk uprightly.'

But remember, if you seek these things, that they become real to you—real in your perception of them, and in your reception of them—only by your receiving the Spirit. It is he that redeems your religion from all unreality. It is he that fills divine doctrines to you with the verities of which they speak. It is he by whom you know the things that are freely given you of God. It is he that takes of the things of Christ and shows them unto you and makes them yours. For it is he who leads you through the Son even unto the Father's bosom—that boundless bosom of redeeming love, where your forgiveness is not a theory but a fact, being there your Father's real and eternal purpose of forgiving grace, the secret of the Lord which is now with you because you fear him. There your religion is real indeed.

There you taste and see that the Lord is good.

Would You Have a Personal Religion?

Would you have a personal religion?—a religion not of mere principle however right and righteous. For, a religion of mere solemn impersonal principle at the best must be stern and comparatively cold and dull; with no variety, or at least but little; no charm; no warm fascinations; no passages of rapture, love and joy. It is the religion of personal fellowship—as when you open unto a loving friend and he comes in and sups with you and you with him (Rev. 3: 20)—that is full of influence to cultivate and gratify and sway the heart, to satisfy and fill its desires.

Between these two types of piety—the piety of impersonal principle, of cold law, and sense of mere abstract obligation, on the one hand; and the piety, on the other hand, of personal adoring friendship with a Heavenly Father, and a present elder brother whose love is limitless, and whose sympathy embraces all our sorrow—one might almost institute Paul's contrast on another, though really kindred theme—scarcely for the former with its stern 'righteousness,' but cold and unattractive, would one die; yet peradventure for the other with its personal 'goodness' and charms of tender friendship, some would even dare to die (Rom. 5: 7).

Test, for instance, their respective values, as in the hour and article of death. Will a religion destitute of personality minister any real comfort to you then? Will you commit your departing spirit, for eternity, on the faith of a mere doctrine, however true—on the strength of a mere principle, however good? Will you not crave the presence of a living person? Will you not hearken for a personal voice—for the promise of his personal presence? Will not the one solitary assurance, 'Lo, I am with you,' be worth all worlds to you then? And will not your ability to say—'Though I walk through the valley of the shadow of death, yet will I fear no evil'—depend on your realizing the personal presence of the living shepherd; while you justify that fearlessness, on your part, by the gracious manifestation of his presence given to you on his—'I will fear no evil; for thou art with me; thy rod and thy staff they comfort me' (Ps. 23: 4).

And if personality in your religion becomes manifestly indispensable in your departure hence, it is as necessary in your pilgrimage here. Your justification is a personal act of God's free grace; and your daily realization of it by faith is an intensely personal thing. The privileges of your adoption are surely all intensely personal. And is not living prayer pervaded by personality? Indeed, it is this element that is the charm of all vital Christianity. And so essential is this element, that it is just the consciousness and comfort of it which we first let slip when we backslide, and cool, and flag, and are ready to die. It is the first, also, which vividly revives when our captivity is turned, our backsliding healed, and our piety quickened to flourish again. The living personality of our piety becomes its charm once more. There is no dulness then; no coldness; no weary sense of sameness, in our religion. We have a personal friend whose thoughts are not as our thoughts, narrow and few; but higher than the heavens, and countless as the sand; yea, 'each thought of thine is a great deep, and if I would declare and speak of them, they are more than can be numbered' (Ps. 40: 5; 90: 5). We have his presence. And the tenderness of his affection, and the breadth of his unflagging sympathy, yield a fresh and ever-varying consolation in all our anxiety and woe.

The religion of the apostle Paul—the religion of the Psalms of David—the religion of intense personality and adoring loving fellowship with God, through a personal and fraternal mediator—is a religion of inexhaustible resources; of ever-varying experiences; instinct with the charms of fresh, unflagging novelty, and of ceaseless variation; echoing joyfully, in its onward march and history, to the harmonious movement, and the continually changing combinations, of all honourable affections. Just because of its personality it is so. By reason of this element or characteristic, its present experiences here are beyond computation, and its expectations multiply into eternity behind them. For 'eye hath not seen, nor ear heard, neither have entered into the heart of man, the things which God hath prepared for them that love him' (1 Cor. 2: 9).

But—'God hath revealed them to us by his Spirit' (v. 10). Yes; in this life he has begun to reveal to us the deep things of God that belong to our forgiveness, our peace, our walk with God, and our purifying of ourselves even as God is pure. And it is by the Spirit that he has revealed them to us; because 'the Spirit searcheth all things, yea, the deep things of God.' For the living personality of your religion, with all the liveliness, and freshness, and variations thence accruing, you must depend on the Spirit. By the Spirit you shall have personal access through the Son, unto the Father (Eph. 2: 18). By the selfsame Spirit the Son finds access to you, and fulfils the promise—'Lo I am with you alway,' indeed, 'my Father and I will come and make our abode with you' (John 14: 23).

9

THE TWOFOLD REVELATION

'My presence shall go with thee.—I beseech thee shew me thy glory' (Exodus 33: 14, 18).

'God, who commanded the light to shine out of darkness, hath shined in our hearts, to give the light of the knowledge of the glory of God in the face of Jesus Christ' (2 Cor. 4: 6).

The presence of Christ to the consciousness of his people resolves itself very much into a manifestation of his glory.

So did the beloved disciple judge (John 1: 14), when speaking of the privilege of fellowship with the Incarnate Word. For he did not attribute anything essential in that privilege to the temporary presence of the Lord with them in the flesh, but to the permanent revelation of his glory which his being made flesh has been the means of once for all accomplishing. Very much in this view, indeed, are we to explain the introduction of the remarkable parenthesis—'and we beheld his glory, the glory as of the only-begotten of the Father.' For observe how it comes in. 'The Word was made flesh and dwelt among us.' 'Full of grace and truth'—he was immediately about to add. But, as if the thought had, on the instant, flashed upon his mind— I am awakening the envy of all future ages; my language will be construed into an assertion of the peerless blessedness of having seen the Lord in the flesh: such is not my meaning, and I will therefore qualify my words; it is the disclosure of his spiritual glory that we have prized as the essence of our privilege (the permanent heritage of the church)—let me express my meaning explicitly. And so, ere the sentence is completed which by itself alone might have favoured the misapprehension, John shuts it out by explaining that what he and his brethren counted themselves blessed in perceiving in the presence with them of the Incarnate Word was not any vision that would vanish with his ascension to heaven, but that glory which he himself so emphatically declared his ascension would only reveal more brightly. This was what he meant to express; and he has expressed it powerfully. 'The Word was made flesh, and dwelt among us (and we beheld his glory, the glory as of the only begotten of the Father), full of grace and truth.' To John's mind, the permanently precious presence of his Lord is the manifestation of his Lord's glory.

So also did Moses judge. For having received the promise—'my *presence* shall go with thee'—surely not misapprehending it, but entering into its deepest import, he pleads—'I beseech thee, shew me thy *glory*.'

In treating of Christ's presence, therefore, the divine scheme or method of revealing his glory must be considered.

In this investigation let the singularly exalted language of Paul be a guide to us. 'God, who commanded the light to shine out of darkness, hath shined in our hearts, to give the light of the knowledge of the glory of God in the face of Jesus Christ.'

The expression, 'the light of the knowledge of the glory of God,' is very striking. The central word is 'knowledge.' But the word 'knowledge' is preceded by the word 'light'—'the light of the knowledge.' And it is followed by the word 'glory'—'the knowledge of the glory of God.' There is, therefore, a certain 'glory' spoken of, and a certain 'light.' And in between these, as resulting from the combination or concurrence of the two, there is interposed that knowledge, the nature and origin of which we propose to investigate.

Surely it appears in a very noble position, looking simply at the terms in which it is spoken of. It is heralded and introduced by light. It is guarded and followed by glory. Light is pioneering its way; glory is following in its train—'the light of the knowledge of the glory of God.' The knowledge conveyed is that of God's glory—'the knowledge of the glory of God in the face of Jesus Christ.' But this knowledge is never given save in God's light—'God, who commanded the light to shine out of darkness, hath shined in our hearts, to give the light of the knowledge of the glory of God in the face of Jesus Christ.'

The doctrine, then, becomes obvious; namely, that the acquisition of a saving knowledge of God demands a twofold revelation; a revelation without the soul—external to it; and a revelation within the soul itself. There must be outwardly presented to us—'the glory of God in the face of Jesus Christ.' There must be inwardly accomplished in us a work of giving light within. It is from the concurrence of these two revelations that a true knowledge of the Lord—a spiritual perception of his presence and glory—springs.

Glory is presented to the soul: light is made to arise in the soul. The glory is the glory of God as revealed in Jesus Christ: the light is the light of God as conveyed by his Holy Spirit. And that glory without being apprehended and appreciated in this light within, the blessed resultant is that knowledge of God which is eternal life—'the light of the knowledge of the glory of God in the face of Jesus Christ.'

Looking, then, to the Spirit of God to give us this light and show us this glory, let us consider, in their order, these two portions of the doctrine: first, that in order to a saving knowledge of God there must be a presentation to the soul of the divine glory in Christ: And secondly, there must be a divine operation in the soul conveying a divine and spiritual light.

Revelation—External or Objective

In order to our obtaining that knowledge of God which is eternal life, there must be a representation made to us of the glory of God in the face of Jesus Christ. And this proposition branches out into the three following: (1) The glory of God must be revealed to us. (2) This glory must be revealed in Christ. (3) The gospel history is the glass in which this revelation is given.

The Glory of God Must Be Revealed to Us

In order to our acquiring a personal and saving knowledge of God, his glory must be set before us. We cannot acquaint ourselves with God and be at peace, till he draw near unto us, and make himself manifest in his glory.

For the knowledge of God now under consideration is not a mere knowledge that there is a God, but a knowledge of what kind of being God is. It is not a mere conviction that there is a great first cause; or even that there is a living and personal creator. It is a personal and intimate acquaintance with him. Hence, no argument from God's works of creation, or of providence can convey it; no rising inferentially 'from Nature up to Nature's God.' That never converted and saved any man. There must be direct revelation of himself, as when friend meets friend face to face, and mutual revelations of character and disposition are given. So must God reveal his moral character which is his glory.

God dwells in light that is full of glory, but which also is inaccessible to creatures. He covers himself with light as with a garment—with light, which for its overpowering splendour, is, to created eye, equivalent to darkness. It remains that the Lord, of his own sovereign pleasure, should come forth from the obscurity of his glory unapproachable, and reveal himself. Especially he must reveal those perfections of his nature which constitute ground for personal confidence in him, and cordial intercourse with him. In a word, his glory must be set before us, as a God of unswerving justice, who cannot do but what is right; as a God of unbounded beneficence, who can never refuse us what is good. In a confidential friend you expect rectitude, that can do you no wrong; kindness, that can wish you no hurt. You demand both these, in infinite perfection, in God.

But an appalling obstacle to any such revelation arises from the fact of our sin. Unswerving rectitude on God's part—calm, impartial, inflexible justice, holding in quiet unrelaxing grasp every transgressor of the law—the glory of this attribute alarms me, a sinner. And again, to strip my God of this glorious perfection, and clothe him with a soft and weak indulgence towards the wrongdoer—to set him forth as very lenient in dealing with iniquity, lowers him in my estimation, robs him of his glory, and renders it impossible for me to repose in him an honourable or joyful confidence.

This Glory Must Be Revealed in Christ

To obviate this, his glory must be set forth in the face of Jesus Christ.

It is the person and work of Emmanuel that afford a true revelation of the glory of God. *He* is the full and express image of God in human nature; *he* is the brightness of the Father's glory. To Philip's prayer: 'Shew us the Father,' Jesus gives the answer—'he that hath seen me hath seen the Father.' And the co-existence of the divine and human natures in the unity of one person in Christ affords a marvellous—(one might almost say, a fascinating) revelation of God—God manifest in the flesh.

Does the human soul of Jesus burn into lofty indignation against scribes and pharisees, hypocrites? It is a holy human affection, in unison with, and revealing, the divine detestation of sin. Does the tender heart of Jesus overflow in tears for Jerusalem? It is a holy human affection, in unison with, and revealing, the divine compassion for sinners. So that the human graces of the man Christ Jesus are an inlet by which we enter on the contemplation of those divine attributes with which these graces subsist in glorious and perfect coalescence. There is no inharmonious jar between godhead and humanity as they are yoked in matchless union in the *person* of the God-man, Emmanuel. And there is no inharmonious jar between the attributes of godhead and the graces of humanity as these are exhibited in the *character* of Emmanuel. We can draw near and contemplate holy justice and unparalleled love in the man Christ Jesus. And, entering by this open door of his character as man—owing to the unison of which I have spoken—we may follow on, without a break, into the depths of his character as God. We see in the man Christ Jesus the glory of God—the glory of God in the face of Jesus Christ.

But especially is the glory of God seen in Christ in connection with the work given him to do, as he himself has emphatically attested. For having said—'This is life eternal, that they might know thee the only true God and Jesus Christ whom thou hast sent' (John 17: 3)—he immediately added an explanatory allusion to his great sacrifice of expiation—'I have glorified thee on the earth; I have finished the work which thou gavest me to do' (v. 4). I have manifested thy glory by finishing thy work.

And assuredly the accomplishment of that work alone presents the glory of God in an aspect suitable for sinful men. Now is the unbending rectitude of the divine character and government manifestly stamped with the seal of absolute immutability; for, listen to the Judge of all the earth—'Awake, O sword, against even the man that is my fellow; smite the Shepherd' (Zech. 13: 7)—while the truly infinite and all-sufficient love of God is brought to light, even as eternity can neither crave nor obtain a higher revelation of it; for now the triumphant and all-satisfied exclamation of the church is this: 'Herein is love, not that we have loved God, but that he hath loved us, and sent his Son to be the propitiation for our sins' (1 John 4: 10).

Here, then, is the full glory of God in the face of Jesus Christ—the glory of a rectitude that cannot move aside a hairsbreadth, though its onward march involves the slaying of the Lord of glory, made sin for us: the glory of a love that, for the sake of heartless adversaries, spares not from the death of shame and wrath that Lord of glory, God's only-begotten and well-beloved Son. 'And Moses prayed unto the Lord and said, I beseech thee, shew me thy glory.' And the Lord passed by before him, and proclaimed: 'The Lord, the Lord God, merciful and gracious, long-suffering, and abundant in goodness and truth, keeping mercy for thousands, forgiving iniquity and transgression and sin, and that will by no means clear the guilty.' Where but in the face of Jesus does this glory shine? Is it not in him—in his visage more marred than any man, in his soul poured out unto death—that we read at one and the same time God's infinite wrath against sin and God's infinite readiness to forgive sin? In the Lamb of God, a burnt offering on the altar of the cross—in the Holy One made sin for us, and suffering sin's entire and unabated penalty—all doubt is eternally precluded as to whether God can clear the guilty. And in the grace of the Father providing even his own Son for a burnt-offering, an unanswerable demonstration is afforded that the Lord delighteth in mercy and is both able and ready to forgive the very chief of sinners. Herein is glory—the glory of a love that compasses the pardon of all my rebellion—the glory of a righteousness that hushes up none of mine iniquity, but sternly reckons with and expiates it all. It is the glory of God in the face of Jesus Christ.

The Gospel History Is the Glass in Which this Revelation is Given

We have not seen the face or person of Jesus as Philip did when he said—'Shew us the Father, and it sufficeth.' Till the restitution of all things, Jesus is at the Father's right hand. And it is expedient for us that he should be there.

But the gospel history which he has left with us is resplendent with the glory of Christ. An instrument of revelation, constructed by the Spirit of light himself, and answering his great idea, the gospel is a radiant mirror, glowing with the powerful beams of the Sun of Righteousness. So replenished with light is the Gospel of our salvation that the Apostle speaks with astonishment, and with something like terror, of those who see no light in it. He takes this as a conclusive proof that they are themselves darkness—that they are altogether lost. 'If our gospel be hid, it is hid to them that are lost' (v. 3). Nothing less than their being in a 'lost' condition can account for the gospel being hid to them. They must be lost creatures who see no light of glory in the gospel. And then, bringing out yet more strikingly the power and fulness of light which the gospel contains and sheds abroad, he adds, concerning those who fail to perceive it—'In whom the god of this world hath blinded the minds of them that believe not, lest the light of the glorious gospel of Christ, who is the image of God, should shine unto them' (v. 4).

It is a marvellous statement. So brilliant is the light of this glorious gospel, that Paul is driven to the fact of satanic agency to account fully for anyone not seeing and rejoicing in it. It must be the god of this world who is blinding the minds of them that believe not. And even he, in Paul's estimation, would seem conscious that it is a very great work he achieves when he succeeds. For it is no glimmering taper, no distant, trembling, flickering star, whose tiny ray he interrupts and turns aside from the unbelieving mind. Little would the great capabilities of the prince of darkness be taxed, were that the extent of his achievement in blinding men's minds to the glorious gospel of Christ. It is very far otherwise. Christ, as the image of God, shines there. Christ, as the brightness of the Father's glory, in the unspotted reflection of his blessed face, or person, or character, stands forth embodied in that gospel history. And so great and overpowering is that revelation—that light—in the glorious gospel of Christ, that it would seem as if it were on the very verge of bursting through all barriers of human ignorance and darkness; as if, one moment more, and its splendours would be glowing in heaven's light and warmth in the souls of them who hitherto have not believed. But, as if to seize his opportunity and prevent this, and 'lest the light of the glorious gospel of Christ should shine unto them'; afraid lest, delay on his part, and immediately the glory must burst in upon his victims' minds and snatch them from his kingdom of darkness into God's marvellous light; as if in haste to prevent what he sees almost inevitable, so great is the fulness of the light that shineth, the god of this world interposes and blinds their minds—'lest the light of the glorious gospel of Christ, who is the image of God, should shine unto them.'

Oh! what an estimate this proves the god of this world to have formed of the gospel as overflowing with the light of the glory of God. He is in terror, he is in haste, 'lest the light of that gospel of glory should shine unto them.' He cannot trust that shining gospel near his victims for a moment, without labouring to counteract it. He will watch narrowly lest it shine unto them. He will preoccupy—he will blind—their minds.

If ever it be lawful to learn from a foe, surely it is lawful and more than lawful here. Nor is it possible we could be more impressively instructed concerning the greatness of the light that shines in the gospel.

Such, then, is the external revelation which is requisite to our obtaining a saving knowledge of God. First; there is a representation given of the moral glory of God. Secondly; his glory is set forth in the face of Jesus Christ. Thirdly; the gospel is the instrument by which this representation is given. The glory of God in the face of Jesus Christ as seen in the gospel, is the complete object with which saving knowledge is conversant.

Revelation—Inward or Subjective

But there are two revelations needed for the actual acquisition of this knowledge. The external revelation must be accompanied with a revelation that is inward. There must not only be a representation made *to* the soul from without. There must be an operation *in* the soul within. The glory of God is the object to be seen. But the light of God is the element in which alone we can see it. For we are by nature darkness, and require to be made light in the Lord.

But the same Spirit of light who has furnished the external revelation of the glory of God in the face of Jesus Christ in the gospel, furnishes an inward revelation also in the case of all those that believe. And there is, perhaps, no grander statement of this latter truth in all the Bible, than this beautiful utterance of Paul.

'God hath shined in our hearts.' And to exalt our impressions of his sovereign pleasure and supreme power in doing so, he is designated from that noble revelation of his glory given when he said—'Let there be light and there was light.' Even he—this 'God who commanded the light to shine out of darkness'—has accomplished a grander work; he—'hath shined in our hearts to give the light of the knowledge of the glory of God.'

This precious saying has been very frequently misquoted, as if it read—'God hath shined *into* our hearts.' But it is not so; and more than half its beauty is lost when we so misread it.

For observe, in the first place, that, when we think of God shining *into* the heart, the idea present to the mind is that of some source of light erected or set up near the soul, outside; the illumination being then supposed to strike into the heart from without. The actual arrangement is unspeakably more grand. There is a shining *in* the heart. The heart itself is taken possession of by the light. The light does not shine from without. It is not outside and apart from the heart, falling upon it externally. It shines within. The heart is not the recipient of an illumination the source of which is external to itself. The heart is made the dwelling-place of the light—the central home of the illumination. He hath not shined *into*, he hath shined *in*, our hearts.

But observe also, secondly, as completing the unparalleled perfection of this arrangement—in the first creation, God simply 'commanded the light to shine out of darkness.' His creative and almighty will was the sole cause of natural illumination. But Paul does not say that in the second and spiritual creation God commands light to spring up[1] in our dark hearts and shine there. But—far more, and far nobler— God himself shines in our hearts. He takes possession of our hearts by his Spirit. He returns to his own rightful dwelling-place—his people's souls; from which he had retired, offended by their rebellion, leaving them to the inevitable darkness which his absence entails. But having brought them to himself with a great ransom, that they might be his rightful holy temple yet again, he returns to them once more. He returns, and takes up his dwelling in them, by his Spirit. He grants them his gracious presence again. And he returns and dwells in them in his glorious character as the light: for God is light, and in him is no darkness at all. He seats himself secretly, yet by resistless, sweet and sovereign power in the inmost heart; and there he shines—'God hath shined in our hearts'—there

---

[1] There is undoubtedly a creative work—'Create in me a clean heart, and renew a right spirit within me.' There is spirit born of the Spirit (John 3: 6)— light of light—'Ye who some time were darkness are now light in the Lord.' But with the new-created spirit, God, by his eternal Spirit, abides for ever; and (being light) there he shines—in the heart.

he throws around him the sweet illumination of his presence and his glory.

He does not tarry without, and aloof from the soul; and rear in its immediate neighbourhood some shining light, whose rays may pierce the gloom of nature's spiritual darkness. Nor does he—still himself abiding without the soul—create some light within. But the glorious procedure is this; God himself is light—light adequate for the souls of intelligent beings, even as the sun in heaven is light suitable for material creation; God himself is light: And seeking to restore light to the darkened heart of man, he makes his way into the inmost soul, having all power over it, and all right to pass through all its chambers or tarry in them at his pleasure. He exercises that right. He takes his seat and throne in the central citadel there; and from within the heart God shines. Not into, but—'out of, Zion, the perfection of beauty God hath shined.' God hath shined in our hearts.

How desirable and glorious is this illuminating work of the Spirit! Seated in the souls of his people, and working in every one severally as he will; restraining or enlarging the light at his pleasure; he shines in their hearts to give the light of the knowledge of the glory of God. A free and sovereign agent; very gracious also at the voice of their cry; and rejoicing in his commission, as the Spirit of wisdom and of revelation, to glorify Christ; he cleanses and purifies the heart; eliminates its self-darkening love of sin; moulds its affections to purer joys, and to an ever-increasing susceptibility of his own heavenly light. Enthroned in the power of his office in the very centre of our intellect and heart, and subduing the carnal mind with its ignorance and prejudice and enmity and error, the Spirit urges back the thick clouds of our spiritual darkness; enlarges the sphere of our spiritual vision; communicates in the soul a measure of the very light in which he himself sees light—the very light in which he himself sees the character and glory and will of God; and realizes in us the amazing assertion of the Psalmist—'In thy light, O God, shall we see light' (Ps. 36: 9).

Such is the unspeakable grandeur, precision, and perfection of God's illuminating work by his Spirit.

He does not command the light to shine out of darkness. That he did once, when, all creation lying in chaos and night, the word of his lips spake light and beauty into being. In creating man anew in holiness and knowledge, he does not act thus. He acts in a manner far transcending his first procedure. He does not call into existence a light that never shone before. He conveys to us a light that has been from everlasting; the light which from everlasting has been his own—the light which from eternity he himself has been. 'The Lord God is a sun'; and he gives himself. He becomes, in sovereign grace, a dweller in our hearts. The Eternal Light takes his abode in our hearts; and there, gradually, and as we are able to bear it, he shines.

Believer; this is the history of your spiritual illumination, and this is the sublime result of it: the Lord light in you; you light in the Lord; *his* Spirit dwelling in *your* spirit, making you a child of light; giving you capacity to see spiritual things as he sees them, in the very light in which he sees them; so that in the measure of your enlightenment, your views of divine things, so far as they go, are his views—spiritual, infallible, divine.

Ah! there is no teacher like the Spirit. He teaches savingly, inwardly, to profit. He gives you the mind of Christ. In thy light shall we see light. God hath shined in our hearts.

And now, such being the inward or subjective revelation; namely, God himself, by his Spirit, seated in the heart and shining there: and such, also, being the outward or objective revelation; namely, the glory of God in the face of Jesus Christ, delineated with unspotted purity in the bright mirror of the gospel: let these two revelations be combined. Let them be considered as co-existing and conspiring, each in its own place and for its own end. And how perfect a scheme have we now for securing a true knowledge of God!

There is the glory of God without. There is the light of God within. There is the glory of God presented outward to the soul—in the gospel. And there is the God of glory dwelling and shining inwardly—in the heart. That glory of God without, and this God of glory within; how can they meet without a mutual recognition? The outward glory in the

The Twofold Revelation

gospel commends itself to the inward light in the heart. The inward light in the heart pours the warm beams of a ceaseless illumination on the outward glory in the gospel. And the result is a knowledge which is no mere human opinion, but a divine, infallible conviction—a conviction on which you can stake your everlasting salvation, and pass in peace into the everlasting world. For you know whom you have believed; because 'God, who commanded the light to shine out of darkness, hath shined in your heart to give the light of the knowledge of the glory of God in the face of Jesus Christ.'

It remains to make some application of the subject.

Have You Seen the Light?

Have you never yet seen this light of the knowledge of the glory of God?

You are invited and commanded, in believing obedience to the gospel, and in believing dependence on the Spirit, to behold the glory of God. Yes: in believing obedience to the word, and in believing dependence on the Spirit. For, always it is the glorious combination of—the word and Spirit.

'The God of glory appeared unto our Father Abraham.'

And it is by his appearing as the God of glory to you, that you will become a child of Abraham, a child of God in Jesus Christ. Now to you also, in the gospel, the God of glory appears; the God of glory, and the glory of God, in the face of Jesus Christ. And his glory appears pre-eminently in this—that his glorious righteousness and glorious love both appear in boundless splendour and perfect harmony.

When God appears to you in the gospel—draws near to reveal himself to you, and reconcile you to himself—his infinite unbending justice and his infinite endearing mercy both appear, comforting you—standing before you, face to face. And they stand before you in covenant alliance, hand in hand; mercy and truth meeting together, righteousness and peace embracing each other. Behold that justice of God that remorselessly assigns eternal death to the very least of sins! Behold that love of God that triumphantly bestows eternal life on the very chief of sinners! In the sacrifice of the cross, God is both infinitely just and infinitely gracious in forgiving iniquity, transgression and sin. And this is his glory in the face of Jesus Christ—the glory of eternal satisfied justice blended with the glory of eternal saving love: divine justice wholly satisfied for sin in the blood of God's dear Son; divine love freely saving sinners by that precious blood. Such is the attitude in which the glory of God appears to you in the gospel.

What can your fitting attitude or answer be, but the full, immediate, free confession of all your iniquity? For, see how safely you may in faith acknowledge all your sin, when infinite justice stands ready to exclaim, 'I am fully satisfied for it all' —and infinite love to say, 'I freely save thee from it all!'

Oh! deal faithfully and frankly with your God in such a case; for satisfied justice can in no wise harm you; saving love can in no wise cast you out. Is not this the glory of the Lord?

Beware that you do not deal falsely with the glory of the Lord. Shame on the hypocrisy that would falsely deal with love so exceeding great and marvellous! Nor can justice tolerate the wickedness: for though justice stands there as satisfied in Christ, it stands there as justice, infinite and unbending still.

But deal truly. Open all your heart. Yes, rend it open. Acknowledge all your sin and enmity to God. Excuse your inexcusable iniquity no more. 'Father, I have sinned against heaven and in thy sight, and am not worthy to be called thy Son.' Then, God is faithful and just to forgive you your sin, and to cleanse you from all unrighteousness. And God is loving and kind to call for the fairest robe for you; to cast his arms round your neck; to command for you a day of gladness and rejoicing.

O taste and see that the Lord is gracious. Behold and see that the Lord is glorious. Believe on the Lord Jesus Christ, and you shall be saved. Believe on the Lord Jesus Christ, and you shall taste the grace and see the glory of the Lord. 'Said I not unto thee, that, if thou wouldest believe, thou shouldest see the glory of God'—'the light of the knowledge of the glory of God in the face of Jesus Christ'?

Have you never yet seen this glory? All your present duty is summed up in the command—behold this glory.

Have You Seen This Glory?

Have you seen this glory? Then all your present duty is summed up in the command—reflect this glory.

Yes: reflect this glory of God which you have seen in the face of Jesus Christ. Let this light (now your light) so shine before men that they seeing your good works may see and admire the glory of your Father which is in heaven. Arise, shine; for thy light hath come, and the glory of the Lord hath arisen upon thee. His glory is to be your glory. You are to reflect the very glory of the Lord.

For what is his glory? It is his unbending justice blended with his unconquerable love. And what is your glory? Is it not like justice incorruptible, blended with love exhaustless; justice, which you resolve in all things to do, whatever expediency or interest may prompt; love, which you resolve on all hands to show, whatever provocation or ingratitude may tempt? Is it not the glory of a man to say (and to act upon it)—let justice be done though the heavens be ruined; and while saying this, to say also (and to act upon it)—let love—let charity suffer long and be kind; let charity bear all things, believe all things, hope all things, endure all things? Let justice never bend; let charity never fail.

It is thus with your God. This is his glory, his excelling glory in the highest; very illustrious in redeeming you. Let it be your glory also. Be like your God.

He hath showed thee, O man, what is good: and what doth the Lord require of thee; but to do justice, to love mercy, and to walk humbly with thy God? And it will be so, if you live in the habit of beholding his glory. 'For we all, with open face beholding as in a glass the glory of the Lord, are transformed into the same image, from glory to glory, even as by the Spirit of the Lord' (2 Cor. 3: 18).

Yes: it is by continuing in the believing contemplation of his glory that you will reflect it. When Moses had spent forty days with God upon the mount, he came down with a countenance radiant with glory. For when Aaron and all the children of Israel saw Moses, behold, the skin of his face shone. But they were afraid to come near unto him. 'They could not steadfastly behold the face of Moses for the glory of his countenance; which glory was to be done away' (v. 7). Yet was it merely an external glory. It was very terrible. Also it was transitory: And above all it was incommunicable. It belonged to Moses only. It did not pass over to those that looked upon it. The glory of God in the face of Moses was not to be diffused among Israel.

Had it been otherwise—had it been communicable and actually communicated and diffused—how marvellous the scene!

Child after child of the many thousands of Israel draws near and beholds with open face the glory of God in him who is 'king in Jeshurun.' The heavenly radiance transfers itself to each admiring countenance; till, the burning glory gleaming on every face in Israel, a million glowing mirrors multiply the pristine splendour, and make the wilderness at midnight a more than sun-lit land. And as their cohorts thus gleamed with the glory of God, well might such a camp, in arising for their onward march, have compelled the exclamation—'Who is this that cometh up out of the wilderness, bright as the sun and terrible as an army with banners?'

It was not to be. And though it had, this was but a glory 'to be done away.' Nor is there room for mourning its departure. To every 'Israelite indeed' a nobler privilege belongs. The glory of God in the face of Moses was itself merely a reflection—a reflection, too, of a mere outward glory; and such as might be caught in the brief period of forty days' communion in the mount. The glory of God in the face of Jesus is the immediate and true glory of the divine nature, the glory as of the only-begotten of the Father. It is the glory of him who has been—not for forty days in the mount with God, but—in the bosom and communion of the Father from everlasting; and who has come forth to reveal—not a glory to be done away, but—an exceeding and excelling glory that remains. And the privilege which a sight of Moses was not able to confer, faith's sight of Jesus secures. The law came by Moses, terrible to Israel, and demanding the concealment of a veil. Grace and truth came by Jesus Christ—revealed with open face. His glory is not external, but spiritual and moral; the glory of righteousness and love, and therefore never to be done away. It is very sweet; not terrifying the true Israel away from it, nor tempting them to call for a veil to shroud it. It is a glory in the highest—*gloria in excelsis*—in blessed unison with their own salvation and their peace; a glory that attracts and allures them to behold it. And as the many thousands of the true Israel behold as in a glass this glory of the Lord, it shines reflected from themselves, and will shine increasingly, from glory to glory, as by the Spirit of the Lord. In the mingled righteousness and charity of their character and conduct it shines.

In that 'righteousness' of theirs for which perhaps scarcely one would die, blended with the attractive 'goodness' for which peradventure some would even dare to die; in the stern rectitude that compels esteem, and in the tender love that wins our cordial, warm confidence; the light of the glory of the Lord shines more and more, in Israel, unto the perfect day.

And that perfect day! A day that knows no cloud; a day that knows no evening! Then shall the righteous shine forth as the sun in the kingdom of their Father. 'Ten thousand times ten thousand and thousands of thousands' of living mirrors shall radiate the unbroken glory of the King. 'For when he shall appear we shall be like him' (1 John 3: 2). We shall be like the brightness of the Father's glory; like the express image of his person.

Oh! surely, every 'one that hath this hope in him purifieth himself even as he is pure' (1 John 3: 3).

10

CHRIST'S PRESENCE IN HIS PEOPLE

'Christ liveth in me' (Gal. 2: 20).

When Christ's presence in the gospel history is savingly revealed to us—and his glory as the only-begotten of the Father—there is a simultaneous revelation of his presence in us. 'It pleased God,' says Paul, 'to reveal his Son in me' (Gal. 1: 16). Nor is this revelation transient but permanent. Henceforth he could say—'Christ liveth in me.'

It may be well, therefore, if we vindicate for the presence of Christ in his people the same characteristics of the veritable, the literal, the thoroughly definite and distinct, which we have challenged and defended on behalf of his presence with them.

Nor is this an unnecessary or superfluous task. For assuredly it is a very singular, almost a stumbling, statement of Paul's—'Christ liveth in me.' One almost needs an explicit reminiscence of the fact of his inspiration, to prevent the notion that this is a high-wrought utterance of religious mysticism. Or, if our veneration for the inspired word be too great to permit of such a view of the apostle's marvellous assertion, we may be in danger, on the other hand, of acquiescing in the most vague and indefinite apprehension of its meaning—as if it were nothing more than a highly figurative (perhaps hyperbolical) expression, such as in all fairness should not be canvassed too minutely nor pressed too far.

Nevertheless we maintain that it can hardly be pressed too far, or canvassed too minutely. We plead for an intense and glorious literality in the avowal—'Christ liveth in me.' We challenge for the experience which it asserts, the place in the kingdom of God due to a literal and fundamental spiritual fact; grander by far than all hyperboles that can be uttered or imagined.

First of all, however, it may be profitable to call to mind that this is far from being a solitary or unparalleled statement in the Word of God.

The truth contained in it is even declared a lie at the foundation of all personal and living Christianity—'Examine yourselves whether ye be in the faith; prove your own selves. Know ye not your own selves, how that Jesus Christ is in you, except ye be reprobates?' (2 Cor. 13: 5).

To convey this astonishing privilege of having Christ living in us, is the great end for which the gospel ministry is established and exercised: 'My little children, of whom I travail in birth again till Christ be formed in you, I desire to be present with you now, and to change my voice; for I stand in doubt of you' (Gal. 4: 19–20).

The realizing of this great marvel among the Gentiles is 'the mystery which hath been hid from ages and from generations, but now is made manifest unto God's saints; to whom he would make known what is the riches of the glory of this mystery among the Gentiles, which is Christ in you, the hope of glory' (Col. 1: 26–7).

It is the great object for the attainment of which Jesus knocks, by his gospel and his Spirit, at the hearts of sinners: 'Behold, I stand at the door, and knock; if any man hear my voice, and open the door, I will come into him' (Rev. 3: 20).

It is the realization of the great covenant promise: 'For ye are the temple of the living God: as God hath said, I will dwell in them and walk in them; and I will be their God and they shall be my people' (2 Cor. 6: 16).

It is the object for which believers are commanded to abide in Christ: 'Abide in me, and I in you' (John 15: 4).

It is the scope of Paul's prayer for the Ephesians: 'For this cause I bow my knees unto the God and Father of our Lord Jesus Christ, of whom the whole family in heaven and earth is named, that he would grant you, according to the riches of his glory, to be strengthened with all might by the Spirit in the inner man; that Christ may dwell in your hearts by faith' (Eph. 3: 14–17).

Nay, it is the grand and ultimate aim of Christ's own intercession. It is the utmost and terminal desire of his heart, as expressed unto the Father on their behalf. It is the resting place of his heart concerning them; where he sees of the travail of his soul and is satisfied. For even thus does his intercessory prayer for them terminate: 'That the love wherewith thou hast loved me may be in them, and I in them' (John 17: 26).

These are a few parallel statements asserting the indwelling of Christ in his people. But it may be questioned if any of them is so beautiful and emphatic as the utterance of our Apostle, at once so bold and brief: 'Christ liveth in me.'

The rich meaning and import of this statement may in a measure open up to us; while its fulness of grace and truth, with its intense and glorious literality, will become manifest; if, with prayer for the Spirit's light, we consider the causes and consequences of Christ living in his people. Doubtless some caveats or cautions may be necessary, to clear this great truth from the risk of perversion. But these it will not be difficult to point out.

Our thoughts, then, may run in these three channels. We shall consider—first, the causes; secondly, the consequences; thirdly, the cautions.

I: CAUSES OF CHRIST'S PRESENCE IN HIS PEOPLE

The immediate causes of this great effect are manifest. They are apparent, conspicuously, on the very face of it. For if Christ lives in me, it must be of his own sovereign pleasure and supreme power. He himself must be the great, leading, efficient cause. This, in the first place. But then, he lives in me, not as in the holy place of the dead material tabernacle of old, but as in a living temple. He lives in me as in an intelligent, consenting, recipient soul. He does not live in me by an exercise of will on his part such as should overbear or exclude the exercise of will on my part. He consults my will, and carries it along with him. He makes me willing in the day of his power. He controls my will, indeed. He makes it act consentiently and subordinately to his own. His will remains evermore the leading cause of his living in me. But it does so in the very way of accomplishing the designed effect by calling forth and consulting my will; insomuch that I myself also am a true and indispensable—subordinate but indispensable—cause in this great and marvellous effect.

Thus, 'Christ' and 'I' are the two immediate causes of 'Christ living in me.'

Christ Himself

Consider Christ himself, then, as the sovereign and efficient cause of his own presence in his people.

And here again it will be found that Christ gives his presence by his Spirit, and according to the gospel history; by the agency of his Spirit, and by the instrumentality of his word.

By the Holy Spirit

Christ lives in his people by his Holy Spirit. This great effect is to be attributed to the agency and indwelling of the Holy Spirit.

Regeneration, which is the Spirit's work, is the implantation in a soul, formerly dead in trespasses and sins, of a new life, a vital principle of holiness. The will is renewed; and from being ungodly and enmity to God, it is turned to choose God, satisfying itself with him as its supreme good, subjecting itself to him as its sovereign Lord. This is a new life—spiritual, God-ward, altogether new—a new creature. With this new principle of life, this new creation in the soul, the Spirit of God, who is the author of it, maintains a vital and uninterrupted connection; thereby dwelling in the believer henceforth as in a living temple. It is in virtue of this in-dwelling, this in-living of the Spirit, that Christ lives in us. For, in all this, the Spirit acts as the Spirit of Christ. For, 'if any man have not the Spirit of Christ, he is none of his.' And, 'hereby we know that he abideth in us, by his Spirit which he hath given us' (Rom. 8: 9; 1 John 3: 2).

Christ, as God the Son, is of one substance, power, and eternity with God the Holy Spirit. Christ, also, as the Son of man, had the Spirit bestowed on him without measure. His human nature was formed, in body and soul, and sanctified from the first, by the special operation of the Spirit. He was anointed with the immeasurable plenitude of the Spirit. By the light of the Spirit, the man Christ Jesus thought all his thoughts; by the grace of the Spirit, willed all his purposes; by the strength of the Spirit, wrought all his works; till finally he, 'through the eternal Spirit, offered himself without spot to God,' thereafter rising from the dead by the Spirit of holiness, and ascending to pour out that Spirit of truth and consolations which he had promised so graciously to his disciples. In his godhead, our Lord is one with the Spirit; and as man—by the Spirit he was what he was.

When Christ, therefore, sends his Spirit, not to speak of himself, but to take of what is Christ's and show it unto us; to create us again in Christ and like Christ; to dwell in us as in a living temple, as ourselves living spirits to which he has given a new and Christ-like life—can we fail to see that there is something here which in no respect falls short even of the great marvel of—'Christ living in us'?

Christ, considered as the eternal Son, lives in us when the eternal Spirit dwells in us; for the Spirit and the Son with the Father are inseparable in their joint possession of the all-fulness of the Godhead. And Christ, considered as the Son of Man, the God-man—the very Christ that tabernacled with men upon the earth; the very Christ of the ever-living history—lives in us when the Spirit, dwelling in us and shining in us, confines himself to revealing Christ, and conforming us to Christ, as the God-man, whose glory disciples saw, in human flesh, as the glory of the only-begotten of the Father, full of grace and truth—a glory still mirrored in the gospel history—the glory of the Lord with unveiled face reflected in the glass of the word (2 Cor. 3: 18).

For it is exclusively as the agent and ambassador, the representative and plenipotentiary, of Christ that the Spirit is present in the shrine of the believing heart. It is Christ whom he there 'reveals,' and 'forms,' and 'glorifies' (Gal. 1: 16, 4: 19; John 16: 14). And in all the putting forth of his light and power there, the Spirit restricts himself, by the rule of his office, even as also by his own consentient will, exactly within the limits of what he first revealed and wrought, according to the covenant, in the living head, the man Christ Jesus. He dwells in Christ's people, in a measure, as he dwelt in Christ himself. He reveals in them progressively the truth which he implanted and developed in unclouded spiritual splendour in the intellect of the man Christ Jesus, he establishes in them progressively the grace with which he replenished the heart of the man Christ Jesus. In a word, he conforms them to the—'firstborn among many brethren.' How then can his indwelling, his in-working, his in-living in them, be more adequately expressed than by the grand doctrine—by the assertion of the marvellous fact—that 'Christ liveth in them'?

Yes; Christ by his Spirit lives in them. By his Spirit he quickens them to new and spiritual life; and by his Spirit he takes possession of them as his living temple. As a *living* temple, he always regards them and acts in them. Their faculties as living men—alive from the dead—He animates and controls. Whatever in their thoughts, affections, purposes, actions, is opposed to his own, he sets himself to suppress; and the faculties themselves he undertakes to sanctify—to form, mould and guide into harmony with his own. Nay; their whole character, their very natures, as living men—spiritually living—he works by his Spirit to assimilate unto his own. So far as this work advances, the very thoughts that he thinks

> Christ by his Spirit lives in them...the very thoughts that he thinks they think; the affections he entertains they entertain; the purposes of his mind are theirs also; his work is their work; his nature theirs.

they think; the affections he entertains they entertain; the purposes of his mind are theirs also; his work is their work; his nature theirs. And up to the limit to which this blessed result has in its onward progress been achieved, how can a better, a briefer, a more perfect expression be found for it, than to say that, to this extent—'Christ liveth in them'?

It is, therefore, literally and profoundly true that Christ lives in his people. It is not the random utterance of enthusiastic mysticism—but a simple fact in the kingdom of God. Christ lives in his people, by his Spirit which he has given to them.

BY THE WORD

But, secondly, while the Spirit is the efficient cause, the gospel history, or more generally the word, is the instrument by which Christ lives in his people.

Without attention given to this, all is left, in reality, vague and indefinite as before; the door open to the spiritualism that rejects all rule, and the pietistic fervour that trembles evermore, in its indecision, between the wildfire of fanatical excess and the pleasing fancies of self-deluding sentimentalism.

We know nothing of Christ save as revealed and set forth in the word—'the word of the truth of the gospel.' God is manifest in the man Christ Jesus. The invisible, inaccessible godhead is brought near and manifested in Christ. But Christ himself is as invisible, inaccessible, unknown to us as the Godhead is, save for the history—the gospel—the word. 'No man hath seen God at any time; the only-begotten which is in the bosom of the Father he hath declared him' (John 1: 18). The only-begotten, the eternal Word, declared the Father by being made flesh and dwelling among us. Thereby disciples saw his glory. But the history of his sayings and doings, as he dwelt among us and manifested forth his glory and his Father's name, is altogether indispensable to us, if the revealing Son is not to remain as inaccessible and unknown as the Father whom he came to reveal. God was manifest in the flesh. But it is by the gospel that the manifestation is made over to us. Take away Christ and you take away the knowledge of God: but take away the gospel and you take Christ away. For he has bound himself inseparably to his gospel in all his dispensations to the sons of men. He has seated himself in the chariot of his gospel, and all his goings forth have been—and to the end of time will be—as seated there. He has clothed himself with his own gospel, and in the robes thereof alone does he appear in his church below. We can, in this life, receive him only as he is offered to us in the gospel.

When another gospel, therefore, was preached in the church at Galatia, Paul felt that *the Christ in them* was endangered: 'my little children, of whom I travail in birth again till Christ be formed in you' (4: 19). When to the church at Colosse he spoke of 'Christ in them the hope of glory'—knowing that by means of the gospel only could Christ be in them—he added, '*Whom we preach,* teaching every man, and warning every man' (2: 27–8). If his word dwell in you, Christ dwells in you. 'Let that, therefore, abide in you which ye have heard from the beginning. If that which ye have heard from the beginning shall remain in you, ye also shall continue in the Son and in the Father' (1 John 2: 24). And if you continue in the Son, he continues in you, according to the sacred oracle: 'Abide in me, and I in you' (John 15: 6).

It appears then that Christ lives in his people by his Spirit and word—in secret power, by the Spirit; in ostensible and intelligent expression, by the word.

Believers Indispensable yet Subordinate

But the believer himself is an indispensable co-operating cause; subordinate to Christ, the sovereign, leading cause; yet indispensable although subordinate.

For if Christ lives in me, it must be with my own consent. And my consent is given and is exercised in faith. Moreover, if Christ acts in this matter by his Spirit and word, my action must be by faith. For my action, though subordinate to Christ's, is to be subordinate in the highest, noblest kind. It is to be responsive to his; the very counterpart of his; fitting in to his; nay, growing out of his. It is to be the very effect of his—the very thing which his action immediately effects. But faith—and faith alone—is at once the immediate effect and the exact direct response to Christ's Spirit and word; faith wrought in me by the power of the Spirit and the instrumentality of the word; faith by which, through the Spirit's secret grace, I read in the word the Spirit's ostensible mind. By such a faith, wrought in me by that very Spirit and word whereby Christ quickens me (that Spirit who lives for ever in Christ himself, and that word in which Christ himself for ever lives) I consent to Christ's coming into me to live in me—to live in me, by that Spirit to whom I now so gladly yield, and according to that written word and gospel history which I now so greatly admire.

And such a faith—in which, manifestly, my will is consulted and called into co-operation (and that in a manner that shields my true liberty unto the uttermost; indeed, stimulates and rules and perfects it) and which exalts me to the lofty honour of entertaining in my poor home the King of glory—does, at the same time, keep me in my own secondary and subordinate place. For in its very nature, this faith is my acknowledgment of Christ's uncontrolled supremacy. His will and mine are the conspiring causes of this great effect. His is sovereign and supreme. Mine, if it act by faith, can have neither a more honourable nor a more humble place in this matter assigned to it. It is at once the most lowly and the most exalted. 'He that humbleth himself shall be exalted.'

The place and operation of faith in this matter are attested emphatically by the apostle in his prayer for the Ephesians— 'that Christ may dwell in your hearts by faith' (Eph. 3: 17). And it is this that reconciles Paul's apparent contradiction, that he himself lives, and yet that it is Christ that lives in him; bringing it about that while he himself lives, and Christ lives in him, these are not two lives, but one. It is by faith that they are really one.

'I live; yet not I, but Christ liveth in me.' Does Paul, then, retract the assertion, 'I live,' by saying 'yet not I, but Christ liveth in me'? Does he deny that he lives, by declaring that Christ lives in him? Nay, he asserts it; he re-asserts it, for he goes on to say, 'And the life that I live in the flesh.' And how does he make these two lives to be really one? By the reconciling medium of faith. 'The life that I live in the flesh

I live by the faith of the Son of God, even him who loved me and gave himself for me.' By the faith of him I live on him; I live his life. By faith I receive and retain the living Christ—living in me, Christ my life. By faith I live the life which Christ lives in me.

Mark also very specially that it is by faith in a dying Christ that Christ lives in his people.

It might have been supposed that it would be otherwise. Naturally we would have expected that by faith in a living Christ would Christ live in us. But it is not so. It is by faith in a dying Christ. 'I live by the faith of the Son of God,' says Paul. Be it so. But under what view of Christ—in what aspect of Christ's relation to you, and his work for you—do you exercise your faith in him? 'Who loved me, and gave himself for me,' is Paul's answer. It is as loving him and dying for him that Paul exercises faith in Christ, in order that Christ may live in him. Indeed, this singular verse, with its rich and unfathomable wonders, both begins and closes with this truth—that it is by faith's communion with a substituted, crucified, dying Saviour, that that Saviour lives in his people; 'I am crucified with Christ: nevertheless I live; yet not I, but Christ liveth in me: and the life that I live in the flesh I live by the Faith of the Son of God, who loved me, and *gave himself for me.*'

It is this great truth that the Lord himself sets forth in his startling discourse concerning eating his flesh and drinking his blood. For it is faith's participation, of his sacrifice of himself in death, in the wounding of his flesh and the shedding of his blood, that he is there describing: 'The bread that I shall give is my flesh, which I shall give for the life of the world. Verily, verily, I say unto you, Except ye eat the flesh of the Son of man, and drink his blood, ye have no life in you. Whoso eateth my flesh, and drinketh my blood, hath eternal life and I will raise him up at the last day. For my flesh is meat indeed and my blood is drink indeed.' And then he comes nearer to the doctrine before us: 'He that eateth my flesh, and drinketh my blood, dwelleth in me, and I in him.' And at last he exactly states it: 'As the living Father hath sent me, and I live by the Father; so he that eateth me, even he shall live by me' (John 4: 51–7).

The apostle Paul, also, in writing to the Corinthians, puts this truth in a very beautiful light—the truth, I mean that it is by faith in a dying Saviour that that Saviour lives in us—when he says—'Always bearing about in the body the dying of the Lord Jesus, that the life also of Jesus may be made manifest in your mortal body' (2 Cor. 4: 10). If I would have Christ living in me, I must be crucified with Christ; if I would have Christ living in me, it must be by the exercise of faith in Christ dying for me.

Nor is this mysterious. For if I would have life reigning in me, I have a prior death that reigns in me to dispose of. I have a judicial death, a death in the anger of God—a wrathful but righteous sentence of death—barring me from all life and blessing; strengthening, also, and rivetting in me the dominion of spiritual death—my death in trespasses and sins. I must, therefore, find a life that shall suppress my death, and that shall not itself die in doing so—that shall not expire in the effort, but shall conquer and live on—the true and only life everlasting. Such a life is Christ's death. Do not marvel at this. Christ's death is vital—Christ's death is life—Christ's death is life eternal swallowing up death in victory—suppressing my death, and living for me and in me—eternal life still. The life that I need is a life that can live in the midst of death, seeing that I am dead—dead under the law of God, and dead in trespasses and sins. Show me eternal life made under the law of God, and giving itself in death for my trespasses and sins. Show me a life in the midst of death, if you would show me a life that can live in me.

A singular demand! But it is exactly met in Christ—the living one—the Life, giving himself a sacrifice in death for me, and living still—living in the inviolable depths of his divine person; never more living than when actively and livingly giving himself in death for me—laying down his human life, that, in the unabated life and living energy of his divine person, and in the legal triumph of his mediatorial office, he might—after the power of an endless life which his death never for a moment interrupted—resume that human life once more. Give me that death of Christ in which, even when dying, he lived and conquered—that death of Christ in which through death he destroyed him that had the power of death—that death of Christ which, far from extinguishing the life which he brought from heaven to me, only broke open for me that 'fountain of life' (Ps. 36: 9) in his godhead which had otherwise been for ever sealed and inaccessible, till there poured forth from it 'a river of the water of life,' sweeping away and swallowing up death in victory. Give me that death of the Prince of life. It is a vital death: it is a real life: it is the very life for me; for it is the life which can live in death—the only life that can live in me. I am crucified with Christ: nevertheless I live. By the faith of Christ dying for me, I have Christ living in me—not otherwise. The life which I live in the flesh I must live by the faith of the Son of God, as having loved me and given himself for me.

Apart from Christ, what am I, and what is my position or place? I am shut up within the gates of death. And apart from me, what is Christ? He is 'the life'—life eternal and inviolable—no death in his lot at all. What, then, is Christ's death, if in redeeming love he dies for me—if he gives himself a substitute, a sacrifice in death for me—if he comes into my place and dies in my stead? What have I here but eternal life bursting open the gates of death, and coming in to adjoin and identify himself with me? And as he bursts them open, and comes in, do they close again, and imprison both him and me? Is the fountain of life—is godhead in the man Christ Jesus—the prey and prisoner of death? God forbid. He is not death's prisoner: he is death's plagues and death's destruction. He has come to me, not in the suppression and defeat, but in the unabated energy and in the glorious triumph of his character and power as the Life Eternal; his triumph being this—that in dying he hath burst the gates of death; Christ crucified, the only life that could ever find its way into me, and that hath done so by dying for me.

Yes; give me life in the midst of death, if you would give me a life that would suffice for me. The cross alone meets my demand. For this is the marvel of the cross, and of the decease accomplished there. It is life in the midst of death. Not life extinguished in death—and by death. But life living in death: life living death down: life, by being crucified, crucifying death dead. I am crucified with *this* life. No wonder, therefore, if—'nevertheless I live.'

Therefore, always as I would have Christ live in me more and more, let me have communion more and more with Christ dying for me. For thus only the death that is always rising up over me, to claim me, through the sin that is always dwelling in me—for sin rises up in me, and death by sin—thus only is that ever-rising death suppressed and set aside, even by my faith ever bringing in the death of Christ for me. For if by sin being ever in me, death enters by sin, by faith there ever enters also death for sin—Christ's perfect death, always conquering death, and always giving life to me. Only by bearing about in the body the death of Jesus, can the life also of Jesus be made manifest in my mortal body. Only as Christ crucified does Christ live in his people. Only as always crucified with Christ do I continue to live. I *am* crucified with Christ. It is my continuous history. I not only get my life—I live it, by the faith of the Son of God, who loved me and gave himself for me. Not only as Christ crucified does he come into my soul; it is as Christ crucified that he dwells and lives there. Faith in Christ dying for me is the means whereby Christ lives in me.

Such, then, are the causes of Christ's presence in his people. The Spirit and the word, on his side; on their side, a living faith.

II: CONSEQUENCES OF CHRIST'S PRESENCE IN HIS PEOPLE

Holiness Secured

If Christ's presence is really in his people, then in the *first* place, their holiness is hereby secured.

For what is their holiness but their likeness to Christ? And how true must that likeness be, if Christ himself actually lives in them! So far as Christ lives in you, so far you will inevitably and exactly be like Christ. For, whether living in his own person or in you, there is but one Christ, unchanged—the same yesterday, to-day, and for ever—the very Christ of the gospel history. He will not contradict himself; he will not misrepresent himself. He will not live in you any otherwise than he lived in the days of his flesh upon the earth, and as the history records. It is just the very Christ whom we read of in the gospels, living just as he lived when tabernacling with men upon the earth, that lives in you; and what he was then in his own person, exactly that will he be in you, to the full extent to which by faith you allow him to live and dwell in you.

In you, as in himself, he will still be the same meek and lowly one; the same kind and condescending one; the 'same dutiful, diligent, obedient Son; the same uncomplaining, unflinching sufferer. In you, as in himself, he will still go about doing good; or you will, when he lives in you. In you, as in himself, he will long after lost souls, and love the souls of the saved; or you will, when Christ lives in you. In you, as in himself, he will say (He will say in you, or you will say in him—the ever same, unchanged, obedient one) 'It is my meat and drink to do the will of him that sent me: Wist ye not that I must be about my Father's business?'—the same submissive one, 'Father, if it be possible, let this cup pass from me: nevertheless, not as I will, but as thou wilt!'—the same forgiving one, 'Father, forgive them, for they know not what they do!'—the same relying one, even in death, 'Father, into thy hands I commit my spirit.' All those utterances of his own he will (as it were) prolong and perpetuate in you. To the full extent to which he lives in you he will be in you just what he was himself in the days of his flesh. For, by the Spirit he was what he was. And in the word he is portrayed as he was. But by that very Spirit and word he lives in you—by the Spirit who lives in him and the word in which he himself lives.

Allow him so to live in you. And he will reproduce himself in you. He will re-present himself in you. Even as he was, so will you also be, in the world. His thoughts will be yours; for the same mind that was in Christ will assuredly be in you, when Christ himself is in you. His will will be yours; for he will work in you to will and to do of his good pleasure. His work will be yours; 'for he that abideth in me, and I in him, the same bringeth forth much fruit.' Surely Christ living in you is the truest and profoundest security for your being like him, for your being made holy even as he is holy.

And mark how holiness on this principle—holiness thus secured—cannot fail to be based upon profound humility and pervaded therewith, as all true holiness must be. You live—you live a holy life; but you have no credit, you have no ground of glorying thereby. For it is really not you that live; it is Christ that lives in you. The thoughts of purity and light and wisdom that you think, are not your own; they are the mind of Christ—they are Christ living in you, thinking his own truth in you, wielding by his Spirit your faculty of thought, and bringing its perceptions of heavenly knowledge into harmony with his own. The purposes of meek obedience and uncomplaining patience which you cherish are not your own; they are the will of Christ—they are Christ living in you, willing his own purpose in you, wielding your will by his Spirit, and bringing its desire and choice into unison with his. Your good works are not your own; they are Christ's—they are Christ living in you, working in you to will and to do of his own good pleasure. You resign all ground of glorying: you renounce all claim to honour. Nay, far more: you renounce, indeed, your very self. It is not I, it is Christ. Christ is all in all. 'By the grace of God I am what I am; and his grace which was bestowed upon me was not in vain, for I laboured more abundantly than they all; yet not I, but the grace of God which was with me' (1 Cor. 15: 10). 'I live; yet not I, but Christ liveth in me.'

Oh! who would not thus renounce himself, that he might be filled with Christ; that he might have Christ reproduced in him, Christ living in him—the chiefest among ten thousand, the altogether lovely, fairer than the sons of men!

Mutual Love

As a *second* consequence, take the mutual love that subsists among the members of Christ.

'Hereby know we that we have passed from death to life, because we love the brethren.' Hereby know we that we ourselves live—that Christ lives in us—because we love them in whom Christ lives. Our love to him inevitably goes forth as love to them. Nay, our love to them is just our love to him, recognizing, receiving, resting on him, as living in them also. For if Christ lives in them, then his word is literally and profoundly true—'He that receiveth you receiveth me.' 'Inasmuch as ye did it unto the least of my disciples, ye did it unto me.' When a Christian brother ministers to me in Christian love, it is not he, but Christ living in him that ministers to me. When I, in turn, minister in love to my brother, it is to Christ living in him that I minister. So that in his people Christ himself ministers to me here; and Christ will own me as having ministered to himself in them hereafter. Therefore, not a cup of cold water, given in the name of a disciple, should fail of being met with gratitude to Christ for it now; nor shall fail of obtaining from Christ its reward at last.

Hence, also, the secret of that pure and exalted feeling of honour and esteem with which the blessed grace of love to the brethren is characterized. For when I truly love a believer, it is with an emotional ascription of honour to him as one of the excellent of the earth. I recognize him as a child of God—as an heir of God. I recognize him as a king and a priest by the appointment and in the estimation of our Father who is in heaven. But, honourable and exalted as this—his recognized rank and renown—must be, my estimate of him rises higher still when I recognize the truth that Christ lives in him, or rather when I recognize Christ himself living in him. Then I not only honour him in Christ; I honour Christ in him. Nor does the element of his earthly rank or estate enter into this consideration at all. *That* dwindles into insignificance, and does not come at all into account. Nay; his nation, kindred, people, tongue, become matters of pure indifference. Christ living in him obliterates all distinctions of social or national estate, throws down all barriers of social or national separation. 'There is neither Greek nor Jew, circumcision nor uncircumcision, barbarian, Scythian, bond nor free; but Christ is all, if Christ is in all—Christ is all in all.' 'Inasmuch as ye did it unto the least of my disciples ye did it unto me.' Well, therefore, may this mutual love be assigned as the grand evidence of discipleship: 'Hereby shall all men know that ye are my disciples, if ye have love one to another.'

Persecution

As a *third* consequence, observe the explanation, the origin, of persecution.

It originates in the world's hatred to Christ, and is directed against him. It must be so, seeing that Christ lives in his people. 'Saul, Saul,' wasting the church, 'why persecutest thou *me*?' And it is no extenuation of the world's guilt in hating the saints, that they do not believe that Christ lives in them—that they do no know or recognize Christ in them. Their rejection of those that are his stands exactly on the same footing with their rejection of him: 'Henceforth the world knoweth us not, because it knew him not.' Depravity blinded the world to the glory of Christ when he came in his own person, and blinds them to the measure of his glory in which he comes in the persons of his people. The bitter Ishmaelitish laugh and jest with which you (the worldling) scorn the Isaac of God, the promised seed; the hard words or hard deeds with which you, born after the flesh, persecute him that is born after the Spirit, will bear no excuse from your assertion that you did not know, you did not think, you did not see, that Christ was living in him—that it was really the promised Seed of the woman—Messiah himself—you were persecuting. For it is only your hatred and bitter prejudice that blind you. If you feared God and loved Christ, you would joyfully recognize him in his people: 'They that fear thee shall rejoice when they see me trusting in thy word'—'they glorified God in me' (Ps. 119: 74; Gal. 1: 24).

Ah! consider, in your dislike of those that are Christ's; in your suspicion of them; your hard thoughts and hard speeches concerning them; your discomfort in their presence when their godliness, their Christliness, comes out; your scornful joy over their infirmities and failures—consider what a proof you have in all this of your deadly enmity to that Christ who lives in them. You cannot but know that as yet Christ lives in them only partially. If Christ is in them, 'the body is dead because of sin, though the Spirit is life because of righteousness.' A body of sin and death is in them, as well as a living Christ. And that body of sin and death is a drawback on the completeness of the life and likeness of Christ in his people. They profess to give no more than a partial, though still a real, representation of Christ. They profess no more, though they long that it were far more—indeed, long that it were unbroken and complete. But were it so—were their infirmities removed their remaining corruption finally suppressed and extinguished; were there absolutely nothing seen or extant in them any more save Christ—'Christ living in them' in the unabated fulness and energy of his holy grace and life—ah! you know that their society would be unspeakably more painful to you still; their Christliness would rebuke you more powerfully than now; your withdrawal from them, if withdrawal were possible, would be more complete. Or if you could not escape their presence and their intercourse—if you found yourself in relations to them which you could not set aside—if you found them a people with whom, in their perfect righteousness, and holiness, and likeness to Christ, you could not but have to do—ah! would not your dislike to them, your rejection of them, your resentment against them and their piety, break out in manifold strength and bitterness? And what is this but just a proof that the more clearly Christ is revealed to you, and the nearer Christ's presence is brought to you, so much the more do you dislike him; and that were Christ, therefore, to come to you, not only in his own personal perfection in his people, but in himself—in his own perfect person—you would fully and finally reject him, and say, 'Depart from us, for we desire not thee, nor the knowledge of thy ways'? Ah! do not forget that it is this, indeed, you do say, when now you reject his people. You reject, you persecute, him in them. For—'Christ liveth in them.'

But let believers know what they are to expect at the world's hands, and why. 'Christ living in you' will not fare any better at the world's hands than Christ sojourning in the world in the days of his flesh. The world is the same now as then. Christ in you is the same Christ as then. To the world, therefore, Christ's presence in the persons of his people in all climes and ages must be as unacceptable and offensive as Christ's presence in his own person in Judea in the fulness of time. If they have kept his sayings, they will keep yours also; if they have persecuted him, they will persecute you. The servant is not greater than his Lord; it is enough if the servant be as his Lord. And it must be so, if his Lord lives in him. Christ in his own person was the object of the world's malice. Christ living in you will be so still.

Hope of Glory

But, *fourthly*, as another consequence of Christ living in you, take the words of Paul to the Colossians: 'Christ in you the hope of glory' (Col. 1: 27).

Christ living in you by his Spirit is the seal, the hope, the earnest of the glory to be revealed. Not the glory itself as yet; the seal only, not the substance; the hope only, not the realization; the earnest merely, not the fulness or completion. And the reason is that Christ lives in you, as yet, not as he lives in his glory: when he does so, that will be your glory realized. When Christ as glorified shall live in you, you also will be glorified thereby. But not yet does Christ live in you as he lives in his glory. Christ lives in you as he lived in his humiliation, in his work and travail, in his sorrows and sufferings; his glory veiled in the tabernacle of his flesh and beneath the thick covering of his deep abasement. The Christ who now lives in you is not the Christ as sitting in the fullness of his blessed reward; but the Christ as labouring in the yoke and toil of his humble service; the Christ as going about Judea and Galilee doing good and suffering evil—overcoming evil with good—enduring the contradiction of sinners against himself; living, indeed, a glorious life in the favour of his Father even then, but with his glory hidden. This is the Christ who now lives in you. Your life, therefore, also, is hid with Christ in God. To suffer with Christ is your portion now, even to fill up what is behind of the sufferings of Christ. Christ, when glory comes, will live in you in glory as he lives in glory himself. Christ, ere glory comes, will live in you in the world even as he himself did live in the world. 'Ought not Christ to have suffered these things, and to enter into his glory?' Ought not you to suffer with him, that you may be also glorified together?

It is, then, only 'the hope of glory.' But it is that hope most sure and blessed—most animating for duty, most comforting for patience. For living in you, and working in you, Christ will perfect that which concerns you. He will gradually suppress, and finally extinguish, all that is not 'Christ in you'; and he will then shine forth in you in the unabated splendour of his perfect image. You know not what you shall be; but you know that when he shall appear, you shall be like him, for you shall see him as he is. There will be nothing in you then but Christ. Already you have said, and do habitually say, 'None but Christ for me'; and, blessed be God, that is already realized in full perfection: Christ for me; Christ, 'who loved me and gave himself for me', Christ who 'appeareth in the presence of God for me.' 'None but Christ for me'—is the watchword of faith; the expression, also, of what is even now most fully true: 'None but Christ in me'—is the watchword of hope; the expression of what shall be most fully true in glory; true in its first-fruits now—true in its fulness then. Meantime, bear patiently the sufferings; for I reckon that the sufferings of this present time are not worthy to be compared with the glory that shall be revealed in us, when the full splendour of Christ's presence in us shall be revealed. The seal, and earnest, and hope of that glory is Christ's living presence in us already. Engage more and more, by faith, by vigilance, by prayer, the Christ that lives in you to mortify and crucify the sin that dwells in you. So will you realize and manifest the inward presence of your Lord. And you will say, with growing faith and wonder, and with deepening apprehension of the rich grace and marvels of the saying—'I am crucified with Christ: nevertheless, I live; yet not I, but Christ liveth in me: and the life which I live in the flesh, I live by the faith of the Son of God, who loved me, and gave himself for me.'

III: CAUTIONS CONCERNING CHRIST'S PRESENCE IN HIS PEOPLE

This doctrine needs doubtless to be handled carefully. For there are inferences that might be hastily drawn from it—specious but utterly invalid. It may be well, therefore, to repel them. Especially as it is scarcely possible to do so, without somewhat more fully elucidating the true state of the case: for not only are these inferences not legitimate; they may be even reversed—to the increased glory of the truth.

It might be thought, then, that if Christ lives in the believer, this might, in the first place, impair or set aside the believer's own *personality*; Christ being really the living person; the believer himself, as a distinct and separate person, being, so to speak, ignored. Or, secondly, that his *responsibility*, or sense of responsibility, might be trenched upon, endangered, or destroyed. Or, in the third place, that, by so glorious a person living in him, his simple *humanity* might be injuriously affected. Or, fourthly, that at least his *individuality* of character would be overborne, cramped, confined, constrained.

All these supposed consequences are imaginary. Neither the personality, nor the responsibility, nor the humanity, nor the individuality of the believer is in the least degree dangerously affected by Christ living in him. Rather they are all acted on happily and healthfully. They are all, indeed, truly perfected.

Its Bearing on Their Personality

Is my personality—my distinct and separate personality—at all endangered, when, hearing Christ's voice, I open the door, and Christ comes in to live in me?

Not assuredly in Paul's estimation; even though he does use language fitted, without its conjoined qualifications, to make one fancy he were renouncing his own personal existence 'I live; yet not I.' No; 'not I; Christ liveth in me.' But mark;

immediately—'the life that I live in the flesh, I live by the faith of the Son of God.' It is a life which I live.

For it is not a personal, but a spiritual union with Christ which the Spirit is the agent in accomplishing and faith the means of maintaining. And the personality of the believer is as distinct from the personality of Christ, as Christ's is from the Father's; according to the wondrous utterance, 'I in them, and Thou in me' (John 17: 23).

What is it that takes place when I 'deny myself' (Matt. 16: 24) in favour of Christ—when I renounce myself and embrace into my soul, as henceforth my life, the crucified Jesus? In the first place, all life of sin I render up to the destroying influence of the cross. To make my denial of myself effectual and true I add the additional commanded exercise; 'I take up my cross'—Christ's cross, now become mine. And 'my old man is crucified with Christ that the body of sin may be destroyed, that henceforth I may not serve sin' (Rom. 6: 6). My old man is crucified that he may die.

I, however, am crucified with Christ that I may live. The oracle runs thus—'I am crucified with Christ, nevertheless I live.' Accordingly, in the second place, all my life of intellect, conscience, affection, will, and active energy, I render up to the sanctifying influences of the cross. All my living faculties I surrender to the crucified Christ who lives in me, asking him—through the righteousness and for the sake of his cross—to purify them by his own Spirit; to strengthen them; to free them from all perversion, and bondage, and degradation; and to mould them into harmony, and wield them in unison with his own. And the Spirit deals with these faculties of mine, in a measure, as he dealt with the same faculties in the man Christ Jesus.

Did his sanctifying and ruling all these active powers in him destroy his personality? And how, then, can it possibly destroy or injure mine?

Nay rather; the very reverse must be the issue. Instead of my personality and personal consciousness being driven into the background and overborne; it might rather be expected that this blessed experience would bring them out in quite a new light; bring them out in far more powerful action; and into far livelier recognition. And in point of fact it is so.

For herein is the saying true—'Whosoever shall save his life shall lose it; and whosoever shall lose his life for my sake shall find it' (Matt. 16: 25). This, indeed, is the Lord's own utterance concerning that very self-abnegation (v. 24) which is impossible save 'for his sake'—impossible save under the 'expulsive power' of the entrance of the crucified Jesus. In the very sense in which danger might be supposed to accrue to the believer's consciousness and standing as a distinct individual person, his denying himself shall not injure but profit him.

He resigns a life most shallow, superficial, transient; most fragmentary also; dream-like and vague—a ruin. And he receives instead, a life—profound, eternal; complete; distinct; not 'trailing clouds of' gradually vanishing 'glory after it'—as if parting more and more with every trace of childhood's beauteous simplicity, and childhood's bounding hope and warm enthusiasm—but hiding in, its heart an ever-growing glory, which, when Christ who is our life shall appear, shall also appear with him, in the glorious liberty and manifestation of the sons of God (Col. 3: 4; Rom. 8: 19, 21).

Ah! this life—Christ living in me—though a hidden life (indeed, all the more that it is a hidden life) sounds the depths, and quickens the powers, of personal consciousness—consciousness of awful personality—as they could not otherwise be fathomed nor called forth. 'Bless the Lord, O my soul; and all that is within me bless his holy name' (Ps. 103: 1).

For thus only are my eyes fully opened to the grand and awful truth, that, on the broad plains of God's eternal government, I am a separately subsisting, distinct, individual person; having my own personal interests, indissolubly united with, but perfectly distinct from, all others; my own personal and endless future to anticipate; my own personal reckoning to render; my own personal eternal career to run; my own personal services to render to my God, even such as none can render for me—no, none in all those multitudes that are without number—but which must be rendered personally by me.

So long as I lived unto myself, my personal consciousness was hemmed in within the narrowest limits. Now, if Christ lives in me, it breathes the atmosphere of the wide kingdom of God, and throbs in sympathy with the feelings and experience of the King. So long as I lived among 'the things that are seen and temporal' my conscious life was cramped and confined indeed. I was little more than half a living person, half a dying dream. It was not for me (poor slave of sense and time!) to know the largeness and the liberty of the kingdom unseen and everlasting. Saving my life, I was losing it. Living for myself personally, my personality was imprisoned, if not impaired.

But now, if Christ lives in me, and I therefore live not unto myself but unto him, I find my personal consciousness emancipated and enlarged. I find my life renewed unto me—a new grant of it given; in better kind; in larger measure; in health and thrilling buoyancy infinitely more intense. And just because I have renounced myself, and owned Christ as my life and as my all, I am free to feel (and do now feel indeed) that I have personality of my own—full of awe, but full of joy too. By the grace of God—I AM. 'By the grace of God I am what I am.'

Its Bearing on Their Responsibility

Is my responsibility—or sense of responsibility—destroyed or endangered or trenched upon, by the inward presence of the King? As if all responsibility now might be devolved on him? Let us see.

Only yesterday, the soldier paced his little beat before yon snow-white tent. And his eye was dull. And his step was negligent. And his weapon was carelessly slung. And his whole carriage was uninspired with dignity or firmness. And his thoughts were manifestly roaming. Or he had a light word to bandy with the passer-by.

To-day, the soldier paces his little beat before yon snow-white tent again. And his eye is clear and keen. And the tramp of his foot-fall is measured. And his carriage is erect and dignified. And he handles his weapon like a man of war, in the hour of honour. And his whole soul and body and spirit are at his post. And every thought (indeed, all that is within him) is stirred up and is on honour, in action and alert.

Yon streaming standard, gracing the snow-white tent to-day, explains the change. It proclaims that the presence of the king is within. And to-day the sentinel is proud to be responsible—even unto death.

What when the king is the King of kings? and when both the king and the kingdom are within you?

But this is a mere illustration; and goes but a very little way to carry us into the heart of our theme, or to satisfy the understanding as to a difficulty.

Let it be observed, then, that a man's sense of responsibility—his clear perception, and habitual, practical acceptance of his responsibility—depends on the true rectification of his conscience and the right ruling of his will. The enlightenment[1] of the understanding is of course presupposed. But the faculties or powers of the inner man with which the element of responsibility more immediately deals, or to which it more directly appeals or applies itself, are the conscience and the will.

How, then, are these affected by the indwelling presence of Christ?

Conscience

And first, as to the conscience. Here it must be borne in mind that if Christ lives in me, it is in indissoluble connection with my being crucified with him. 'I am crucified with Christ, nevertheless I live: yet not I, but Christ liveth in me.' Not otherwise can Christ enter my heart to live in me, than as crucified for me. And not otherwise can I receive Christ to live in me than as crucified with him, my 'denial of myself' in his favour; or 'for his sake' (Matt. 16: 24–5)—my renouncing of myself that Christ may be my life, is incomplete; rather, it is ineffectual; nay, it is impossible; unless I 'take up my cross.' I must make Christ's cross my cross. I must be crucified with

---

1 See Chapter 9.

him. With him I must enter intelligently and acquiescingly into the spirit and import of the cross. As a guilty soul, ill-deserving, I am to appropriate the well-deservingness, the merit of the cross. But its merit in its marvellous response to the law—its magnifying of the law and meeting all its demands, making it honourable. My insight, therefore, into the very power of this cross to save me from condemnation and to justify me before God—the end which I contemplate and design more immediately in believing on Jesus Christ and him crucified (for with the heart man believeth unto righteousness, that is, with the design of obtaining justifying righteousness, and not with the design only, but with success)—my very power of appreciating the cross, and appropriating the righteousness there wrought out, presupposes and implies an insight into the honourableness of the law, the righteousness alike of its commandments and its curse; the rightful authority of him who has imposed it; and my own unconditional, unchangeable responsibility under it. I cannot read the cross except in the light of the Law. If I see anything in the cross precious to me, it is because I have been awakened to my responsibility, and recognize in that cross a holy provision for meeting it.

To embrace Christ's cross, therefore, as mine, is the most intense recognition and acknowledgment of my responsibility. It is to stand before the eternal holy law of God, adoring the justice, and bowing down to the authority, of the lawgiver; while I express my loyalty by 'submitting myself to the righteousness of God' (Rom. 10: 3), proffering and pleading an obedience whereby many are made righteous. And in this very acceptance of justification in the righteousness of the cross—when the cross becomes mine, and I am crucified with Christ—my 'knee doth bow' at the throne, and my 'tongue sweareth' fealty to the King. And my oath of allegiance is but the echo of his oath of sovereignty—sovereignty both in law and in grace—'I have sworn by myself, the word is gone out of my mouth in righteousness and shall not return, that unto me every knee shall bow, every tongue shall swear. Surely shall one say, in the Lord have I righteousness and strength. In the Lord shall all the seed of Israel be justified and shall glory' (Isa. 45: 23–5). So intimately is my justification unto life through the cross bound up with my swearing to the King—my recognition of that sovereignty of his which he hath sworn by himself shall be recognized.

The provision of the cross is designed in infinite wisdom and with glorious adequacy and precision, to enable the conscience to feel—nay, to meet—its responsibilities. 'The blood of Christ, who through the eternal spirit offered himself without spot to God, cleanseth the conscience from dead works to serve the living God!' (Heb. 9: 14).

So is the conscience affected by 'Christ living in me.'

The Will

And now, secondly, as to the will. How does the in-living Christ deal with it?

Let the memorable appeal of the apostle speak on this point—'Work out your own salvation with fear and trembling, for it is God that worketh in you to will and to do of his good pleasure' (Phil. 2: 12–13).

Yes! the in-living Christ works in you. But his very work is to set you working; he works in you 'to do.' And yet he does not so work in you as to set you working mechanically—as if the operation of his power set aside your responsibility, dispensing with it either in whole or in part. All the work which he works in you is preceded by your willing to work that work. He works in you 'to will' everything that he works in you 'to do.' He carries your will along with him. Secretly—by sovereign, creative, controlling grace—he does so. And, what is more, the very fact that he does deal sovereignly and subjectively with your will, he makes an objective ground of appeal to your will itself. He stirs all the energy of your will by this very motive. He calls on you to work—'for'—because—on the ground that—'he worketh in you to will.' So that whatever repugnance has been fancied between efficacious grace and moral suasion, the Lord himself speaks of them as beautifully consistent and harmonious. For he makes the fact of his efficacious work upon your will the very topic of a moral suasion; and the ostensible or objective exhortation or moral suasion becomes the occasion and the channel through which the effective work of subjective grace upon the will is secretly performed.

Having cleansed your conscience from dead works by his atoning blood, and made it powerful and peaceful and pure—alike, and in equal measure, delicate and strong to own your responsibility to law, even the sovereign and absolute law which commands your perfect love—Christ, the priest, living in you thus as Lord of your conscience, lives in you also as king and ruler of your will. And he truly rules it; not by mere command from without, but by the power of his grace within. And he brings the demand or your conscience and, the choice of your will into perfect harmony—into a unity. 'Unite my heart to fear thy name.'

Nor is there in all our glorious Christianity anything finer than this arrangement.

For the great problem of the rectification of my moral nature is not met, unless I can feel that I am at once under the most stringent and rigorous responsibility, and in the enjoyment of the sweetest and largest freedom. I must be brought to own and accept the absolute supremacy of moral law, and to find my very freedom in doing so.

For I cannot think that the honour due to my own awful attribute of distinct personality is rendered to it, unless the Great Supreme abstains from dealing arbitrarily with me, and gives me all the immunity and privilege and confidence implied in ruling me by known and published law—law most righteous and immutable. Far am I from cherishing pride in making this demand or entertaining this desire. The very essence of pride is in the reverse desire—the desire to be under no authority, but to 'be as gods.' The carnal mind is not subject to the law of God, neither indeed can be. But in choosing this exemption, it dishonours and degrades itself, according to the sure and inevitable process, 'He that exalteth himself shall be abased.' It is an honour due to my nature, as a creature of God made in his image, that I should be under law to him that I be not arbitrarily dealt with by my maker, but be ruled by an ostensible, intelligible, moral law. I can escape from arbitrary treatment—with all its haphazards and uncertainties, and all the paralysing influences of its utterly undecipherable prospects, its utterly unimaginable contingencies—only by being under law. I am emancipated from the fear of despotism just by betaking myself to the sovereignty of law.

Moreover, if I am under law to God at all, it must be law absolute and unconditional—eternal, unchangeable, and perfect. For exactly as the existence of any cause logically infers a first cause, absolute and everlasting, so the sense of any obligation implies an ultimate obligation, unlimited and unconditional, most perfect and unalterable for ever. And the expression and assertion of this obligation—not one jot or tittle of which shall pass away, even though earth and heaven should pass away—I find in the two great commandments—'Thou shalt love the Lord thy God with all thy heart, and thy neighbour as thyself.'

If I am crucified with Christ, it is because my conscience has been brought to honour this law; to own my inexcusableness and ill-deservingness in breaking this law; to prize and appropriate the cross as magnifying this law and making it honourable, and as putting me in a right relation to it. My crucifixion with Christ—while most obviously it secures my deliverance from the curse of the law and my acceptance by the lawgiver as righteous in his sight—is also subjectively and simultaneously the rectification of my conscience towards that very law which must be the recognized standard in justification, recognized both by my lawgiver and by me. Therefore I am now placed on a new vantage ground for owning my responsibility to law—responsibility most rigorous to law most stringent and righteous.

But if this were all—were I simply brought to own my responsibility without accepting it—a career of intense wretchedness would be opening up to me. I am under law, but I am destitute of liberty. 'O wretched man that I am!' I am under overwhelming conviction of what is right, but sold under sin to what is wrong. And in the struggle between my quickened conscience and unrenewed will there are elements of misery and the consciousness of self-degradation, to sting me in growing agony, and haunt me with growing sense of shame.

Never can my immortal soul be emancipated and ennobled truly; never can my religion exalt and strengthen me; never can it make me the honourable, upright, true and gladsome subject of the King of glory—until it be a religion of liberty as well as law; a religion of the will as well as of the conscience; of choice as well as of conviction.

But let me be not only crucified with Christ; let Christ live in me. Let him so live in me that his will shall inform, actuate, rule mine; moulding it into the form of the law, and filling it with the contents of the law, even love. Let him plant in me a living and indestructible germ of a new life (1 Peter 1: 23), in vital connexion with which he himself shall for ever dwell, thereby living in me. And let this germ of new life, on being developed and manifested, exhibit—as the now fixed habit of my heart and native tendency of my will—just the tracery and tenor of that sovereign and absolute law; so that it is now as much an inward prompting law to my will, as it was formerly only an outward authoritative law to my conscience; which I discover in my own consciousness by finding that disobedience to the law now is as much a thwarting of the native bent of my will as it is a violation of the native function of my conscience. In a word—Christ the priest being seated on the throne of my conscience, Christ the king touching and guiding the springs of my will—let it come to pass that my will delights in the selfsame things that my conscience demands. My responsibility now is as welcome to my heart as it is undeniable in my convictions; while, in the reconciliation between my conscience and my will, I have found a liberty as unreserved and absolute as the law of God is; a liberty which I will now enjoy just in proportion as I walk according to the law. For I can be brought into bondage and constraint now, not as formerly, by striving more and more to render obedience, the obedience of mere conviction. I will be conscious of bondage now, only if I turn aside from the law. In fact the sphere of my liberty is now identical with the sphere of my responsibility, which is the sphere of law—'I will walk at liberty, for I seek thy precepts' (Ps. 119: 45). The realm of bondage is outside the law. Within the law, I am free. And the law is within me, also; in my heart, even as it is in Christ's

(Heb. 8: 10; Ps. 40: 8). For Christ, in whose heart the law is, himself 'liveth in me.' Therefore—'I delight to do thy will, O my God.'

If the conscience and the will are thus affected by Christ living in me (those faculties which share between them, on the one hand, the righteous and revering acknowledgment—and, on the other, the loving and loyal acceptance—of responsibility), surely not only is my responsibility itself deepened, but my sense of responsibility is enhanced incalculably, by the inward presence of Christ.

Its Bearing on Their Humanity

It may seem unnecessary and superfluous even to hint at the idea of Christ's in-dwelling trenching, in any sense, upon our humanity—on the essential and distinguishing characteristics of our nature as human nature; as if that nature by being inhabited by so glorious a person as Christ might thereby become something more or something else than human. Nor would we tarry to indicate a caution here at all, save for the completeness of this short series of considerations; and for the clearer view of the full glory of the case which every false conception, when dissipated, presents to us.

Were it one whose higher nature was less than divine, or his created nature else than human, that claimed to enter in and live in me, doubtless acquiescence in his claim might operate injuriously on the essential elements of my nature. And obviously a great incongruity would take place. Did I 'deny myself' in favour of an angelic being—did I 'lose my life for the sake of' such an one (if such a supposition is indeed intelligible or conceivable)—the result, possibly, might be a submerging of the fundamental characteristics of my humanity, and the substitution of something superhuman or extrahuman—something, perhaps, neither human nor angelic—in its room.

But he who dwells in me is the man Christ Jesus; and he dwells in me by his Spirit, who is God. His Spirit is God—the creator of my human nature. He understands it. He will respect it. He will not violate it. Nay, rather, he will perfect it. For he dwells in me, in a measure, even as he dwelt in the man Christ Jesus. And when he finally expels all that is not 'Christ in me,' He will have trained me up 'unto a perfect man, unto the measure of the stature of 'the fulness of Christ' (Eph. 4: 13).

Yes, Christ's own created nature was not superhuman. It was humanity and nothing more; humanity and nothing less; humanity and nothing else. It was humanity most true, genuine, unperverted, perfect. And by dwelling in you he conforms you unto himself—'the first-born among many brethren.' He emancipates your nature from all that perverts and degrades it. He gives it free play and full scope. He brings it out in its true capacities and capabilities. He shows you, in himself, what, by the in-dwelling of the Spirit, it may be made; what, under the guidance of the Spirit, it may achieve. And he gives the same Spirit to achieve, in a measure, in your human nature, what he achieves in his; to make yours, in subordination to him, what the Spirit has already made his. For by living in you, on the one hand, he puts the same law in your heart which the Spirit placed in his own. And, on the other, 'if the Spirit of him that raised up Jesus from the dead dwell in you, he that raised up Christ from the dead shall also quicken your mortal body by his Spirit that dwelleth in you' (Rom. 8: 11). So that he renews your mind, and he fashions your body, like unto his own gracious mind, and his own glorious body. He redeems and glorifies your entire humanity.

But a more interesting question remains.

Its Bearing on Their Individuality

Is the in-dwelling presence of Christ fitted to act injuriously on the individuality of the believer's character? The same Christ living in each and all—will not all diversity be sacrificed, and personal, distinguishing peculiarities submerged or set aside?

Now let it be distinctly understood what the in-dwelling of the same Christ in all his people is fitted to set aside and submerge. All diversities that are not of Christ's own prior creation must unquestionably disappear. Diversities that are formal, false, factitious, of man's formation—these assuredly must all give way before the presence of the Lord. Powerful barriers of separation though they be in the moral world—even as seas, and mountains, and rivers, in the natural—theirs shall be a discomfiture and 'removal fitted to remind one of the exulting question—'What ailed thee, O sea, that thou fleddest? thou Jordan, that thou wast driven back? Ye mountains, that ye skipped like rams; and ye little hills like lambs?' And the reason given in reply is to the point. It was—'at the presence of the Lord, at the presence of the God of Jacob' (Ps. 64: 5–7).

Separations by space and time; by the diameter of the globe or by millenniums of its history; separations by rank or caste, tongue or nation; by family feuds or national antipathies; all must give way before the life-giving power of Christ's one Spirit, and under the commanding supremacy of all-harmonizing redeeming love. In this sense 'there is neither Greek nor Jew, circumcision nor uncircumcision, Barbarian, Scythian, bond nor free; but Christ is all, and in all' (Col. 3: 11).

Moreover, the perversities of individual temper; the affectations of singularity; the sharp and sore angularities of character, by which, often, brother rasps on brother, unto mutual discomfort and unto the creation of a wariness more raw than tender, and more akin to suspicion than to mutual consideration or care—these, too, the more that Christ dwells in all, will give way, or be submerged. 'I beseech you that ye walk worthy of the vocation wherewith ye are called, with all lowliness and meekness, with long suffering, forbearing one another in love; endeavouring to keep the unity of the Spirit in the bond of peace' (Eph. 4: 1–3). Such is the apostle's call for harmony. And he grounds it on unity—'There is one body and one Spirit' (v. 4).

But does he set aside diversity? Does he advise the Ephesians to labour and strain after an absolute and tame uniformity? Does he recommend to keep in view the desirableness of every brother being a perfect copy and exact repetition of every other? Does he hint that the oneness of the body or the oneness of the Spirit must render any such result either desirable or likely? And (yet more exactly in point and to our present purpose) when he tells them not only of one body and one Spirit, one hope, one faith, one baptism; but of one God and Father of all being above all, and through all, and *in them all*; does he admit or recommend, as either the issue or design of this indwelling, that every trace of individuality—of peculiarity of gift or grace, or taste or talent, or tendency—must be resigned by the several members of the body? Is this his inference?

Very much the reverse. For he immediately adds, as if with special design to forestall any such conclusion—'But unto everyone of us is given grace according to the measure of the gift of Christ' (v. 7). At times the train of thought may require the statement: 'There are diversities of gifts but the same Spirit' (1 Cor. 12: 4). At other times, it may be well to reverse the order of these clauses, and diversify the prominence given to them respectively: It is the same Spirit, but there are diversities of gifts.

And why should it be supposed that the in-dwelling of him who gave them should cramp them, or constrain them, or in any way affect them injuriously? Surely your exact individuality of character—so far as it is not an affectation or a perversion, and therefore to be got rid of as soon and thoroughly as possible—will not be injured by him who actually created it. Your admission of him into your inner man will surely not endanger any specific bent or characteristic whereby he who loves variety has diversified you from others. You bring your individuality to him. 'Just as you are'—not merely as a sinner, but as his creature—'you come.' Your own individual soul you give to him, believing that he has redeemed it. You believe that in all that discriminates you from others—not merely as numerically a different unit from them, but a distinct member in a boundlessly varied organism—you are an object of love and care to your redeemer. You believe that you have a place in the body, and services both in time and (Oh! how countless and inconceivably grand) in eternity—services before you which demanded, not merely in you, numerically one more member, one more agent—but the very member and agent which exactly your individuality makes you to be; and you believe that, by the gracious in-living of the Lord in you, your individuality, far from being injured or suppressed, is now for the first time, in a sense, necessary; that it is necessary now, because the Lord hath need of it (Matt. 21: 3). Now, in fact, the chief end of its existence will come forward into view—and be fulfilled.

For, the in-living Christ emancipates it from all perversion. Your entire surrender unto him, your abnegation of self and acceptance of Christ instead, brings it back to its creator—to the author of it; who will be the finisher, the perfecter of it, too. You put it into his hands who impressed its original features upon it. You put it at his disposal. And he will bring it out in its true and unperverted form and actings, its native bent and tendencies, its own specific features. He will perfect in you his own original idea of what he desired and decreed your individuality to be. On the other hand, the surrender of your individuality—your slavish imitation of any man—trenches on the fulness of your communion with Christ. It is a limitation, to that extent, of what should be your unreserved surrender to him. It is a partial revolt from him.

'Whom God foreknew he also did predestinate to be conformed to the image of his Son that he might be the firstborn among many brethren.' But the perfect conformity of every brother to the elder brother will be on conditions, or with qualifications, that shall not destroy diversity among themselves. They shall be conformed to the Son in all that relates them to the Father, consistently with the preservation and the perfecting of all that discriminates and diversifies them—in point of natural endowments, providential disciplines, and gracious communications—from one another.

And Christ, accepting all these their diversities, 'fills them all' with himself.

Why should this be thought a thing incredible? Were it a human person that lived in each and all of the faithful—supposing the idea to be self-consistently conceivable—one can hardly see how the free and natural development of endlessly varied individualities could be provided for. But this is a divine person. He is God. He is God manifest. He is God manifest in the flesh. By his Spirit, who is one God with him, he lives in his people. And the Spirit dwells in a measure in their human nature, as he dwelt without measure in his. And should not the immeasurable indwelling of the Holy Ghost in the God-man convince you that he can dwell in a measure in you and fill all your humanity; and yet keep your special type of character and individual gifts and powers all and wholly inside of what was really immeasurable in the Christ? For it hath pleased the Father that in him should all fulness dwell. There was nothing one-sided in him; nothing peculiar; no grace forcing itself specially on our notice; no predominant characteristic; nothing of what we mean by individuality when we speak of the various characters of mere men. Peculiarity and predominance of gift or grace or talent among the faithful is the result of *measure*: 'To each is given grace according to the measure of the gift of Christ.' This cannot be in him who is 'above his fellows' (Ps. 45: 7), precisely in respect that in him is no measure: 'The Father giveth not the Spirit by measure unto *him*' (John 3: 34). No. 'We beheld his glory as of the only-begotten of the Father, full of grace and truth. And of his fulness have all we received and grace for grace' (John 1: 14–16).

Hence when he ascended up on high, receiving gifts for men—it is expressly added that 'he ascended far above all heavens that he might *fill all things*' (Eph. 4: 9–11). And in beautiful keeping with this is the Apostle's other allusion to the ascension, in the same epistle: 'God raised him from the dead, and set him at his own right hand in the heavenly places, far above all principality and power, and might, and dominion, and every name that is named, not only in this world but also in that which is to come; and hath put all things under his feet, and gave him to be head over all things to the church, which is his body, *the fulness of him that filleth all in all*' (Eph. 1: 20-3).

He ascended that he might fill all things. He filleth all in all. His church, his body, is his fulness. It is especially his fulness in respect that he filleth all in all. It is his fulness as the result of his filling all in all.

It will take, therefore, all the individualities of all the hundred and forty and four thousand sealed ones (Rev. 14: 1) and all the numbers without number whom that special number symbolizes; it will take them all, in all their divinely decreed combinations, and in all their gloriously perfected organization; all filled with Christ; Christ living in them all—it will need them all to exhibit what he shall be content to 'shew unto the ages to come' as a representation of 'his fulness.' The glorious company of the apostles; the goodly fellowship of the prophets; the noble army of the martyrs; the patriarchs and pilgrim fathers of every dispensation; the confessors and reformers of every age; all the hidden ones also, brought to light (in a word, the whole seed of Abraham)—'tell the stars, if thou be able to number them; so shall thy seed be'—Ah! in their gathering together at the last, what a heaven these stars will make! But of that heaven also shall this saying be true, 'One star differeth from another star in glory.'

It would be a tempting theme to launch out upon, the marvellous diversity in the church considered as a single organism—Christ the living head and life of it. Assuredly in this light the indwelling Spirit of Christ makes no war on the special tastes and powers and places of various members; nor does he charge you to aim at any such conformity as would stunt you into anyone rigid type or form; or put the free development of your own particular gifts under any bondage whatsoever. Nay, he charges you to keep the place, and fulfil the service, for which just your own individuality, under his instructing word and informing Spirit, qualifies you. He forbids you to resign your own place or function. He commands you to abide in it with contentment. He tells you there will be schism in the body if you do not. And to make this plain he represents the ear saying: Because I am not the eye, I am not of the body:—and the foot saying: because I am not the hand, I am not of the body. And he asks, are they therefore not of the body? And he asks, further, what or where would the body itself be, if these individual powers resigned their individual functions and distinctions? 'If the whole body were an eye, where were the hearing? And if they were all one member where were the body?' And it is by one Spirit that the body is one, and the members many. 'By one Spirit are we all baptized into one body.' So that it is just the in-living Christ, by his Spirit, who preserves the individualities, calls them into requisition, shields and defends them, perfects them, gives them fullest scope and freest action—abundant and comely honour also—tempering them together into the promptitude and concert of individuals numberless and endlessly diversified, yet acting under his own one Spirit as a single organism, thrilling with one life, and all holding the head—Christ the life of all; Christ 'all in all.'

There is one very plain but precious application of the point now in hand which I cannot resist indicating. I refer to the completeness which the view just given confers on personal Christian liberty.

No doubt the great and fundamental elements of Christian liberty were under our notice when speaking of the in-living Christ as not superseding but quickening our sense of responsibility. The law of the tables of stone being by Christ's Spirit written on the fleshy tables of our hearts, immediately we are subjectively free. For the renewed heart then delights in identically that which the enlightened conscience demands. The prompting law within you is the same as the commanding law without you and above you. And this sweet harmony, in the main prevailing, sheds over all your inner man a joyful sense of liberty and amplitude, and the bounding hope of ever onward and unfettered progress.

But this new life, if it is to be one of full enlargement, must embrace—appropriate—afford scope and field and unhampered action for—every personal endowment you possess, and every defensible taste and tendency that may characterize you.

The demand for liberty in this secondary sense, which is just a protest on behalf of personal individuality—is sometimes met with in its most imperious force, and (it may be) not always in very well-regulated action, in generous and lovable young men; high-spirited perhaps; perhaps, also, somewhat heady. Nor is it a case that can be safely dealt with without generosity and wisdom, and somewhat in a sense of high-spiritedness too. Would that it had been always so dealt with; and that one were always near to show how, within all good and righteous limits, a living religion—the religion of Christ living in us—gloriously meets this demand!

For it is quite a possible thing that Christianity may have been pressed on your acceptance in unjustifiably close, or too exclusive, connection with the actual specimens of Christianity with which you come in contact. And in these there may have been somewhat to irritate and revolt you. There may have been a narrowness; a want of symmetry; a want of fire or force, on the one hand, or of calm and steady regulation, on the other; a stuntedness or ill-proportion; a firmness of principle passing over into sternness and severity for want of an element of geniality; or a geniality degenerating into tame effeminacy for want of an element of strength and vigour. And, in particular, in these realized exhibitions of the religion urged upon you, there may have been to your view no scope, no indulgence—no quarter, one might almost say—for the very pursuits in which you find your innocent and invigorating recreation; or to which perhaps you purpose dedicating yourself as the leading business of your life.

Now, doing you the justice, or exercising towards you the charity, to believe that in this you are not seeking to cloak over and conceal, to justify or excuse, an enmity to the essential spirit of Christianity under the guise of your dislike to some mere form of it, might it not help you to remember that there is no obligation laid on you whatever to embrace the particular form which you dislike? Christianity never proposes to force on you, for instance, who are in the bud and bloom of opening manhood—it may be, also, in the conflict with sincere and earnest doubts; it may be, also, in the possession of individual special gifts; with endowments that may fascinate you towards the keen severities of science or the bold scopefulness of speculation; with tastes that turn you to the fine arts; or tendencies that prompt to energy and business—Christianity does not propose to force on you, and no wise pleader of its claim will urge upon you, a style of piety, let us say, suited to your godly aged grandmother. And yet, young man, you may have been deaf to her kind expostulations, merely because conscious that a form of piety like hers would never do with you. You have your individual character, your individual career. And while she, good soul, may all the day long croon her quiet hymn beside the hearth, you have to face, with brave uplifted hand, life's opening battle, or follow out, with trembling thought, inquiries and fears that never cross her simple mind.

Be it so. But there is as little need for you to follow the type or form of her piety as there is room for you to despise the spirit and substance of it. All honour to the spirit that breathes in it: you need not be in bondage to the form. I say, all honour to the spirit of her piety:

> She, for her humble sphere by nature fit,
> Has little understanding and no wit,
> Just knows, and knows no more, her Bible true,
> A truth the brilliant Frenchman never knew;
> And, in that charter, reads, with sparkling eyes,
> Her title to a treasure in the skies.

Ah! well might you lay all your tastes and gifts and tendencies—all your sciences and arts and speculations, with all your progress and all your pleasure in them—at her feet. And wisely might you barter them all for a portion of her spirit. Yes: wisely and well—were it needful.

But it is not. You may be baptized with the same Spirit wherewith she has been baptized: and you may keep all your tastes, and gifts, and arts, and sciences, and speculations, too; and all the laurels of the schools that you may have gained—provided you can wear them humbly. The Spirit of the Lord can baptize you and all your individuality of character besides. The Christ living in you can fill and sanctify you wholly. There was nothing cramped and stunted in his own character when he dwelt among men, visible in his own person. And there is no stunting, cramping influence in his presence and indwelling in his visible church which is his body. And he can dwell in you, 'a member in particular,' filling all your heart and all your soul with his presence, and animating with his own healing, hallowing power every endowment he may have assigned to you. He is the author and giver of every good and perfect mental gift which you possess. He knows and understands them all. He knows what education they are susceptible of. He knows what perfection they are capable of reaching; what service in his kingdom they are capable of rendering. He will have a just regard for them. He will respect them with a tenderness and care which none like the very author of them can feel. No repressive action will he exert upon them: very much the reverse. Only let him wholly possess your inner man. And will he not wholly sanctify you, soul and body and spirit; giving all warrantable scope—and all free, healthful movement; giving firmer action, and fuller fruit, and grander prospect of future fruit and future action—to every trait of individuality which, seeing the end from the beginning, and contemplating your history into eternity, he himself from the first bestowed upon you?

In this sense also, 'where the Spirit of the Lord is, there is liberty.' And the word rules all, most definitely. For it is the Christ of the gospel history that lives in you.

11

THE VIRTUAL CONTEMPORANEOUSNESS OF ALL SAINTS

'The Fulness of the Times' (Eph. 4: 10).

'Abraham rejoiced to see my day: and he saw it and was glad' (John 8: 56).

'He turned the sea into dry land: they went through the flood on foot; there did we rejoice in him' (Ps. 66: 6).

'Then we which are alive and remain shall be caught up together with them in the clouds, to meet the Lord in the air: and so shall we ever be with the Lord' (1 Thess. 4: 17).

If Christ's presence is with his people in all ages as in the gospel history, all saints are thus virtually contemporaneous with the day of Christ. But if this be so, and if, moreover, Christ's presence is in his people also, then all saints are virtually contemporaneous with one another.

This is a singular result and worthy of being rigorously tested, lest any element of fancy and illusion be allowed to enter where we are anxious to set forth the indefeasible warrants and undoubted functions of faith.

We have already had occasion in the course of our inquiries to see that faith has an intrinsic power of casting out the element of time. And the fact is that the whole realm of faith is supra-temporal.

For our entire salvation belongs to a world, or realm, or sphere above time and sense; a realm such, that whosoever liveth in it, has life eternal. He is no more a child or denizen of time. Like the king of that realm, 'he was dead and is alive again, and, behold! he liveth for evermore.'

This sphere or kingdom receives various designations in Holy Scripture. It is indicated by the single word 'above.' Its messenger is—'he that cometh from above' (John 3: 31); its treasures are—'the things which are above' (Col. 3: 1); its metropolis is—'Jerusalem which is above' (Gal. 4: 26); and 'Jerusalem which is free,' being 'the mother of us all,' the children of this kingdom are 'born from above' (John 3: 3, marg.). Doubtless we have here a true transcendentalism. 'The heavenly places' is another name for this home and realm of the eternal; where Christ's mediatorial throne is (Eph. 1: 20), and where his quickened people that have been raised together with him sit by faith with their forerunner (2: 6), enjoying all spiritual blessings (1: 3), and illustrating to powers and principalities the manifold wisdom of God (3: 10). It is 'the tabernacle of God,' where the psalmist vows that he will abide for ever, trusting under the covert of God's wings (Ps. 61: 4). It is 'the house of the Lord'—'his temple'–'his pavilion'—'the secret of his tabernacle'; as it is written—'One thing have I desired of the Lord, that will I seek after; that I may dwell in the house of the Lord all the days of my life, to behold the beauty of the Lord, and to inquire in his temple. For in the time of trouble he shall hide me in his pavilion; in the secret of his tabernacle shall he hide me' (Ps. 27: 4–5). It is the hiding-place of the hidden life, whereunto the children of the kingdom may continually resort: 'Thou shalt hide them in the secret of thy presence from the pride of man; thou shalt keep them secretly in a pavilion from the strife of tongues' (Ps. 31: 20). They are often summoned into it, as into an ark of safety, when the Lord comes out of his place to punish the inhabitants of the earth: 'Come, my people, enter thou into thy chambers, and shut thy doors about thee: hide thyself as it were for a little moment, till the indignation be overpast' (Isa. 26: 20). And 'he that dwelleth in this secret place of the Most High shall abide under the shadow of the Almighty' (Ps. 91: 1).

Here is the native home of our salvation. All that appertains to our redeemed and spiritual life transpires and is transacted here; in a realm transcending time and sense, and the world and the body, even the kingdom of heaven; the heavenly places; the secret place of the Most High. What wonder, then, if time be lightly accounted of here; vanquished; disregarded; eliminated? Shall it seem a thing incredible—such being the supra-temporal and transcendent sphere of our salvation—if 'God that cannot lie' is said to have 'promised us eternal life before the world began' (Tit. 1: 2)?—and even to have 'given us his grace in Christ Jesus before the world began' (2 Tim. 1: 9)? Yes; the dwelling-place of our salvation is the bosom of the everlasting Father, where the Son has never ceased to dwell; where he dwelt (it is very carefully testified) even while dwelling among us in the flesh (John 1: 18; 3: 13). While living here that life which the gospel history records he was living in the bosom of the Father; inhabiting at one and the same time, as God-man, the eternal realm and the temporal, the transcendental and the sensible. Even in dying on the cross he died in his Father's bosom, tasting in its infinite sweetness the love wherewith his Father loved him because he laid down his life for the sheep. And is it not into the Father's bosom that the returning prodigal is received, when, taking heart of grace from that very death of Jesus, he commits his own spirit—as with Christ's departing spirit, and in the righteousness of his one offering—into the Father's hands, and the Father falls on his neck and kisses him?

Our salvation is all in the Father's bosom, and our being brought personally to possess it is our being brought home to our Father's bosom.

But while it was there from everlasting—there, in the Father, with the Son who 'was as one brought up with him, daily his delight, rejoicing always before him, rejoicing in the habitable parts of his earth, and his delights were with the sons of men' (Prov. 8: 30–1); and while it was there given to us in the Beloved 'before the world began'—a conjunction had to be effected between the eternal realm, the secret home of our salvation above, and the ostensible platform and scene of our temporary pilgrimage here below. The supra-temporal promise and gift had in 'due times to be manifested.' Accordingly, they were 'made manifest by the appearing of our Saviour Jesus Christ.' So do those remarkable passages (Tit. 1: 2–3; 2 Tim. 1: 9, 10) which speak of that gift and promise as being, in their first bestowment, independent of time, indicate the divine procedure in bringing them at last into conjunction with time in the 'due times'—the 'fulness of times'—the 'day of Christ.'

The incarnation of the eternal Word in time—in the fulness of times—was the bringing of that eternal salvation, 'that eternal life which was with the Father,' into contact and connection with time. But it remained eternal, and in the supra-temporal realm, notwithstanding. It certainly was not thereby limited to time's conditions; not incased within the narrowness of things that are seen and temporal; not subjected and subordinated to time's transiency and vanity; or stunted into the littleness of earth's limited horizon. No, time is not capable of embracing in its narrow arms the boundless contents of the Father's bosom—full of the exceeding riches of his grace in his kindness towards us by Jesus Christ—nor the fulness which it has pleased the Father should dwell in our Emmanuel for us—nor the all-sufficient stores of the everlasting covenant. These treasures of the realm that is unseen and eternal may be connected with time, but they must abide eternal; even as the eternal Word made flesh and voluntarily conversant with the implications of time—an infant of days—continued nevertheless 'the Father of the ages,' 'whose goings forth have been from of old, from everlasting' (Isa. 9: 6; Micah 5: 2).

The incarnation of the eternal Word is the personal union of godhead and humanity—each remaining purely and perfectly distinct. Is it not also the yoking of eternity with time? On the humanity of the God-man, as on a divinely perfect index, we read the character of God. On 'the day of Christ,' as an index quite analogous, may we not read the interests and implications of all time—the events and the issues of eternity?

Is there anything permanently precious or purely good pertaining to human nature which is not embraced and glorfied in the humanity of him who is God? Is there anything permanently precious pertaining to all human time which does not run up into 'the day' of him who is the Father of the ages—or issue forth from it?

In the person of Christ, God and man meet and are at one; all of man that shall not be reprobate for ever. In the day of Christ, eternity and time meet; all of time that shall not be for ever cast away. The person of Christ is the head of the body. The day of Christ is the fulness of the times. Is not this an analogy that may fairly be questioned as to the lessons it is fraught with? And, in particular, may we not most safely judge, that if the infinite love and care of the Holy Ghost, according to the purpose and good pleasure of the Father, framed a human organism for the eternal Word such as should worthily fulfil the destined function, namely that in him, God might gather together, recapitulate or head up, all things which are in heaven, and which are on earth, even in him: so the same divine wisdom chose for the central epoch of this 'dispensation,' a day not unworthy to be called 'the fulness of the times'—a day in which all 'the times' might find themselves gathered together and recapitulated; standing to it in a relation analogous to that of the members of the body to the head?

It is a thought not easy to fix into definite expression. But it assigns 'to the day of Christ' among the days, a place of supereminence and influence which the intuitions of spiritual faith must be not slow to sanction and to welcome joyfully. Save for that day, well might I abandon all interest in every other day; and, in special, well might I cry with Job—'Let the day perish wherein I was born; let darkness and the shadow of death stain it.' But neither Job nor I can have cause to say so, however painful our probation, since Job's better utterance has found its fulfilment—'I know that my Redeemer liveth and that he shall stand at the latter day upon the earth.' The day in which the Son of God finished the work given him to do, has cast a radiance of eternal heaven on every other day, and left an impress and signature of hope and glory on all the times besides. We will marshal 'the times' under the leadership of this day. We will make the day of Christ the head and soul and heart of all the days. Nor is it a passive or honorary relation this, but full of mighty influence and of controlling command; as when the head and soul of some establishment, governmental or commercial, seated in his central bureau of management, by means of mirrors, telegraphs, and various devices of communication, reads in central record and rules from seat of power unquestioned, every movement of the far-extending mechanism; while nothing can originate save under his own regulating hand, and nothing transpire but must repeat and register itself beneath his ever-watchful eye.

Some such relation, it is conceived, of central position and supreme importance, does the gospel history bear to all other history, or the day of Christ to the entire period of God's dispensation with the world. The 'times' are intelligible, in connection with eternity, only as marshalled in one compact body under that day of Christ as their head. The ages stand all alike related to the Father of the ages; and the salvation which he achieves is 'prepared before the face of all people'; who may therefore be seen, in their successive generations, coming forward and passing on in front of the day of Christ, its cloudless and unsetting sun lighting them along, in their silent march, to the other great day of the Lord. Until that great day arrive and time shall be no more, from its place of high command, throned in the central seat of time, the day of Christ, which Abraham saw and was glad, pours forth in endless plenitude influences such as those that gladdened Abraham and gladden all his children; and back on that selfsame central day the faith of all saints refers itself continually. Nor is it wonderful. For, as from the person of Christ the love of godhead flows to men, and men by faith betake themselves in Christ to 'bone of their bone and flesh of their flesh,' finding a support divine for their frail humanity where godhead and humanity are conjoined for ever; even so, from the day of Christ the light of eternity flows over upon time, and the ages betake themselves into it to find there an everlasting support, that they may not die away in their transiency but register themselves into everlasting permanence where eternity and time are one. O day of Christ! Thou art the fulness of the times. Thou art the gate of the bright eternity. The ages all meet in thee. By thee they pass out into the kingdom.

The thoroughly unique relation, in respect of position and supreme control, which subsists between the day of Christ and the ages, may be represented somewhat strikingly, if a geometrical illustration be forgiven. Conceive of all time—the entire period of God's dispensation with this world—as represented by the figure of a cone. There, before you, is a symbolic representation of the entire history of time; the Christian era, we shall say, represented by the portion of the surface fronting you, while the pre-Christian ages are symbolized by the portion on the other side and in the shade—from your point of view invisible. Your own day on earth may, on this scheme, be fitly indicated by the slanting line, from the apex to the base, immediately in front of you. Now, that line of yours—your day—would be redeemed from darkness were a luminous point—shall we say the star of Bethlehem?—to settle on it anywhere between the apex of the cone and its base. But your day is not the fulness of the times; and if the star of Bethlehem seat itself anywhere but in the fulness of times—anywhere down the slope of this mystic cone on the side of it confronting you—yours may be a glorious privilege, but it is confined to you and your literal contemporaries. The ages concealed from view behind are left in outer darkness. Abraham cannot see the day of Christ.

But let the star of Bethlehem choose the apex of the cone— that singular and only point in which the slanting lines all meet—and settle in its radiant beauty there. Let there be a day into which all the lines of history may be found recapitulated and gathered together into one. For the dispensation is to be one of entire recapitulation. Let the day selected for it correspond with it. If it is to be a dispensation of the fulness of all things, let it also be 'the dispensation of the fulness of times.' If in Christ's person God shall recapitulate the fulness of the Godhead (Col. 2: 9) and the fulness of humanity; the fulness of the church also (Eph. 1: 23), including both the fulness of Israel (Rom. 11: 12) and the fulness of the Gentiles (v. 25)—for in Christ's person it has pleased the Father that all fulness should dwell (Col. 1: 19)—then it would appear that all lines of history should recapitulate and gather themselves together into one in Christ's day; like as when all electric lines of telegraph gather, in their messages and meanings, on the face of some central dial where alone they become intelligible and tell their tale.[1] Let all the times thus congregate into the day of Christ. Let the epoch of Christ's appearing be so chosen as to constitute, in the wisdom of God, a central home into which the times may all congregate until they find themselves there, literally in 'the fulness of times.' Let the apex of the symbolic cone indicate the day of Christ; and there let the star of Bethlehem shine. Is it not the light of the world—even from the foundation of the world to the world's end? Does not its radiance flow down all the sides of time—past, present, and to come—alike? Does it not shine down behind—on Abraham's day—as it shines on ours? Does it not make Abraham's day contemporaneous with the day of Christ? And can our day be better than contemporaneous with Christ's own day?

Are not you and Abraham thus virtually contemporaneous? Let Abraham look up from behind those millenniums that divide us; let him look up unto the hills whence cometh our aid—unto 'the mountain of the Lord's house established on the top of the mountains.' Be it yours also to look up. That star of Bethlehem shining there—'the root and the offspring

[1] It is in some such way as this—is it not?—that, according to Paul's beautiful idea (1 Cor. 10: 11) we may conceive of 'the ends of the ages'—τὰ τέλω τῶν αἰώνον—as 'come down upon us'; bringing with them and writing off before our eyes the telegrams (ἐγράφη, τέλη) which, ages ago and far away, were 'written for our admonition' and in 'our types'—τύποι ἡμῶν; telegrams that are purposeless as written merely yonder, and that yield up their full import only as read off here—here, where the true key of their cipher in our hands opens the message or meaning of the Spirit more fully to us than it was patent to the patriarchs or prophets who transmitted it (1 Pet. 1: 10-11)—for 'these all, having obtained a good report through faith, received not the promise: God having provided some better thing for us, that they without us should not be made perfect' (Heb. 11: 39-40).

of David, the bright and the morning star'—dwelling in the eternal realm, which he never leaves, even when seated on this most commanding central throne of time—is just the reconciling medium between eternity and time, through which the faith of Abraham, travelling upward from behind the mountains of Bether—the mountains that divide us—passes out into the realm from which time with its conditions is eliminated. Upwards through the same star of Bethlehem your faith travels too, carrying you also out in spirit into the same kingdom of the things unseen and eternal: and as you enter it, time to you also is eliminated and cast out, as with Abraham. You and your father Abraham find yourselves victorious over time's limiting and separating influence. He and you are virtually contemporaneous in the kingdom.

Therefore, not the gospels only—thus have we oftener than once had occasion to resume and extend some inference from the leading thought of these pages—not the gospels only, but the entire Scriptures are 'the Galleries of the King'; and in them all, by the Spirit, we find the presence of the king with his friends. To the eye of faith his presence is with us also in the self-same manner as with them; and the revelations of his glory to them survive and are being prolonged to us. For we are virtually contemporaneous with them: and, by the Spirit, we are present at the interviews the king vouchsafed unto them; and, present, not as spectators, but parties, identified with our believing fathers. I do not need to look on with envy when I hear Abraham called of God and blessed with the blessing that is irrevocable and eternal (Gen. 12: 1–3). If I am 'of faith,' I have shared in all that is of spiritual efficacy and eternal import in Abraham's call, and am 'blessed with faithful Abraham' (Gal. 3: 9). In that case, I am no intruder on the secrecy of his fellowship with God; but, by the presence of the Lord with me and the Spirit's ever-living history of his presence with Abraham, I share in that fellowship and all its solemn recorded interviews. Soon as I have come forth at the Lord's separating call (2 Cor. 6: 17), I am virtually sojourning with Abraham, as in a strange country, dwelling in tabernacles with Isaac and Jacob, they and I heirs with him of the same promises; all of us alike looking for a city which hath foundations, whose builder and maker is God; indeed, desiring a better country, that is, an heavenly: wherefore God is not ashamed to be called our God, for he has prepared for us a city (Heb. 11: 8–16). And from the time I assume the stranger's guise and the pilgrim's staff, as a child of Abraham; wherever my tent may be pitched and my altar reared (Gen. 12: 6–9), it is to me practically as if I worshipped with the household of the pilgrim-father, 'with Bethel on the east and Hai on the west'; while his orisons and mine ascend together into the transcendent realm of faith within the veil. And when I have gone down to Egypt, it may be, and (alas!) not wholly kept my integrity there, but compromised my faith through cowardly fear, yet the Lord has rescued me from snares, and restored my soul, and reiterated and enlarged his promise (Gen. 12: 10–20; 13). And when, after some victorious conflict with my foes, Melchizedeck, on my return (and in him a Greater than he), meets and blesses me in the name of the Most High God, possessor of heaven and earth, and blesses the Most High God who has delivered my enemies into my hand (Gen. 14)—the eternal royal priest of Salem and of righteousness has thus mediated my peace and blessing more and more as my pilgrimage advances. Having heard the word of the Lord in a vision (Gen. 15) saying, 'Fear not, I am thy shield and thy exceeding great reward,' I have gone forth with Abraham beneath the midnight vault, and listened to his God and my God, that tells the number of the stars, speaking of the promised seed, and testifying my irrevocable justification through faith in him—for it was not written for Abraham's sake alone, but for us also to whom the righteousness is imputed, if we have the faith of our father Abraham (Rom. 4). Then again I may have heard the reviving call (Gen. 16)—'I am God Almighty; walk before me and be thou perfect.' Yet again, I may have learned the holy art of being an intercessor (Gen. 18) for others. In a word, when I have passed through great variety of pilgrim-life, till the 'hope against hope' that kept my 'heart' from being 'sick' is 'deferred' no more, but Isaac is born (Gen. 21) and laughter fills my heart and home; and when, further still, Isaac may have been asked from me (Gen. 22) again by the Lord, and grace may have enabled me to say, Let the Lord deal with his own as it pleaseth him—'Jehovah-jireh'; and in an hour of terrible probation I may have seen Christ's day more clearly than I ever did before: Oh! may I not, in such manifold experience as this, perceive that—as 'no prophecy of the Scripture'—so no promise to the saints, and no interview ever granted by the king to any of them, 'is of any private interpretation,' but all are mine in Christ the Lord? and being Christ's, and thereby Abraham's seed, and an heir according to the promise, I find something much more precise and specific than once I looked for—much more full of meaning and rich with ample stores of spiritual blessings in the heavenly places—in that word of God to Abraham his friend—'In thee,' O Abraham, 'and in thy seed'—'In thee and in thy seed shall all the families of the earth be blessed'; and in that other word of the Spirit commenting on his own earlier utterances—'They that be of faith are blessed with faithful Abraham.'

And then, too, when I go on to identify myself with Isaac, the child of promise—the child of the free woman, of Jerusalem which is above; born after the Spirit and persecuted of him that is born after the flesh—I find that exactly 'as then, so it is now.' The essentials are the same; for I also am born of the same mother, a child of the promise and the Spirit. And the circumstances are the same; for I too am persecuted of him that is born after the flesh. There is really no change. So that, if what philosophers tell us be true, that, without some change, lapse of time is not cognizable, in this transcendental realm of Jerusalem which is above, I am entirely contemporaneous with Isaac; and the Scripture is sounding in my ears—'Cast out the bondwoman and her son, for the son of the bondwoman shall not be heir with the son of the free.' I will therefore stand fast with Isaac the free-born son and rightful heir, in the liberty wherewith the Seed of Abraham has made Abraham's children free (Gen. 21: 9–10; Gal. 4: 22–31; 5: 1).

Jehovah's glorious interviews with Jacob, whom he named Israel—from these also I am not excluded. Jacob's vision belongs to me, and to Nathanael, and to every 'Israelite indeed' (Gen. 28: 10–22; John 1: 51). For Bethel, and Mahanaim, and Peniel are lifted up by the inspired history, and the revealing Spirit, into a realm where no desecrating hand, whether of sin or of time, can mar their holy beauty; even up into 'the house of God and to the gate of heaven'—where 'the angel of the Lord encampeth round about them that fear him'—and where 'the house of Jacob walk in the light of the Lord' as when their father passed over Peniel—halting on his thigh, but a prince with God—and 'the sun rose upon him.' But why specify more of these long withdrawing sacred halls of 'the Galleries of the King?' It is enough. We see that these 'ivory palaces' are in a realm transcending sense and time; they are in the heavenly places, in no mount that might be touched, but in the city of the living God, the heavenly Jerusalem; in a kingdom into which no alien can intrude and from which no son can be excluded; for if the Son hath made you free, you have the freedom of the Lord's house indeed. By the word and Spirit I can see Abraham and Isaac and Jacob sitting in the heavenly places in him who is bone of their bone and flesh of their flesh, the King of Israel; and I can join them there in all their experience of faith and love and joy, if I also am raised up together with Christ. For faith is the key and the Spirit is the guide into these Galleries of the King, which are truly in the kingdom of heaven. And, if I only feel in very truth that 'I am not worthy that 'the king' should come under my roof,' yet believe that he has 'but to speak the word only' and I shall have all my salvation and all my desire; then, in virtue of such faith given me by himself—and he has not found greater faith, no, not in Israel—He admits me into these galleries of the sacred scriptures to 'sit down' there 'in the kingdom of heaven with Abraham and with Isaac and with Jacob,' and tells me that many more 'shall come from the north and from the south and from the east and from the west,' all blessed with faithful Abraham, all virtually contemporaneous with him in his interviews and intercourse and walk with God (Matt. 8: 8–11).

    What a wealth of spiritual experience—what a crowded life of faith—what a boundlessness of fresh variety in the history of the hidden man of the heart, and of the holy walk with God—does this single principle of contemporaneousness with all saints place within our reach! Read in this light—and in this manner *live*—the eleventh chapter of Hebrews; and if 'the time failed' the writer to tell of the experiences and exploits of those who obtained a good report through faith, much more will time fail you to pass through with them and appropriate all their believing joys and sorrows, works and warfare. Yet, in every trial of your faith, you may surely find a precedent in some conjuncture of the history of one or other of them, and with the blessed assurance that it is not a precedent in the sense of being past, but a prelude in them prolonged in you. Is Joshua, for instance, brevetted of the Lord in the room of Moses exalted to his rest? Is the 'young man' that 'departed not out of the tabernacle' (Exod. 33: 11)—but 'ministered' there with veneration and love to the veteran 'king in Jeshurun' (24: 13)—is he now inaugurated Generalissimo of all Israel; and is Jehovah giving him military instructions on the plains of Moab beneath the shadow of Nebo? How utterly unlike your history and circumstances, O hidden child of God! Nevertheless, assert, without fear, your place side by side with this mighty man of war, as Jehovah designates him to his fight of faith and makes him stronger with his word than all the Canaanites that are in the land. Hark to the promise given him! 'I will be with thee; I will not fail thee, nor forsake thee.' Is that promise not alive and abiding for ever? May you not embrace it as God utters it to Joshua, and spiritually carry over all your warfare to the plains of Moab, and identify triumphantly all your apparently impossible or hopeless duties with the passage of the Jordan? Is this a fancy or illusion that would thus appropriate the promise and the power given to Joshua? Not if the writer to the Hebrews, or rather the inspiring Spirit, is to be permitted to advise us. For he expressly tells us that the conjuncture, and the promise relative to it, as it were, are still surviving; or, virtually, we are gathered back to the day of the promise and the circumstances in which it was given—contemporaneous, in a word, with the warrior of Israel—'For he hath said I will never leave thee nor forsake thee: So that we may boldly say, The Lord is my helper, and I will not fear what man shall do unto me' (Heb. 13: 6). Fearlessly, therefore, be counselled; take your stand among the many thousands of Israel; and if some impossibility is assigned to you, pass over Jordan with them before the Lord.

The sweet singer of Israel would not hesitate so to counsel you. Hark how he identifies himself with Israel even at an earlier period, and in, perhaps, a grander passage. He does not shrink from asserting his virtual contemporaneousness with Moses, and his fellowship with those that were baptized into Moses in the cloud and in the sea. For in these noble strains does the King of Israel claim faith's victory over the centuries that have elapsed since then—'Come and see the works of God: he is terrible in his doing towards the children of men. He turned the sea into dry land: they went through the flood on foot: *there did we rejoice him*' (Ps. 66: 5–6). The glorious exodus, O church of the living God, is in all ages yours; and the glory and the power of your God are not gone out of it. If you have the perpetual passover, you have the perpetual exodus too. Often times you have by faith to achieve impossibilities. Synchronize them by faith with the exodus; and pass on through the flood on foot. The kingly word of your God commands you—a word ever living in the realm that transcends time and the wilderness, and sounding out into the wilderness to you at this present time, unabated in its might—'Speak unto the children of Israel that they go forward.' 'Forward'—O church, O child of God! The waters that shall overwhelm your enemies shall be a wall unto you on the right hand and on the left. Pass on through the flood on foot. Pass on with the voice of song. 'Sing unto the Lord for he hath triumphed gloriously: the horse and his rider hath he cast into the sea.' Evermore he is the Lord your God that has brought you out of the land of Egypt and out of the house of bondage; and he is bringing you to 'the land that is very far off.' Claim all the grace of the past as thine; claim all the glory of the future. For, hark how Paul, 'by the word of the Lord,' claims a victory over millenniums of prophecy, analogous to that of David over centuries of history; making the second advent the present[1] and perpetual heritage of the church, as David in Spirit makes the exodus—'We which are alive and remain unto the coming of the Lord shall not prevent'—shall not anticipate or be beforehand with—'them that are asleep'

---

1 See page 117.

(1 Thess. 4: 15), Therefore, let no child of him who is Alpha and Omega, the first and the last, be in bondage unto time. For on you are come down all the ends of the ages. And all things are yours—whether Abraham, or Isaac, or Jacob; Moses, or Joshua, or David; Paul, or Apollos, or Cephas; the world, or life, or death; things past, or things present, or things to come—or the exodus of Israel, or the advent of the Lord. Christ's presence with you and with all saints—in you, also, and in them—achieves this great result. In him, in the dispensation of the fulness of times, are all things thus recapitulated. In him, also, are all the ages recapitulated; both the ages that are past and those that are to come. He is the head of the body: and he is the father of the ages. In his presence, therefore, one day is as a thousand years and a thousand years as one day: and in his presence you are in the presence of 'the whole family in heaven and in earth.'

Such is the privilege of faith. 'Now,' indeed, 'we see through a glass darkly.' The hour comes when we shall 'see face to face.' But the object seen shall be the same, the method of the revelation alone being changed; and rapturous shall be the saints' recognition of it. For as grace passes over into glory, by no rude shock, but of very ripeness; and faith merges sweetly into full fruition; so—while the heavens shall pass away with a great noise and the elements shall melt with fervent heat, the earth also and the works that are therein being burned up—Christ's presence as in the gospel history, preserving beautifully its identity, shall blend into the brightness of his coming and be transfigured into—Christ's presence as in the glory of his Father.

'Surely I come quickly.' 'Amen. Even so, come, Lord Jesus.'

The Glory of Christ
His Office and Grace

JOHN OWEN

'*Take time to read this book. Savour each page. Appreciate the depths of what Owen says. Allow yourself to be analysed, searched, exposed, deconstructed, edified, enlightened, engraced, and refocused on the glory of Jesus Christ.*'

Sinclair Ferguson

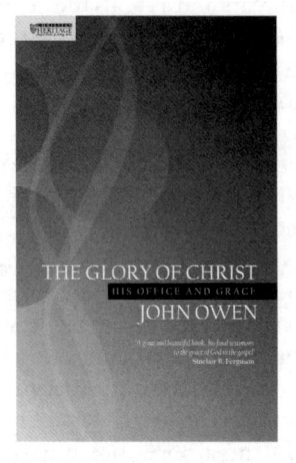

To see the glory of Christ is one of the greatest privileges that a Christian can enjoy. Anyone who does not see his glory in this world, will not see his glory in heaven, and no one should look for anything in heaven that he has not experienced in this life. Just as looking directly into the sun darkens our vision, so Christ's heavenly splendour is too brilliant for our mind's eye, but in seeing it by faith, we are prepared for heaven. In his immense essence, the infinite God is invisible to our finite human eyes, and will remain so for eternity. Only 'in the face of Jesus Christ' can we see God and be filled with peace and rest.

Read this book, and may God by his Word and Spirit give you such a sense of his uncreated glory, blazing forth in Christ, that you will be satisfied and filled with joy.

This is the orginal text with a new layout and is fully subtitled which makes it more accessible to a new generation of readers!

ISBN 978-1-85792-474-9

Christ Crucified
A Puritan's View of the Atonement
STEPHEN CHARNOCK

'Sentence after sentence in Charnock's ordered march lights up and glows in your heart'
J. I. Packer

In this stimulating work Stephen Charnock links the Old and New Testaments with this classic explanation of how the sacrifice of Jesus Christ fulfils the Old Testament sacrificial system. He particularly illustrates the importance of the Passover, and opens up our understanding of the differences which characterise the New Testament Church era. He shows that Jesus willingly submitted to the pain he knew he would go through, in order to bring us the blessings of a new covenant with God.

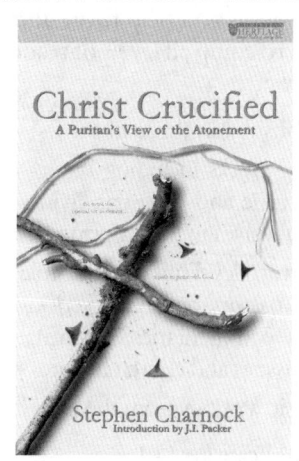

The Puritans were brought up on the Bible; for a Puritan mind a clear text from the Bible settled all controversy. It is this discipline and clear sightedness which makes their work so valuable to today's generation.

ISBN 978-1-85792-813-6

Christian Focus Publications
publishes books for all ages

Our mission statement –

STAYING FAITHFUL
In dependence upon God we seek to impact the world through literature faithful to his infallible word, the Bible. Our aim is to ensure that the LORD Jesus Christ is presented as the only hope to obtain forgiveness of sin, live a useful life and look forward to heaven with Him.

REACHING OUT
Christ's last command requires us to reach out to our world with His gospel. We seek to help fulfil that by publishing books that point people towards Jesus and help them develop a Christ-like maturity. We aim to equip all levels of readers for life, work, ministry and mission.

Books in our adult range are published in three imprints:

Christian Focus contains popular works including biographies, commentaries, basic doctrine and Christian living. Our children's books are also published in this imprint.

Mentor focuses on books written at a level suitable for Bible College and seminary students, pastors, and other serious readers. The imprint includes commentaries, doctrinal studies, examination of current issues and church history.

Christian Heritage contains classic writings from the past.

Christian Focus Publications Ltd
Geanies House, Fearn, Ross-shire,
IV20 1TW, Scotland, United Kingdom.
info@christianfocus.com
www.christianfocus.com